Rela Boyd

The Next
American Century

The Next American Century

Essays in Honor
of Richard G. Lugar

Edited by
Jeffrey T. Bergner

ROWMAN & LITTLEFIELD PUBLISHERS, INC.
Lanham • *Boulder* • *New York* • *Oxford*

ROWMAN & LITTLEFIELD PUBLISHERS, INC.

Published in the United States of America
by Rowman & Littlefield Publishers, Inc.
A Member of the Rowman & Littlefield Publishing Group
4501 Forbes Boulevard, Suite 200, Lanham, Maryland 20706
www.rowmanlittlefield.com

PO Box 317
Oxford
OX2 9RU, UK

British Library Cataloguing in Publication Information Available

Library of Congress Cataloging-in-Publication Data

The next American century : essays in honor of Richard G. Lugar / edited by Jeffrey
    T. Bergner.
        p. cm.
    Includes bibliographical references.
    ISBN 0-7425-2788-3 (hardcover : alk. paper)
    1. United States—Foreign relations—21st century. 2. United States—Foreign
relations—Philosophy. I. Bergner, Jeffrey T. II. Lugar, Richard.

E895 .N49 2003
327.73—dc21

                                                                    2002151627

Printed in the United States of America

∞™ The paper used in this publication meets the minimum requirements of
American National Standard for Information Sciences—Permanence of Paper
for Printed Library Materials, ANSI/NISO Z39.48-1992.

To Richard G. Lugar

Contents

Acknowledgments

There are many people to thank in an enterprise like this book of essays. First and foremost are the contributors themselves. Each contributor is deeply engaged in a variety of activities—public service, administration, teaching, writing, and speaking, to name but a few. It is a tribute to Dick Lugar that they would add to their full schedules the preparation of an essay for this book. It is also a tribute to their continued willingness to engage in the difficult, but stimulating, work of thinking anew about American foreign policy. For that I am grateful.

I would also like to thank a number of current and former colleagues for their assistance and/or indulgence along the way. Chief among them are Marty Morris, Dan Diller, Chip Andreae, Mark Helmke, Bob Tyrer, Vin Weber, Chuck Brain, and Dave Bockorny.

As every author knows, one's publisher can make the creation and production of a book a more or less pleasant undertaking. Jed Lyons and Jon Sisk of Rowman and Littlefield deserve thanks for making this task both as pleasant and as professional as it could possibly have been. Finally, this volume would not exist—literally—without the assistance and persistence of Maia Comeau, who helped at every stage of its production.

Introduction: The Lugar Style

Jeffrey T. Bergner

This year marks the twenty-fifth year that Richard Lugar has served as a U.S. senator. During this quarter century (twenty-three years of which he has served on the Foreign Relations Committee), he has become one of the most thoughtful, influential foreign policy leaders in the Senate's history. This is so not simply because he has been immersed in many of the leading events of the past quarter century. More so, it is because he has approached these issues with a deeply consistent and thoughtful orientation. His views have found expression in cutting-edge positions in U.S. foreign policy, including the SALT II Treaty debate, South African sanctions, Philippine elections, NATO expansion, and the Nunn-Lugar legislation, to name but a few.

His contributions to the many issues he has touched (a chronology is listed in the back of the book) have evidenced a set of underlying principles which have guided his thinking. These principles offer sound guidelines to address the difficult issues the United States will face in the new century. They can be expected to inform the work of Dick Lugar in the years to come. And they inform the thinking behind the extraordinary contributions that the contributors of this volume have made.

What are the hallmarks of the Lugar view? First, that American leadership in the world is absolutely critical. Everyone is fated to be born somewhere. Those of us privileged to have been born as U.S. citizens at this time must play an unambiguous leadership role. The United States is today the indispensable nation—because our institutions, our history, our power, and our values make it so. Like everyone, we can play the hand we are dealt well or poorly; but we must play the hand we are dealt. To play our hand well is to play it energetically, even enthusiastically, knowing that not only America but all the world will be a better place if we do. On that score, Dick Lugar has never wavered.

1

What is the premise of American leadership? What makes it possible? Dick Lugar has never doubted that national power is the source from which we draw our strength. This strength comes from many places, above all the American people and the reservoir of courage we have witnessed since September 11, 2001. But it also includes economic power and it includes—unashamedly—military power. Military power is the cornerstone of successful foreign policy; without it, American concerns and hopes remain impotent. To be credible, this power must be employed when necessary. Failure to deploy power when it is required erodes both power and credibility. No responsible leader advocates the indiscriminate use of force. That would be an obvious, and costly, mistake. But there is no room for sentimentality in American foreign policy either. Dick Lugar stands squarely in the line of Theodore Roosevelt, for whom the "big stick" was not a substitute for good sense, but an expression of it.

Even with its many strengths, however, America is little likely to succeed all on its own. America needs friends in the world who share its belief in liberty and self-government. America's strength never consists simply in the export of stability; it also consists in the export of goods and services and, above all, of ideas. It is in America's interest to encourage and to foster a worldwide system of open trade and investment among democratically governed nations. America must be open to every opportunity to press the case for popular government and for constitutional protections for liberty. At the same time, America must take every chance to press for liberalization of the world trading system. America must be a leader for openness, resisting superficial calls to hamper the world trading system with well-intentioned, but ultimately counterproductive, sanctions, embargoes, and trade barriers. Indeed, too often these measures are a weak substitute for serious action. To the extent the United States is prepared to take real measures, policymakers will be less tempted by the menu of empty trade restrictions which are so frequently advocated. Dick Lugar holds solidly to the view that a robust political and military stance goes hand in hand with an open economic system.

What supports these principles for Dick Lugar is a deep faith that the world and our policy responses to it are accessible to thoughtful analysis. It *is* possible to understand, and even to some degree to predict, our environment if we are prepared to study the world and to think hard about it. This is the premise of Dick Lugar's work in the Philippines, in South Africa, and in the years following the breakup of the Soviet Union. It is the premise of the Nunn-Lugar legislation. And it is the premise of Dick Lugar's early and too-often ignored warnings about terrorism and the threat of weapons of mass destruction. A successful democracy must find ways to attract talented people to think deeply about the world and about American foreign policy choices. Dick Lugar's forty years of public service offer a strong model for that.

This rather forward leaning, not to say aggressive, set of views cannot succeed if it is simply imposed on the American people (or on people abroad for that matter). A successful foreign policy requires the support of the American people. Broad American foreign policy goals must be shared, explained, discussed, and taught, however unconventional that thought may seem today. This requires that each of us must assume the best of one another, and of the American people generally. If a policy fails to persuade the American people, perhaps the fault lies in the policy, not the people. Or perhaps it lies in how well one has argued for that policy. Maligning the motives of others is no substitute for patient, dispassionate explanations of foreign policy goals. In this regard, successful foreign policy initiatives cannot be founded on the narrow ledge of partisanship. Successful foreign policy must be able to command support among reasonable people of both major political parties. Disagreements and compromises are not disastrous. One should never be surprised that if one treats others well, common ground can be found with others who hold many opposing views. Firmly held views and a graceful, open style comport well with one another. This is Dick Lugar's style.

SETTING THE COURSE

It is on these premises that Dick Lugar sets out to work each day. And it is on this general framework that the contributors to this volume have made their own signal contributions to thinking about American foreign policy. In the first section, the contributors address the broad contextual principles within which American foreign policy operates. William J. Bennett sets the tone by addressing the importance of rooting American foreign policy into the goals which informed and continue to inform the American polity. He subtly transcends the sterile debate between "idealism" and "realism" in American foreign policy. Because of the universalistic demands of liberty, he concludes there is no conflict between the ideals of democracy and the arsenals of democracy.

Because foreign policy is often preoccupied with day-to-day crises in which the urgent drives out the merely important, it is easy to lose sight of the broader demographics which will shape the choices that this new century' s leaders will be called on to make. William G. Lesher takes the long view, arguing that a world pressed by scarcity of food, water, and energy will be a turbulent place, full of hard choices, and difficult to govern. He makes the point that we are not fated to live in this kind of world; human ingenuity and good policies can shape our choices for the better. The increase of agricultural productivity per acre—and the resulting benefit to the environment—makes this point in spades. And as he concludes, we have barely scratched the surface of possibilities.

In this regard, Senator Chuck Hagel stresses the importance of international economic policies that can create prosperity—not only for Americans, but also for the entire world. America cannot enrich itself by beggaring its neighbors; to the contrary, American prosperity depends directly on the success of our trading and investment partners. And as Senator Hagel—himself a leader in shaping U.S. international economic policy—suggests, the United States will inevitably be the engine either for openness or its opposite. He offers clear guidance for resisting the politically seductive, but disastrous, course of inwardness and protection.

But economics does not operate in a vacuum; sound economic policies are most often a result of political choices. It is in America's interest—not to say the interest of citizens of other nations—to live in a world of democratic, limited governments which value liberty and individual rights. Carl Gershman addresses the often knotty issues that surround American efforts to foster democratic government, and to aid democratic movements around the world. It is all too easy to offer up one-sided criticisms of democracy-building; the fair-minded reader will agree that Gershman patiently builds a persuasive case for why we must continue to toil in this vineyard.

Finally, it is a certainty that American foreign policy will not succeed unless it is able to achieve a broad consensus within the American polity itself. Lee H. Hamilton offers a road map to generate needed consensus in American foreign policy. He addresses the related issues of bipartisanship and of legislative and executive cooperation. He argues that Congress—often rightly criticized as the fountainhead of partisan bickering—has a special constitutional role in mediating and melding the diversity of American opinions into policies that can command support over time.

CHALLENGES AND OPPORTUNITIES

Within these broad parameters, American policymakers confront the day-to-day regional challenges which preoccupy them and around which American foreign policymaking institutions are organized. Perhaps in no region has the end of the Cold War meant rethinking our relationships more than with Europe. Zbigniew Brzezinski deftly outlines these fundamental changes, without resorting to the "sky is falling" tendencies of so many commentators on U.S.-European relations. Arguing that the perfect should not be the enemy of the good, he sees much that is workably good in the persisting democratic values that bind the United States and Europe together. And with regard to Russia, this can only be reemphasized in the aftermath of September 11.

Casimir A. Yost summarizes the U.S. role in Asia with a stark and arrestingly simple formulation: the United States has gained power, but lost influence. How can this be? He argues that American policy toward Asia over the past decade suffered from two deep-seated problems: an inability to define clearly U.S. goals in Asia, and a commensurate failure to listen to what is on the agenda of Asian countries themselves. After analyzing U.S. interests in Asia, regional and subregional Asian dynamics, and countries of special importance, Yost concludes with six deep questions to challenge U.S. policymakers in coming years.

James Woolsey turns his sharply focused lens on the Middle East. He notes that excluding oil exports, the 260 million people of the Middle East export less to America than does Finland. How, he asks, can the U.S. diminish the leverage which the oil-producing states hold over the United States? His solution is equal parts common sense and farsighted thought about the promise of alternative fuels. Here, he echoes several of the themes of Lesher's essay. His analysis aims to give America the latitude to deal forcefully with the Islamic fundamentalist threat that grows out of several oil-producing nations of the Middle East.

William Perry argues that the Western Hemisphere has far too long been the underappreciated region of American foreign policy. He points to trade, immigration, and cultural influences in arguing that the time for reevaluation is long overdue. Perry sees a democratized, economically successful Western Hemisphere as a bulwark against the spread of terrorism. He argues forcefully that opportunities during the first decade after the end of the Cold War were squandered and that a gradual reemergence of persistent problems pushed democratic and economic institutions backwards in some cases. He sketches a series of steps to put democratization and economic openness back on track at a time when that effort is both more difficult and more imperative.

Finally, Congressman Charles B. Rangel builds on the cooperation which he and Senator Lugar enjoyed in crafting and passing the Africa Growth and Opportunity Act. He argues that while there remain legitimate and pressing needs for assistance to Africa, the African continent's future ultimately depends on the creation of sound economic and political institutions and trade and investment with the rest of the world. There are many reasons to be hopeful that Africa, while beleaguered by problems, is on the cusp of positive new developments. The United States is the natural catalyst to help realize this promise.

THE ROAD AHEAD

That September 11 changed everything is a staple of the media; to craft America's continuing response is more difficult. In assessing the threat of terror, Kenneth L. Adelman argues first that we must identify without any self-delusion or sentimentality, the true nature of the threat. Only then is the American response likely to be effective. Adelman offers strong support for the doctrine of "preemption" which President George W. Bush enunciated in his West Point address of June 1, 2002. He suggests that this approach, however necessary, will be more difficult to sustain politically than the more passive doctrine of "containment" which informed our policy during the Cold War. Undaunted, he concludes by advancing a series of additional proactive steps against those who sustain and harbor terrorists.

Congressman Robert R. Simmons argues that intelligence is the first line of defense in the war on terrorism. Drawing on his background as a former CIA operative and a staff member on the Senate Intelligence Committee, he argues for a series of reforms to strengthen U.S. intelligence gathering and analysis. Mindful of the balance between intelligence gathering and American constitutional freedoms, he suggests that the former can be strengthened without harming the latter. To Secretary Stimson's dictum that "gentleman don't read each others' mail," he responds with clarity: We are not living in a world of gentlemen.

However good our intelligence, it will not avail us if we do not have the military capability and political will to respond to terror. Former defense secretary William S. Cohen authors a practical set of considerations to shape the American military into the strongest possible force to combat today's threats. He offers specific guidance about how to create a military force capable of rapidly responding to both the conventional and the asymmetric threats we will face in the twenty-first century.

This theme is taken up by Sam Nunn, Senator Lugar's former colleague and coauthor of the Nunn-Lugar legislation to dismantle, safeguard, and destroy Russian nuclear, chemical, and biological weapons. Senator Nunn argues that terrorists with weapons of mass destruction are the clearest threat to American security today. He argues forcefully that we need a tiered defense, and that our best chance of security is to prevent terrorists from obtaining nuclear, chemical, or biological weapons in the first place. He concludes by summoning Russia and the United States to lead the world in building a coalition against catastrophic terrorism.

In the end, one suspects that if our democracy can create competent foreign policy leaders when they are most needed, we will prevail. But how is this possible? Why would talented individuals dedicate themselves to the work of foreign policy whose goals are so distant, so diffuse, and so little connected with narrow self-interest? Mark Blitz argues that the answer lies in the modern democratic notion of "responsibility." This ideal is the modern counterpart to the ancient ideal of the great-souled man; the responsible man is one who takes on the burden of the common weal, whose playing field is extensive, but a man who does so without the sense of rank or personal aggrandizement of the great-souled man or the tyrant. The responsible leader is a tall tree, but one which grows in an egalitarian forest.

We come full circle to Bennett's opening argument that the responsible leader finds a way to reconcile and press forward the ideals and the practical interests of the country in a coherent way. The man who is honored in this collection of essays is no doubt the very model of this responsible leader.

I

SETTING THE COURSE

Introductory Remarks:
The Bases of National Strength

William J. Bennett

"We hold these truths to be self-evident, that all men are created equal, that they are endowed by their Creator with certain unalienable Rights, that among these are Life, Liberty and the pursuit of Happiness." Citing these ancient morals, the Founding Fathers gave birth to a new nation—our nation. And before Thomas Jefferson put the final sentences in our Declaration of Independence, he identified these "truths" as "ends" of government and not merely means.

America, in short, was born of a vision: A vision of human flourishing, human rights, and human freedoms. Our history is not spotless; it is a story of the struggle—sometimes bloody—to realize that vision in full. But never have we lost sight of the ideals that animated the men in Philadelphia in 1776. Throughout history, our leaders—political, spiritual, and civic—have appealed to the Declaration's timeless truths in their efforts to make concrete the promises and ideals contained therein. The men who have called America to live up to those ideals are our greatest heroes.

It was no accident that Martin Luther King Jr. led his most famous march and delivered his "I Have a Dream" speech in front of the Lincoln Memorial, at the feet of the man who himself had reified these principles. In turn, of course, Lincoln had written: "All honor to Jefferson—to the man who had the coolness, forecast and capacity to introduce into a merely revolutionary document, an abstract truth, applicable to all men at all times, and so to embalm it there, that today, and in all the coming days, it shall be a rebuke and a stumbling block to the very harbingers of re-appearing tyranny and oppression."

When tyranny and oppression reappeared as they did during the dark days of Nazism's march through Europe, Franklin D. Roosevelt laid out his "Four Freedoms." The world, he said, was founded on freedom of speech, freedom of every person to worship God, freedom from want, and freedom from fear. Roosevelt concluded, "Freedom means the supremacy of human rights everywhere," and he led America and her allies in a war to ensure that those freedoms were protected.

In our own time, we have come face to face with a similar threat. Thus, most recently, in his first State of the Union address, President George W. Bush proclaimed that

> we have a great opportunity during this time of war to lead the world toward the values that will bring lasting peace. All fathers and mothers, in all societies, want their children to be educated and live free from poverty and violence. If anyone doubts this, let them look to Afghanistan, where the Islamic 'street' greeted the fall of tyranny with song and celebration. America will lead by defending liberty and justice because they are right and true and unchanging for all people everywhere. America will always stand firm for the non-negotiable demands of human dignity: the rule of law; limits on the power of the state; respect for women; private property; free speech; equal justice; and religious tolerance.

These principles are those that have animated the American experiment. And while America is unique in her dedication to these principles, these principles are not unique to her. Rather, they are the birthright of every man, woman, and child around the world—rights that must be defended, rights for which we must often fight.

In the wake of September 11, 2001, the age-old debate over the role of morality and principle in foreign policy has taken on new urgency, relevance, and importance. How should we balance maintaining fidelity to our ideals on the one hand, and pursuing policies that protect our national security and self interests on the other? This is a vital subject to which many thinkers, writers, and political leaders have devoted a great deal of thought and attention. And it is now appropriate to mention Senator Richard Lugar, a man who fits into each of these categories. Above all else, Senator Lugar is a man not only of political action but a man of ideas and ideals. It is in his honor that I have the pleasure of introducing this impressive collection of essays.

I will argue that the true base of our national strength—the underfooting of our foreign policy—is secure only when it is based on and guided by those explicitly moral tenets so clearly outlined and established by men like Thomas Jefferson, George Washington, Abraham Lincoln, and Martin Luther King Jr., and, in foreign policy, Franklin D. Roosevelt, Ronald Reagan, and George W. Bush.

The American Founding Fathers understood the essential truth about their young nation's place in the world and about the uniquely American conception of the "national interest." Washington, concluding forty-five years of public service, offered the best statement of this truth in his elegantly composed farewell to the nation. As a nation, he wrote in 1796, we must be able to "choose peace or war, as our interest, guided by our justice, shall counsel." As Washington's words imply, when Americans grapple with the problem of how best to promote their "national interest," they dare not neglect the principles on which America was founded.

It has become commonplace to speak of American "exceptionalism," but the fact is that the American nation itself was founded in exceptional circumstances and on an exceptional statement of timeless, unalterable principles. Put simply, the United States was the first nation ever to base its very claim to nationhood on an appeal to universal principles derived from natural rights. The ideas embodied in the Declaration of Independence—that the purpose of our nation is to protect our God-given liberties—lies at the heart of the American experiment in self-government, and it lies at the very base of our foreign policy. Or at least it should.

In *Federalist* no. 2, John Jay described his fellow citizens as "no less attached to union than enamored of liberty." This correctly summarizes the Founding Fathers' implicit expectation that the Americans would be attached to their country because it protected their rights and thus gave them the best opportunity to lead better and more fulfilled lives. This would, above all, be the root of our patriotic affections.

Alexis de Tocqueville compared older, more traditional forms of patriotism he had known in Europe with the new variety he found in America. Of European patriotism he wrote, "This natural fondness (i.e. for one's birthplace) is united with a taste for ancient customs and a reverence for traditions of the past; those who cherish it love their country as they love the mansion of their father." Something very different, according to Tocqueville, was to be found in America: "But there is another species of attachment to country which is more rational than the one I have been describing. It is perhaps less generous and less ardent, but it is more fruitful and more lasting; it springs from knowledge; it is nurtured by the laws; it grows by the exercise of civil rights; and in the end, it is confounded with the personal interests of the citizen."

No sentiment besides patriotism speaks more directly to the question of how citizens think of their country and see its purpose in the world. All states aim to survive and prosper, but their commonality ends there. The Nazis sought the triumph of what they called the "master race." The Milošević regime sought to expand the territory under the control of a particular group of people united by language, ethnicity, and religion.

And now we are confronted with a similarly nihilistic and xenophobic enemy: radical Islam. Osama bin Laden and al-Qaeda, the Taliban, Hezbollah, and their affiliate networks of global terrorists seek nothing less than a purification of the Middle East of foreign influences and a restoration of the medieval Islamic caliphate. They reject the modern notion of the separation of church and state and demand that Islamic law be the charter of all nations.

They hate the Western nations for their free and open societies, and they reserve a special hatred for America which is at the forefront of promoting and protecting the liberties they loathe.

Needless to say, the philosophical underpinnings of the United States are very different from those of radical Islam. The human rights that we cherish so highly are all but unknown in that ideology. The Taliban, which ruled Afghanistan in accord with sharia, the strict Islamic law, was exceptionally repressive. In the words of the BBC,

> Women were strongly discouraged from leaving their homes, denied schooling and jobs, and forced to fully cover themselves. Women found guilty of adultery were stoned to death, homosexuals crushed under brick walls, thieves' hands amputated and murderers publicly executed by victims' families. Edicts from Mullah Omar [the leader of the Taliban] included the death sentence for anyone converting to another religion, as well as the infamous orders to destroy the country's ancient Buddha statues at Bamiyan.

It is no wonder, then, that the American liberation of Afghanistan was a cause for celebration. Women cast off their burqas; men shaved their beards. One enterprising former burqa vendor prepared to open a video and CD store. The U.S. commitment to human rights might be unique, but wherever offered, these rights are loved and appreciated. There is a reason, after all, that when antirepressive protest movements take shape in other countries, against their leaders, they march with American symbols of democracy: with drafts of the Declaration of Independence, with papier-mâché replicas of the Statue of Liberty. We should be proud of this international achievement of symbolism and hope and we should support those movements that honor human flourishing and despise human tyranny.

When we promote human rights, however, we also promote our national self-interest. Americans believe that all men and women, by virtue of their birth, are endowed by their Creator with certain unalienable rights, and that the progress of other governments toward this ideal completes the natural order of things, even as it ensures our own safety. To put it bluntly: Nations that subscribe to the rule of law and importance of human rights tend not to be territorially ambitious; they tend not to be warmongers. They tend to enjoy the benefits of liberty and the protections afforded by their governments.

Those who argue that Americans have no business trying to advance American ideals abroad, who consider it to be hubristic, the act of an arrogant empire, either do not know their country very well, have lost confidence in their nation's leadership, or (most likely) both. After all, the history of American involvement abroad has been characterized by its generosity and humane acts. Our noblest and most consistent export has been the defense of freedom and liberty. The historical record shows, and is now being elaborated in places like Afghanistan, that time and time again America has been a liberating force from oppression. America seeks neither territorial conquest nor subjugation of others; we shirk from world domination. Behind our attempt to advance American ideals abroad has been the belief that these rights are not simply American, but rather that they are unalienable, universal, and God-given and that all people, wherever they may be, are deserving of them.

"It is a piece of idle sentimentality that the truth, merely as truth, has any inherent power denied to error, of prevailing against the dungeon and stake." So said John Stuart Mill, one of the greatest theorists of liberalism. All of which means that the citizens of democracies must be willing to support the arsenals of democracy. Talk, even right talk, counts for far less than right action. Few recent statesmen understand this fact better than Senator Lugar.

Indeed, principles alone are not enough. The real test is whether we act on those principles, or whether we fall prey to indifference, inattentiveness, or a persistent disregard for basic military and diplomatic facts. America has a tendency to "move on," to "get over it." Sometimes, this serves us well, but in the challenge we now face, moving on will be fatal. We must be willing to maintain our defenses in a manner consistent with our role in the world and the threats posed against us. In the end, our survival and the survival of all we care most about—the defense of Western civilization and the nurture and protection of our children—will depend on whether we are vigilant, strong, and committed to purpose. The president must lead us in this effort, and we the people must respond.

So long as we stay true to the principles of America's founding, our self-interest as a great power will be inextricably linked to mankind's universal interest in life, liberty, and the pursuit of happiness. The American founders clearly understood the unique character of the nation and what it could mean to the world. Two hundred years later, Reagan was able to apply their wisdom to the great challenge posed by the Soviet Union. At a critical moment in our nation's history, Reagan was the embodiment of Americans' noblest aspirations. He was an American patriot, which is to say he believed in America's destiny to be a force for good in the world. Calling the Soviet Union what it was—an evil empire—Reagan brought to bear the wisdom of Washington and Lincoln. George W. Bush follows in that path by identifying the "axis of evil," states that pose a threat to the civilized world and to the liberties of their own citizens.

George Washington's commitment to a foreign policy of "interest, guided by justice" remains the best prescription for our foreign policy in times both troublesome and idyllic. At present, the danger to ourselves and to our principles comes not from acting forcefully on their behalf but from diffidence, lack of confidence, fear, and an unwillingness to rise to the great challenges of our time. That posture will not only put us in harm's way; it is antithetical to what it means to be American.

Today, despite the devastating attacks of September 11, America sits at the summit. Our military strength is the envy of the world, and our accomplishments as a world power would elicit awe and admiration from every nation that has gone before us. America has "the command of its own fortunes," as Washington wrote in his official farewell to his young nation. It would be tragic indeed if we did not use this extraordinary, historical moment to promote the ideals at the heart of our national enterprise and, by so doing, take the steps that will ensure stability and the steady growth of freedom throughout the world.

1

Natural and Human Resources

William G. Lesher

As one thinks about America's role in the world, the foreign policy issues surrounding weapons of mass destruction, terrorism, military strength, and human rights are examples of issues that normally come to mind. Yet, as we move forward in this new century, it seems clear that for the world to be a safer and more peaceful place, its growing population must be fed and clothed in a way that is both sustainable and environmentally friendly. Stated differently, the world's natural and human resources must be mobilized in a manner to make this a reality. This is a truly daunting challenge, and one which can succeed only if the United States takes the lead. This essay focuses on the most appropriate role for the United States in meeting this challenge.

THE SITUATION

Over the last fifty years, the world's population has gone from a little over 2 billion to 6 billion. Projections are that 2 billion more will be added by the year 2025. Of the 8 billion people living on the face of the earth about 20 years from now, three-fourths will reside in developing countries, where natural and human resource problems will be severe. This is especially true for Africa, where the population will likely double by 2025—rising to 1.5 billion people. Recognizing that African food production has been declining for over 10 years and that close to 30 million children are malnourished on the continent today, the International Food Policy Research Institute called this a "building catastrophe."

It is clear that with this population growth, food production will have to more than double by 2025 if everyone is going to have enough to eat. Today, at least 800 million people are chronically malnourished, with as many as

40,000 deaths annually related to hunger. Worse yet, 80 percent of these are children. If we do not meet this challenge, the level of human suffering and death, not to mention extreme environmental degradation, will be enormous.

THE CHALLENGE

What makes this challenge so difficult is that the most productive and sustainable agricultural land is already in cultivation. Adding more land to production means cutting down rain forests and draining wetlands, causing significant environmental degradation. The habitat loss due to agriculture is the greatest threat to earth's biodiversity. According to Nobel laureate Norman Borlaug, writing recently in the *Wall Street Journal,* if we had no greater productivity than existed in food production (crops and livestock) some forty years ago, "at least half of today's 16 million square miles of global forest would already have been plowed down, and the rest would be scheduled for destruction in the next three decades."

A further reason concerns the availability of water. According to the United Nations Food and Agriculture Organization (FAO), in the next quarter century irrigated crop production will need to increase by more than 80 percent to meet future demand for food in developing countries. Water supplies, however, likely will increase by only 12 percent. It is estimated that the nonagricultural demand for water will be exponential, and that the cost of developing new sources of water will be substantial. This is not unlike the situation with farmland. The best and cheapest sources are already developed.

This tremendous challenge has not escaped some experts on food, environmental, farming, and forestry issues. Just a few months ago, on April 30, 2002, Borlaug, Greenpeace cofounder Patrick Moore, and George McGovern, former U.S. senator and ambassador to the FAO, signed a declaration endorsing high-yield farming and conservation practices. The declaration states that modern high-yield farming (biotechnology is a major component) is an "environmental and humanitarian triumph" and will alleviate the need to clear forests for food production and prevent the malnourishment of billions of people. They are urging others to join their effort. Their slogan, "Growing more food per acre leaves more land for nature," has it just right. We must meet the challenges of increased food production without placing much more land in cultivation, while more effectively using increasingly scarce water supplies for food production.

THE ROLE OF THE UNITED STATES

Knowledgeable experts have identified the situation we confront. However, more than good intentions will be required to meet the world's future food and fiber needs. What should the United States do about this impending human and environmental catastrophe?

Free Trade

As an agricultural economist, I believe in the benefits of free trade. Adam Smith laid the groundwork for free trade in talking about absolute advantage, which allows countries to produce what they are best at and to buy the rest. He argued that increasing efficiency flows from competition and specialization. This idea was challenged with the question: What would happen if one country were better at producing everything? What would happen to the other countries? Some forty years after Adam Smith, David Ricardo developed the principle of *comparative* advantage. He made the case that even though one country may be better at producing everything, countries could all be better off if they produced the product(s) they were the very best at producing and traded with other countries (even though other countries were not as efficient at producing any of the products). Incomes of each of the countries would be higher. What free trade does not do, however, is to equalize incomes when productivity differs among nations.

This brief discussion of economic theory makes the point that we should be very comfortable with the direction that freer trade will take the world. As trade barriers are reduced, economic resources are reallocated to more productive uses. This, in turn, increases income, which leads to increased demand for most products and services. As these economic forces ripple through the world economy and savings and investment increase, even further gains are made. Increased incomes are the primary reason that agriculture is impacted positively. Moreover, income increases will be greatest in developing countries—most increases will go first to greater purchases of food and clothing.

Moreover, freer trade will lead to food being produced on land that is most suitable for cultivation. One way or another, the world's growing population will be fed—either by nurturing intensive agricultural production on productive land or by ripping out more rain forests, plowing up fragile lands, and draining wetlands. Freer trade allows food production to occur primarily through more intensive farming of fertile soils. This suggests the need for a greater emphasis on agriculture biotechnology.

Can we truly achieve free trade for farm commodities and food products? The answer is "yes," but the road to freer trade through the adoption of new trade rules contains many sharp curves and large potholes. No one gives up protectionism easily, including the United States. Perhaps a bit of history will prove illustrative.

The General Agreement on Tariffs and Trade (GATT), which has evolved into the World Trade Organization, is the recognized international body for resolution of trade disputes. Concerned about high tariffs after World War II,

U.S. officials invited several nations to begin work on an international trade agreement. In 1948, twenty-three industrialized nations signed the GATT. Today, there are 144 members (the newest being China and Taiwan), with several other nations (including Russia) seeking to join. The main purposes of the GATT were to resolve trade disputes, to treat all members equally with regard to tariffs, and to negotiate lower trade barriers. The GATT was a great success for nonagricultural commodities and products as trade expanded and standards of living grew. It was under GATT auspices that the historic Uruguay Round was negotiated, the first time that food and agriculture was included on the agenda.

Before 1947, the average tariff rate for nonagricultural goods exceeded 40 percent. By 1979, when the Tokyo Round was concluded the rate for these goods was just 5 percent (the Uruguay Round further reduced these to 3.5 percent). Yet, agricultural trade did not benefit as much because negotiations under the auspices of the GATT had not disciplined agricultural trade measures as it did others. Instead, the agricultural policies that emerged after World War II were a haphazard mix that limited and distorted trade. Over the last twenty years, close to 80 percent of trade disputes have revolved around agricultural trade issues—primarily between the United States and the European Union.

Over the last thirty years, world trade has grown from $292 billion in 1970 to $6.2 trillion in 2000—a twenty-onefold increase. Yet, over the same period, world agricultural trade has grown only from $52 billion to $558 billion— less than an elevenfold increase. Paralleling this growth in world agricultural trade has been a tremendous increase in the protection that both exporting and importing countries provided for their domestic agricultural sectors.

The Paris-based Organization for Economic Cooperation and Development (OECD), in a report entitled "Agricultural Policies in OECD Countries: Monitoring and Evaluation 2002," has estimated that support provided to agricultural sectors in the industrialized countries now totals about $311 billion per year. This represents about 1.3 percent of the total OECD countries' combined GDPs. This support generally raises consumer costs, increases government involvement in the farm and food industry, and negates the role that efficient farmers can play in providing an abundant supply of reasonably priced farm and fiber products in the world marketplace. Government supports to producers accounted for about 31 percent of total farm receipts. The report goes on to say that three-fourths of support to producers is carried out in a manner which distorts production and trade.

Thus, lagging trade flows, increased consumer costs, and high budgetary costs of farm programs around the globe were the primary reasons the Uruguay Round addressed agricultural trade rules. The Punta del Este Declaration set the goals for agricultural negotiations. It stated, "Negotiations shall aim to achieve greater liberalization of trade in agriculture and bring all measures affecting import access and export competition under strengthened and more operationally effective GATT rules and discipline."

After eight long years, on December 15, 1993, 117 countries reached a historic agreement to reduce barriers to world agricultural trade in a significant way. The agriculture agreement covers four areas, including export subsidies, market access, internal supports, and sanitary and phytosanitary rules. The agreement was implemented over a six-year period, from 1995 through 2000. The Uruguay Round was the first global trade round that was positive for agriculture—primarily because it prohibited nations from increasing trade barriers and began the slow process of reducing them for the very first time.

After this round was concluded, the GATT was succeeded by a new structure called the World Trade Organization (WTO). A new round of negotiations, the Doha Development Agenda, was launched in November of last year to build on the progress of the Uruguay Round. It was a difficult round to launch, and there were significant setbacks along the way. Antiglobalization forces that aborted the launch of a new trade round in Seattle 2000 added to the inherent complications of launching so ambitious a round. This new round is to be completed by 2005, a date seen by many as overly optimistic. After all, the Uruguay Round required eight years to negotiate and six years for full implementation.

All this argues that a successful Doha Round is far from a foregone conclusion. The Europeans and the Japanese do not seem to have a great amount of enthusiasm for it, and the developing counties are expecting more than ever before. The United States must vigorously and aggressively pursue free trade in the Doha Round, or it will fail. Its negotiating position should be total elimination of all protectionist trade barriers. In return, the United States must be prepared to eliminate its own trade barriers. Such an aggressive negotiating position is more important now with the enactment of the new farm act, the Farm Security and Rural Investment Act of 2002, which continues U.S. production incentives.

Moreover, the United States should insist on speeding up the still lengthy dispute settlement process and making the cost of violating WTO rules much greater. Today, the costs of violating trade rules are not great. It takes years to finalize a dispute, and the compensation awarded is equal only to the extent of the damage. Trade infractions should be settled in a year (including all appeals) and the damages levied should be at least double or treble the damages sustained. Without tightening up the dispute settlement process, the Doha Round will fail because of a lack of confidence about the enforceability of commitments.

Even if the United States pursues this course of action, the Doha Round still may not yield results. As the old saying goes "it takes two to tango" and we may not have many dance partners. Antiglobalization forces seem to be growing while the fervor for free trade appears to be on the wane—even in the United States—leaving one to wonder if there is sufficient resolve for another successful global trade round.

To ensure that no time is wasted while negotiating this new multilateral trade round, the United States should simultaneously pursue free trade agreements through bilateral and regional trade negotiations. The members of the Asia-Pacific Economic Cooperation Council (APEC) are a top priority—APEC's members have a combined gross national product of $13 trillion and conduct 40 percent of the world's trade. Perhaps even more important would be the Free Trade Area of the Americas (FTAA) that involves 850 million consumers living in the 34 democracies of the Western Hemisphere. There are others, as well. As a matter of fact, Secretary of Agriculture Veneman frequently notes that of the more than 130 bilateral and regional trade agreements, the United States is a party to only three of them. The United States clearly needs to do much more. Perhaps over time bilateral and regional trade pacts will put pressure on other nations to negotiate a serious global trade pact.

Some suggest that more food aid is needed rather than more trade. This appeared to be the case during the World Food Summit in Rome in June 2002, as demonstrators from developed countries called for more food aid and less trade. While one can make a case for more food aid, it is not the long-term answer to reducing hunger and improving living standards. The answer is economic development and that is spurred by investment, not by donations. The United Nations Food and Agriculture Organization (FAO) estimated on June 3, 2002, that $24 billion annually would be needed for poor countries to cut hunger in half by 2015. FAO estimates that such a food aid effort would yield additional benefits worth at least $120 billion a year, resulting from longer and healthier lives.

While the benefits of such a food aid package might be significant, the costs are unrealistic and probably not sustainable. The United States is the largest single contributor of food aid today, consistently providing one-half the global total. It is not clear how much more the United States government can do, particularly over the long run. Worse yet, this does not address the self-made impediments to increased food production in the recipient countries. The International Policy Council on Agriculture, Food and Trade (IPC) suggests that in recipient countries macroeconomic and fiscal policies are biased against farmers, investment policies exclude rural areas, land-tenure is uncertain, and access to credit is limited. Many of these policies are designed to keep food prices low for politically volatile urban consumers. But, as has often been said, a cheap food policy eventually leads to a no food policy.

Biotechnology and Research

Free trade in farm commodities and food products is a necessary, but not a sufficient, condition to meet the challenges of feeding the world's population. And, food aid only offers temporary relief. Trade and aid together will not be enough; more must be done.

Agricultural research and the further development of agriculture biotechnology are important avenues to address the world food problem. The United States should provide leadership in increased research in the agricultural sciences, especially biotechnology. Strong arguments for this can be made. About 13 percent of the U.S. GDP, roughly $1.3 trillion, is comprised of the food and agriculture sector. Yet, less than 2 percent of the federal research budget goes for agriculture research. Competitive research, which is the quickest way to achieve scientific advances, is funded at less than $500 million annually. By contrast, the National Institutes of Health spend over $20 billion annually on health research.

The potential benefits from expanded agricultural research are enormous. Science has just begun to tap the vast resources of the plant world. Health benefits could be enormous. Many life-saving changes have come from plant-based sources. It is estimated that up to one-third of the prescription pharmaceuticals in the United States contain at least one plant-derived ingredient. For example, pain-relievers such as aspirin and certain major heart and chemotherapeutic compounds are derived from plants. New techniques allow for easier screening of plants for previously unrecognized compounds that have potential pharmaceutical and therapeutic value. Already this has led to the discovery of new antimalarial, anti-HIV, and anticancer compounds that are under study for uses in relieving diseases in humans and animals. The challenge is to develop plants that will produce pharmaceuticals more cheaply and efficiently.

Nutrition benefits could also be large. Providing more food per acre to feed the world will enable children to grow up better nourished and less susceptible to infectious diseases. The causes of crop loss that can be attacked by modern science include viruses, fungi, insects, drought, depleted soil, and silted soil. Vitamin and mineral deficiencies occur in developing countries. UNICEF estimates that vitamin A deficiency affects more than 100 million children and is responsible for 1 out of 4 deaths in regions where problems exist. Using plant science to increase the natural antioxidants, vitamins, and essential minerals of foods can have a direct and measurable impact on human health.

Food safety is another area that needs additional research. Plants can be made less vulnerable to disease, thereby reducing or eliminating the fungal toxins that are known to cause liver damage and other conditions. Research can also lead to the identification and elimination of unwanted substances from plants, such as natural toxins and allergens.

Sustainable agriculture would also benefit from greater research. As noted earlier, one in seven of the world's population is malnourished. While food and fiber production has greatly increased, continued growth is not sustainable without fundamental new scientific breakthroughs. Traditional plant breeding has afforded many improvements in crop yields and plant quality, to be sure. But many modern agricultural practices deplete the topsoil and cause problems in water quality. Advances in modern plant science can address these problems by providing the methods to grow better and more healthful crops for an expanding population, while ensuring good stewardship of natural resources.

Other ancillary benefits would follow from increased agricultural research. The U.S. farm economy would be more competitive. Value-added crops would increase the profitability of farms. For example, enabling farmers to grow plants that can produce new sources of inexpensive drugs and other high value-added products could supplement income from traditional products.

Despite the enormous potential benefits, achieving a significant increase in agricultural research is a major political challenge. The present approach to funding agricultural research—the annual appropriations process in the U.S. Congress—does not lend itself to optimism about increasing competitive research funding over the long term.

It is time to consider a new paradigm for research funding. The Congress should establish a National Institute of Food and Agriculture (NIFA) modeled after the National Institutes of Health (NIH). NIFA would provide competitively (peer-reviewed) awarded funds for investigation-initiated, novel, and collaborative research open to all scientists. Administratively, NIFA could be located in the U.S. Department of Agriculture (USDA) but, like the NIH, NIFA should have the authority to make independent judgments about the quality and importance of the research that it supports and to develop the mechanisms for funding that are necessary to produce the highest quality research. The director of NIFA should report to a senior USDA official.

This is not a new idea. In fact, a 1992 report of the National Research Council found that the NIH system of comprehensive support for basic biologic research has been successful and that its elements are applicable to the problems facing the plant sciences. The report concluded that a program in basic plant sciences, constructed on the NIH model, should support research and teaching to improve the competitiveness of U.S. plant science.

Moreover, the farm act approved in May 2002 requires the secretary of agriculture to create a task force to conduct a review of the Agricultural Research Service and to examine the merits of establishing a national institute for food and agriculture sciences. The task force is required to issue two separate reports no later than May 2003. The conference report states, "Together, these two separate reports should provide a roadmap for the future of the federal government concerning plant and agriculture research and the potential benefits that could be realized." This guidance presents an unparalleled opportunity for President Bush and Secretary Veneman to provide much needed leadership in both improving the quality of life for 6 billion persons and improving the natural environment globally.

Finally, agriculture biotechnology offers perhaps the most promise of all. For thousands of years people have been selecting, sowing, and harvesting seeds, as well as selectively breeding animals, to increase the quantity and quality of food. It is said that in 2500 B.C. Egyptians began to domesticate geese to make larger, tastier birds for cooking. Human progress from hunter-gatherers to modern civilization has depended on the domestication and selected breeding of plants. Nevertheless, we began to understand the science of genetics only 150 years ago when Gregor Mendel experimented with pea plants to learn that traits (genes) can be passed on through generations. This led eventually to the hybridization of seed corn that farmers began using in 1922. Corn production grew sixfold over the following four decades.

In the 1950s, James Watson and Francis Crick discovered the structure of DNA, which allowed scientists to understand how genetic information is stored in living cells, how this information is duplicated, and how it is passed from generation to generation. By the 1980s, scientists were able to move pieces of genetic information (genes) from one organism to another. Modern plant breeders can now select a gene for a specific trait and move it into cells of another plant. This ability to transfer genetic information is known as genetic engineering—or biotechnology.

Thus, we now have the ability, through modern agricultural and food science, to improve plants (there are over 300,000 kinds of plants in the world) in ways that conventional breeding cannot. Biotechnology allows very precise, efficient, and economical ways to provide solutions for tomorrow's world. In my view, we have only glimpsed the tiniest tip of the iceberg regarding the benefits of biotechnology. Thirty years from now, history will record biotechnology as a revolutionary advance.

Some of the benefits of agriculture biotechnology include:

- Improved crop yields through insect and disease resistance, and weed control (the European corn borer destroys about 7 percent, or 40 million tons, of the world's corn every year, the equivalent of enough calories for 60 million people)
- Higher vitamin and mineral content in food (as many as 100 million children worldwide suffer from vitamin A deficiency that causes blindness and some 400 million women of childbearing age are iron deficient, leading to premature births, retardation, and natal mortality)
- Higher protein foods
- Modified fats
- Longer lasting fruits and vegetables
- Significant reduction in pesticide use (according to a National Center for Food and Agricultural Policy study unveiled on June 10, 2002)

- Protection of biodiversity through intensive agriculture (not planting on fragile lands)
- Special new crops that are drought and heat tolerant and nitrogen fixing for semiarid lands and nutrient-depleted soils that farmers in the developing world routinely face
- Nutraceuticals and edible vaccines (a banana that potentially delivers the vaccine for hepatitis B for 10 cents a dose versus $200 today)
- Biofactories where plants become efficient "factories" and can be used to produce a variety of chemicals, including energy fuels and biodegradable plastics, as well as microorganisms that dispose cleanly of waste and oil spills
- Decreases in soil erosion and greenhouse gas emissions

The benefits of biotechnology can lead to feeding and clothing the world in an environmentally sound way. There is also a huge potential for the energy sector. Renewable fuels, such as alcohol from corn, are being produced now. To make a significant contribution to our energy independence, however, new grasses and other crops will have to be specifically designed for energy production so that large volumes of renewable energy can be grown efficiently on the millions of acres of marginal land in the United States. The potential for energy production and rural development is enormous. Reducing our dependence on Middle East oil is critical for American national security. The United States had its first warning in 1973–1974 with the Arab oil embargo. After a brief and inconclusive flurry of activity, that warning was largely ignored. The events of September 11, 2001, were a clarion call. This time the nation must respond. Our farmers can help.

Besides food and energy production, the benefits of biotechnology can extend to reduced water use. Over the next fifty years, water shortages for agricultural purposes will be commonplace. Agriculture is a high-volume user of water, but other demands will likely outbid farmers and ranchers in the future. The development of crops that can grow in semiarid areas will increase food production while using less water. Some estimates are that we could reduce agricultural water use by as much as 50 percent with the development of crops suited to require less water.

How can the United States play a role to help biotechnology fulfill its potential? First, the United States should fund more research. Over the last thirty years, more and more of this research has been funded by private businesses and less has been done by the federal government. I am not suggesting that private companies funding research to develop patented biotechnology crops are harmful. To the contrary; some corporations have even released important information for public researchers to use free of charge (rice genome sequence data). But there is a public-sector role for the areas of biotechnology research that corporations will not undertake. Important projects may cost too much up front or take too long to develop to satisfy corporate shareholders; yet that research may yield large, long-term dividends for mankind. The whole area of genomic mapping comes to mind. In this case, the federal government could and should play a more significant role.

Also, the United States needs to be ever-vigilant concerning the road-blocks that nations around the globe are erecting in the name of "food safety." The European Union, for example, has suspended its approval process for biotechnology crops for more than three years. Furthermore, the EU is mandating labeling and trace-back requirements that are costly and of little or no public value. Other countries like China seem to be following the European lead. These measures will not enhance food safety; they are simply blatant forms of protectionism. Unsubstantiated fears of biotechnology are often the guise to establish protectionist trade policies. In addition, the United States will need to ensure that new trade agreements that are supposed to open up trade do not become vehicles to diminish trade. For the Doha Round, the "precautionary principle" is a good candidate for such abuse. This "guilty until proven innocent" approach would permit serious trade distortions on products if any risk was alleged, not proven, about the safety of a commodity or food product.

These abuses will stifle new research and the development of new products. These protectionist measures put in place under the rubric of enhancing food safety and the consumers' right to know are nothing short of immoral. They will retard and perhaps stymie altogether advances in agricultural production that will be needed to feed the millions that will otherwise starve. The United States should combat these efforts at every turn. The United States also must press to phase out current restrictions and loopholes that militate against free trade.

In addition, global intellectual property rights must be a priority so that private corporations will continue to invest in research that will help to realize the full potential of biotechnology. U.S. consumers and farmers will not continue to pay more for pharmaceuticals and seeds and let the rest of the world benefit as free riders. If the risks involved in scientific research are not rewarded, there will be no more wonder drugs and miracle crops.

Finally, human capital is also important. In the United States, the education of producers (both formal and through USDA's Extension Service) has been a priority for over a century. This has allowed our farmers and ranchers to use technologies to maximum benefit, both because they know how to use the technology and because they are better managers of their operations.

To reduce world hunger, it is important that the issues of technology transfer and education are addressed. This is of particular importance concerning women living in Sub-Saharan Africa. Fortunately, there is growing awareness of this issue. The following is from the 2002 World Food Summit statement:

> We call on the FAO, in conjunction with the CGIAR (Consultative Group on International Research) and other international research institutes, to advance

agricultural research and research into new technologies, including biotechnology. The introduction of tried and tested new technologies including biotechnology should be accomplished in a safe manner and adapted to local conditions to help improve agricultural productivity in developing countries. We are committed to study, share and facilitate the responsible use of biotechnology in addressing development needs.

The United States should push this issue within each of the international organizations to which it belongs. It should also make certain that biotechnology education is a priority in all of its appropriate development assistance programs conducted by the U.S. Agency for International Development (AID).

SUMMARY

As a nation, we must certainly maintain our military strength. We must combat terrorism at home and abroad. But we should also realize, through careful thought and additional resources, the role food and fiber production can play in promoting world peace over the long term. In particular, freer trade, expanded research, and especially agriculture biotechnology are essential ingredients to stability over the long run. As former President Jimmy Carter has stated, "Responsible biotechnology is not the enemy: starvation is. Without adequate food supplies at affordable prices, we cannot expect world health, or peace." It is not enough to be aware of the problems of hunger and disease; these problems are well-known. At the World Food Summit in June 2002, some 182 nations renewed their commitment to reduce by half the number of hungry people in the world no later than 2015. Let us hope that with leadership from the United States, those nations go beyond rhetoric and take active steps to address these problems.

2

Leadership in the Global Economy

Chuck Hagel

American leadership is essential for global stability and prosperity. Our economic interests are directly connected to the development and expansion of a global system of open trade and investment. America's interest in promoting a more liberal world trading system not only creates economic growth at home, and among those countries with which we trade, but also reinforces our core values of democracy, transparency, and rule of law in economic and political affairs. Our economic power reinforces and complements our political and cultural power. They cannot be separated.

The benefits to the United States from trade are clear. On average, from 1980 through 2000, U.S. exports accounted for over 10 percent of the U.S. gross domestic product (GDP). From 1990 to 2000, export growth created 23 percent of all new U.S. jobs. These jobs paid 13 percent more than the average national wage. Exports of manufacturers alone support about 8 million jobs. Since 1987, over 95 percent of all U.S. firms that exported goods were small or medium-sized enterprises having fewer than 500 employees.[1]

Our trading partners also benefit from trade. They, too, find that economic integration attracts foreign resources into their economies and creates new business opportunities that increase productivity and result in economic growth. As Alan Greenspan, chairman of the Federal Reserve Board, observed, "[T]he evidence is impressively persuasive that the dramatic increase in world competition, a consequence of broadening trade flows, has fostered markedly higher standards of living in almost all countries."[2]

Economic integration also can spread openness, rule of law, integrity, democracy, and other values that Americans hold dear. Open market economic systems are strongly correlated with higher levels of economic development, technological advances, and democratic freedoms. Where there is more competition, individual opportunity, incentives, and access to customers, innovation and foreign investment follow. In the process, our trading partners learn the American way of doing business: transparency, an appreciation of markets, and respect for the rule of law.

On the other hand, in governments with command economies, opportunities and rewards focus on the government sector where political motivations and patronage networks are the primary sources of decision making and power. In this environment, bureaucratic authority is paramount and subject to abuses by officials up and down the bureaucratic scale. These societies are characterized by stifled creativity, lack of innovation, and, ultimately, political repression.

GLOBALIZATION'S DISCONTENTS

Globalization, or the expansion of international networks of interdependence, may not be new, but it has taken on the complexity of our age. In the past, the spread of Christianity and the establishment of transoceanic trade contributed to the globalization of the world community. Today, the process has taken on an even greater universality. The information and communication revolutions, the profusion of technology, and the speed and expansion of international financial flows mark a new era in the interconnectedness of our world. The state system itself has been changed through the rise of transnational actors, including multinational corporations and terrorist organizations such as al Qaeda. Traditional notions of borders and sovereignty are in transition.[3]

There are a growing number of international organizations and individuals that aim to turn back globalization and to limit economic integration. These movements include the antiglobalization protestors at the annual International Monetary Fund (IMF) and World Bank meetings, workers of industries that have lost their comparative advantage, foreign producers of goods that are barred from entering the U.S. market, and isolationists who do not value or understand the importance of U.S. assistance to developing countries.

These critics characterize globalization as either the institutionalization of American economic hegemony or the "Americanization" of world culture. Such a description misrepresents the world as it is. The globalization process is dynamic and interactive, and the United States gets as much as it gives, through trade, immigration, and culture.

That said, globalization does not ensure an equal distribution of benefits within and across countries, even in those countries that benefit from economic integration and growth. Economic dislocations within developing countries will occur as economies undergo transition and change. Political instability, unemployment, and recession are all possible outcomes of these adjustments. In meeting the challenges of leadership in the global economy, America must address the legitimate concerns of those who believe their societies and cultures are not benefiting from globalization.

DOMESTIC OBSTACLES TO ECONOMIC INTEGRATION

Critics of globalization are not only found in developing countries. Some Americans also question our role in promoting liberalization of the world trading system by questioning the benefits of free trade. The arguments they present for turning away from economic integration and freer trade include: (1) job protection, (2) national security, and (3) the desire to hold the benefits of economic integration hostage to other goals through sanctions and embargoes.

Loss of Jobs

The perception that trade diminishes U.S. jobs can create strong pressures to invoke protectionist measures. Opponents of economic integration argue that imports reduce U.S. jobs, that the United States is losing its manufacturing base, and that unfair trade practices distort competition and result in the loss of high-paying U.S. jobs. This fear of job loss fuels opposition to expand economic integration through international trade and economic liberalization. These are powerful political arguments.

National Security Concerns

The second reason often cited to justify limiting economic integration is national security. There are legitimate fears about what can be transported in cargo containers—from suitcase bombs to viruses in our foods. On the export side, controls on dual-use technologies also create potential barriers to trade in the name of national security. Countries which receive sensitive and highly sophisticated U.S. products, it is argued, may use these products against us or reexport them to third parties in volatile regions. Complicating the equation, the United States has no monopoly on many high-technology items which can be used for military as well as civilian purposes.

Sanctions and Embargoes

The third category of antitrade pressure comes from those who believe that the benefits of trade can be used as leverage to bring about changes in the policies of other countries. Economic sanctions or embargoes, it is argued, can force changes in the political, military, or human rights policies of other nations.

ADDRESSING THE DOMESTIC OBSTACLES

When Americans believe that jobs, national security, or certain rights and protections will be lost as a result of trade, they will do their best to erect barriers to economic integration. This is only natural, and these outcomes will be expressed through the democratic system. That is why it is vital to address each of these concerns directly and thoroughly.

Protecting Jobs

Misunderstanding and a lack of information among our workforce about economic integration contributes to the escalation of antitrade sentiment. Antitrade groups are able to fill this void with misinformation. Basic principles about economic integration, specifically international trade, must be shared more aggressively with the public, the media, and organizations representing workers.

The first principle is that trade is not a zero-sum game. Trade makes it possible for people in different nations—with vastly different skills and resources at their disposal—to specialize in those areas where they are low-cost producers, while trading for those items where they cannot compete as well as others. This specialization makes it possible to produce a larger total output than would otherwise be possible. In turn, the larger output allows each country to achieve a higher standard of living as more higher-paying jobs are created. This has been referred to as the rule of "comparative advantage."

The second principle is that imports are not inherently bad for the U.S. economy. Every consumer knows this. Consumers and consuming industries purchase imports because they prefer the lower cost or better quality of the imported product. Consumers are not forced to buy these products; they have choices. By paying less for a quality imported good, a consumer can spend the extra money on a good that will generate more economic growth here at home. Consuming industries use cheaper inputs to manufacture competitive products, thus strengthening the U.S. economy.

Employment losses due to the growth of imports are generally offset by employment increases in other productive activities resulting from the lower interest rates accompanying the capital flow of net foreign investment. In the 20 years of increasing imports from 1980 to 2000, U.S. export-related job growth almost doubled, from 6.8 million to 12 million jobs.[4] The overall economy benefits from more efficient systems and new technology that trade and competition produce.

Protectionism also arises from the belief that cheap imports will eventually eliminate the competing American industry. It is not quite that simple. As Adam Smith said, "If a foreign country can supply us with a commodity cheaper than we ourselves can make it, better buy it off them with some part of our own industry, employed in a way in which we have some advantage."[5] Less costly imports also create competition that propels American companies to constantly innovate and increase efficiencies.

The United States has established antidumping laws to combat serious predatory trade practices.[6] The exercise of these laws, however, can be contagious. As select industries are protected from the competition of foreign rivals, others will seek similar treatment. Moreover, foreign nations are likely to respond in kind. For this reason, common rules to address predatory trade practices are preferable to a cycle of ever-deepening protection. For example, a loud cry for protection in the 2002 farm bill arose from American farmers who face blatant trade-distorting agriculture subsidies in the European Union. If other WTO members continue to trade unfairly, antitrade sentiment in the United States will grow stronger and U.S. lawmakers will respond with our own trade-distorting laws. The elimination of trade distorting practices should be the task of the World Trade Organization.

In addition to better enforcement of WTO rules, U.S. leaders can help to build a consensus on trade by addressing the needs of those who do lose their jobs as a result of trade-liberalizing agreements. We need to deal with these job losses in the same manner that companies deal with job losses associated with technological change. The advent of the computer made the typist's job obsolete. Instead of keeping computers off the market, however, employees were retrained to do other jobs. We all know that certain labor-intensive sectors of the U.S. economy are not going to grow again. It is in our interest to educate the workers in those industries so they have skills that are useful in today's world economy. An educated workforce forms the basis of our comparative advantage. We ought to adopt policies that foster that advantage.

Businesses, unions, and government all can do more to help workers make the transition into more productive jobs. Instead of negotiating higher wages that are not commensurate with the market value of the work, unions should negotiate new programs for worker retraining. State and local governments should support forward-looking community development programs that address the economic dislocations that result from economic integration and trade. The U.S. government has a Trade Adjustment Assistance (TAA) program in place that provides temporary income support, college-level training, and health care assistance to those who lose their jobs as a result of new trade agreements. The program was expanded and overhauled in 2002 to establish new levels of support.

Protecting National Security

U.S. leaders also must address the complex linkages between national security and trade. Policies regarding cargo containers, food safety inspections, and dual-use export controls should be improved to better meet security goals and to facilitate trade. Cargo container security, for example, affects almost all U.S. trade. Last year, the world's total movement in containers amounted to 72 million TEU (twenty-foot equivalent units). The container industry is already experiencing very low profit margins because of vessel overcapacity and the demands of consolidation. Consequently, this industry will find it difficult to invest in new security devices. If governments want trade to become more secure, they may need to foot part of the bill. If we expect to detect components of a bomb in a ten-minute check of a container that has stopped in three different countries before it arrives at the U.S. border, we need more customs officials who employ technologically advanced systems.

The same is true of border controls for food and product safety. Guaranteeing the safety of food for Americans is an important national security goal. The solution is not to block imports of food. We should improve our inspection services, provide technical assistance to developing countries for their inspection services, and establish more detailed international standards on food safety within the World Trade Organization. These responses may require additional government funding. In addition, we need to educate American consumers so that they understand the scientific basis for inspection decisions.

Export controls or dual-use items should be coordinated with our allies to ensure that these technologies do not fall into the wrong hands. It is not reasonable or effective to adopt unilateral controls on dual-use technologies if our allies are selling these very same items. A coordinated export control system will ensure that truly dangerous goods are blocked, without disadvantaging U.S. producers vis-à-vis those in other friendly countries.

Economic Sanctions and Embargoes

Unilateral economic sanctions—whether they are aimed at changing policies that support terrorism, improving human rights, or toppling a regime—have a poor record of success in advancing U.S. goals. These "feel good" policies, which end up harming American producers and workers, are no substitute for serious action. For example, the United States has employed unilateral economic sanctions against Cuba and Iran to bring about change in these countries. These steps have isolated the United States and alienated the people of these countries, making them more responsive to anti-American sentiment. And they have not harmed the leadership of these countries, nor have they caused desired changes to come about. These policies have left the U.S. government without the tools or incentives to bring about desired changes in these governments.

U.S. sanctions have neither forced Cuba to open its political system nor have they encouraged a transition to democracy. Four decades is a long time to maintain a policy without success. With regard to Iran, past and present U.S. administrations have blocked discussions regarding Iranian admittance to the World Trade Organization. This decision has been a result of the U.S. policy to isolate Iran economically. Encouraging Iran to undertake the economic reforms necessary for WTO admittance is clearly in America's interest, just as it was with regard to China's admittance to the WTO. The structure and requirements of WTO compliance would force the Iranian government to make the hard choices of opening its economy and society to the requirements of a liberal global economic order. While this is put on hold because of the unilateral policies of the United States, nearly every U.S. European ally has diplomatic relations with and trades with Iran.

Other methods are far more effective at encouraging countries to embrace policies that the United States supports. Economic integration itself is likely to produce more positive reforms than are sanctions or embargoes. China offers a good example. When China opened its borders to trade with the United States under the 1979 Memorandum of Understanding, the Chinese people experienced greater contact with Americans. The improved relations between our countries and significant policy changes resulted in progress toward a more open Chinese society, while improving the lives of the Chinese people. Today, the Chinese learn about the outside world through the Internet—technology brought by foreign companies. As a result of its accession to the WTO, China worked to harmonize its laws and regulations to create a more transparent business environment. While much remains to be done, China continues to improve its implementation of these international norms and laws.

U.S. leaders can promote worker rights without using economic sanctions by sending a clear message with regard to labor standards. These messages can come from U.S. multinational corporations that invest overseas and bring improved labor practices to other countries. For example, in China General Motors (GM) has established a forty-hour workweek for all employees, prohibits child labor, and applies stringent standards for worker safety. GM's manufacturing facilities in China have surpassed 4 million hours without time lost due to an injury. GM provides extensive employee training and comprehensive health and pension plans. It also offers special benefits such as a housing fund and reimbursement for MBAs.

Stronger U.S. government support of the International Labor Organization (ILO) can also influence positive changes in policy. The ILO does not have an enforcement mechanism because its members have not reached consensus on what standards should be enforced. The ILO can facilitate better labor standards if there is strong support from member countries such as the United States. Under the May 2001 partnering program with China, the ILO provided advice on workplace safety, collective bargaining, and labor disputes. As the first project under the new cooperative program, Switzerland provided $1.9 million for an effort to improve labor-management relations and human resource policies in companies in Shanghai, Chongqing, and Dalian.[7]

The same holds true for improving environmental standards. With more support from the United States, the United Nations' Environment Program could enhance its efforts to formulate standards and technical assistance programs to help countries attain those standards. Developing countries could also be encouraged to open their markets to pollution-preventing technologies and services offered by U.S. companies.

Our goal should be to help developing countries attain political freedoms, human rights, and strong labor, environmental and governance standards. There should be no doubt about this. But requiring these nations to enforce unreachable standards or face economic sanctions is a recipe to harm the economies of both the United States and the sanctioned country, reducing rather than increasing our leverage to achieve positive change.

ADDRESSING INTERNATIONAL OBSTACLES
TO ECONOMIC INTEGRATION

To create a stronger global economy, we must also address international obstacles to trade and investment. While increased trade liberalization in poor countries is correlated with improvements in per capita income, some countries are not able to take advantage of trade liberalization because of corruption, barriers to foreign markets, inadequate internal infrastructure, and other harmful internal economic policies.

Increasing Export Opportunities

To succeed, developing nations must have access to the markets of other nations. This means opening up our markets to foreign competition. Alan Greenspan has said that "probably the best single action that the industrial countries could actually take to alleviate the terrible problem of poverty in many developing countries would be to open, unilaterally, markets to imports from these countries."[8] In that spirit, the United States has sought to negotiate bilateral free trade agreements with a number of developing countries. This work should continue. Regional trade blocs also help to encourage trade among neighboring countries. Jagdish Bhagwati, professor at Columbia University, points out that "the trade barriers of the poor countries against one another are more significant restraints on their own development than those imposed by the rich countries."[9]

Another way to increase export opportunities is to assist with infrastructure development that will directly enhance trading capabilities. Higher transportation costs and weak infrastructure explain much of Africa's poor trade performance.[10] The median transport cost for landlocked countries is 58 percent higher than the median cost for coastal countries. Poor availability of communications and energy can also constrain exports. Unreliable service can be even more damaging to competitiveness than high costs. Production stoppages, missed delivery dates, and a lack of reliable communications make it difficult to compete. U.S. agencies such as the Agency for International Development (USAID) and international organizations like the World Bank, should focus on developing infrastructure projects that enable these countries to enhance their ability to trade.

The export potential of developing countries is also limited by inadequate business community infrastructure. The World Bank funds private voluntary development organizations (PVDs) to provide business development consulting to communities in developing countries. These PVDs help to build sustainable businesses that can grow and lead to trade with neighboring countries. They also help to build local business development services that can continue consulting services when the mission leaves. Such practices help developing countries to understand how market economies work and to see the benefits of rules-based market systems. This aid also brings our aid workers into contact with people in more oppressive societies so that those societies are exposed to the norms of a country where human rights and worker rights are respected and guaranteed.

Increasing Investment Opportunities

The United States must also address the ability of other countries to absorb imports and investment. U.S. support of the efforts of the WTO to improve and enforce international norms with regard to transparency, nondiscrimination, and judicial practices in the trading regimes of developing countries moves the world toward these goals. WTO members should continue to pressure developing countries to adhere to commitments on investment and intellectual property rights protections. Foreign investment in developing nations depends on an environment that allows predictability and protection of accepted business norms. We cannot expect private investment to enter into an environment where there is no hope of financial success.

Technical Assistance

Modern economic systems are complex and sophisticated. There is a role for technical assistance to developing nations. The WTO umbrella provides some technical assistance, much of it rendered by individual member countries. The U.S. government has a role to assist in such areas as banking, agriculture, and judicial systems. Technical assistance in the areas of customs systems and tax administration is also important if developing countries are to become integrated into the competitive international economy.

Domestic Policies

Finally, developing countries need to eliminate their own high import and export barriers. These governments should lower their tariffs, especially on inputs. Bhagwati writes that "even if the doors to the markets of the rich countries were fully open to imports, exports from the poor countries would have to get past their own doors."[11] It is true that developed countries must allow the developing countries the ability to sell to them. But developing countries, too, must overcome their own internal resistances to openness if they are to succeed.

CONCLUSION

The fundamental challenges for U.S. foreign policy today are much as they have been in the past: to secure our global interests and to promote our ideals in an imperfect and dangerous world. In reflecting on the influence of Wilsonian idealism on the American experience in world affairs in the 20th century, Henry Kissinger observed:

> America found that it would have to implement its ideals in a world less blessed than its own and in concert with states possessed of narrower margins of survival, more limited objectives, and far less self-confidence. And yet America has persevered. The postwar world became largely America's creation, so that, in the end, it did come to play the role Wilson had envisioned for it—as a beacon to follow, and a hope to attain.[12]

The terrorist attacks on September 11, 2001, may cause many Americans to yearn for a seemingly less complicated and more innocent time. But, in adversity comes opportunity, and our potential to lead the world during this critical time in history calls for creativity, boldness, and vision rather than nostalgia. America has the reach, the ability, and the responsibility to help establish a consensus for economic growth and political stability throughout the world. It is our future.

Dick Lugar has embraced the imperative of American leadership in foreign affairs for twenty-five years. His leadership has caused Americans to understand more clearly the connections between our economic and military power and our democratic values. By promoting a more liberal global economic order, we promote our own interests and the interests of all peoples seeking democracy and prosperity. Dick Lugar has been the embodiment of this wise course. I have been privileged to serve with and learn from him.

NOTES

1. All statistics in this paragraph from the U.S. Department of Commerce, Bureau of the Census and the International Trade Administration's Office of Trade and Economic Analysis, June 2002.

2. Testimony before the Senate Committee on Finance, April 4, 2001.

3. See the excellent discussion of globalization in Joseph S. Nye Jr., *The Paradox of American Power* (Oxford: Oxford University Press, 2002), 77–110.

4. U.S. Department of Commerce, Census Bureau, April 2002.

5. Adam Smith, *An Inquiry into the Nature and Causes of the Wealth of Nations* (1776; Indianapolis, Ind.: Liberty Fund, 1981), 457.

6. Dumping is selling a product in another country at a price that is lower than the home production cost. Theoretically, the dumper hopes to eventually raise prices to high monopoly levels after competition is eliminated. Others argue that monopolies that charge high prices would not exist for long, if at all, because other firms would enter the market once the prices started to rise again.

7. Eric Eckholm, "China Accepts UN advice to help Labor Strife," *New York Times,* 20 May 2001, 5.

8. Alan Greenspan, Chairman Federal Reserve Board, before the Senate Finance Committee Hearing on Trade Policy, April 4, 2001.

9. Jagdish Bhagwati, "The Poor's Best Hope," *The Economist,* 20 June 2002.

10. Nuno Limao and Anthony Veneables, "Infrastructure, Geographical Disadvantage and Transport Costs," Policy Research Working Paper 2257, Development Research Group of Trade, World Bank, Washington, D.C., December 1999.

11. Limao and Veneables, "Infrastructure, Geographical Disadvantage and Transport Costs," 25.

12. Henry Kissinger, *Diplomacy* (New York: Simon and Schuster, 1994), 55.

3

Building Democratic Friends

Carl Gershman

For the United States, democracy has always been more than simply a system of governance. It has been a national philosophy and a source of national identity and purpose. Analysts of the United States, from Alexis de Tocqueville to Seymour Martin Lipset, have been consistent in pointing to the core democratic values that have shaped the unique American national character—values of equality, achievement, individual rights and responsibility, and social pluralism. The Swedish sociologist Gunnar Myrdal called this value system "the American Creed" which was the root, he wrote in 1941, of both "the American dilemma" over the unequal treatment of the black minority, and of the national feeling "of the historical mission of America in the world." That mission has been to affirm and uphold the democratic idea. "Other nations have been rich and powerful," the historian Frederick Jackson Turner wrote. "But the United States has believed that it had an original contribution to make to the history of society by the production of a self-determining, self-restrained, intelligent democracy."

Inherent in the American value system has also been the idea of universalism—the belief that all people should be treated equally, according to the same standard. This belief has naturally applied to all *Americans,* but since they were entitled to equal treatment because they were *human beings*, it implicitly has applied to all people everywhere. This was the inescapable logic that shaped the American view of society and the world.

The American mission has thus always had a universalistic dimension. From its very founding, long before the United States had the capacity to play a significant international role or to influence events beyond its immediate vicinity, the nation has had a sense of its global mission. That mission has been to enlarge, albeit gradually, the sphere of democracy in the world and to look toward a time when people everywhere would enjoy self-government and democratic freedoms.

This democratic mission has been the lodestar that has guided the United States throughout its history and shaped its world role at every juncture. George Washington saw "the destiny of the republican model of government" as "staked on the experiment entrusted to the hands of the American people," the success of which could change history by proving for all time the falsity of the contention that men were "unequal to the task of governing themselves and therefore made for a master." Abraham Lincoln appealed to the same sense of global mission in decrying the "monstrous injustice of slavery," saying that it "deprives our republican example of its just influence in the world and enables the enemies of free institutions with plausibility to taunt us as hypocrites." Woodrow Wilson called the United States into World War I to make the world "safe for democracy," and a generation later Franklin D. Roosevelt enunciated the Four Freedoms that he hoped to see secured everywhere in the aftermath of World War II. At the start of the Cold War, Harry Truman declared it the policy of the United States "to support free peoples who are resisting subjugation," and toward its end Ronald Reagan called for a campaign to affirm the American "conviction that freedom is not the sole prerogative of a lucky few but the inalienable and universal right of all human beings." And just recently, speaking at West Point about the new war against terrorism, George W. Bush said that "America stands for more than the absence of war" and would support the development of societies around the world "based on nonnegotiable demands for human dignity, the rule of law, limits on the power of the state, respect for women and private property and free speech and equal justice and religious tolerance."

While the American sense of democratic mission has remained constant throughout the country's history, it would be misleading to suggest that there have not been skeptics, such as John Adams or George Kennan, who have urged that Americans place the national interest and the health of American democracy before any desire to advance democracy in foreign societies. This view argues for a clear distinction to be drawn between a practical focus on the pursuit of self-interest in American foreign policy and a more idealistic approach that seeks to promote democratic values. But that distinction is increasingly hard to draw in a world where American interests and security are closely tied to the progress of democracy.

There is powerful evidence, for example, to support the proposition, first advanced by Immanuel Kant in his essay on *Perpetual Peace,* that there is a connection between the way a state is governed and its international behavior. States, Kant wrote, whose authority derives from the consent of the governed, and in which there is a separation between executive and legislative power, are less likely than despotisms to act aggressively in their international relations. This idea was convincingly confirmed after World War II when the former Axis powers of Germany, Japan, and Italy became peaceful democracies. And it was further reinforced decades later when the collapse of the communist systems within the Soviet bloc brought the Cold War to an end and made it possible for the United States to negotiate far-reaching arms control agreements with the noncommunist successor states.

While threats to the United States are far more likely to emanate from despotisms than from countries that are democratic or trying to become democratic, it is also true that the United States has established alliances of convenience or cordial relations with nondemocratic states in the interest of countering more despotic enemies. It allied with the Soviet Union against Nazi Germany during World War II and subsequently cooperated with a variety of anticommunist authoritarian countries during the Cold War against the Soviet Union. Today, in the war on terrorism, the United States has once again been driven to establish relations of security cooperation with nondemocratic countries.

Nonetheless, the United States will never be able to establish enduring relations of friendship with autocracies. During the Cold War, U.S. relations with such authoritarian countries as Chile and South Korea were constantly plagued by criticism of their human rights violations and policy conflicts over whether to impose economic sanctions against these countries. It was only when these and other "friendly tyrants" became democracies that it was possible to establish a consensus favoring normal and friendly relations. The U.S. faces a similar dilemma today in managing its relations with the countries with which it is now allied in the war against terrorism.

The U.S. interest in seeing democracy take root abroad extends beyond the issue of countering threats to the national security or developing friendly relations with new democracies. The U.S. also has a stake in countries becoming viable and self-reliant participants in the international system. Since "democracy has promoted growth far more effectively and consistently than any other political system," as *The Economist* has pointed out, it advances the interest the United States has in helping poor countries develop economically and become politically stable trading partners. It also provides the best governing environment in which countries can develop systems of accountability and transparency that are needed to fight the pervasive corruption that threatens their legitimacy. In addition, the inclusiveness of democracy makes it possible for countries with a high degree of ethnic diversity to manage and prevent debilitating internal conflicts.

Even if one concedes that the advance of democracy serves U.S. interests in a variety of ways, there is still the critical question of whether and how democratic institutions can be effectively promoted in foreign countries and cultures. The situation the Allies faced after World War II in Germany and Japan, when democracy could be imposed on willing countries that had been militarily defeated, was unique and is unlikely to be repeated. The challenge we face today is more complex and difficult. It is to promote democratic *development,* the process by which diverse countries throughout the world can develop the capacity for self-government and the effective management of their own affairs. Aiding such a process will take time, resources, and institutions staffed by people who have commitment and expertise. In addition, since democracy is a multifaceted political, social, and economic system, the assistance needs to take a broad approach that simultaneously addresses different aspects of the democratization process. For example, it is insufficient and potentially counterproductive to strengthen civil society institutions as a pressure on government if, at the same time, nothing is done to build effective political parties that can offer different policy options and accountable governance. It is also necessary to strengthen the rule of law and the professionalism and independence of the media, to encourage policies that foster economic growth and control corruption, and to aid decentralization and local government.

Since the end of the Cold War, these and other objectives have been served by a growing array of democracy-assistance programs sponsored by governments and multilateral agencies. A central and critically important role is also being played by international democracy foundations—publicly funded, nongovernmental agencies or party foundations committed to strengthening democratic institutions and values internationally. Such foundations, which existed only in Germany and the United States before 1989, have now been established in a growing number of other leading democracies, including the United Kingdom, Canada, the Netherlands, France, Sweden, and Australia, and including even such newer democracies as Poland. Other countries, including Ireland and Norway in Europe and Taiwan and Japan in Asia, are also in the process of establishing foundations or seriously exploring whether to do so. This overall trend reflects a new international consensus that strengthening democratic institutions and promoting good governance are indispensable to the achievement of peace and economic development. This consensus has been reinforced by the need to counter the new threat of terrorism and to meet the difficult challenge of rebuilding political institutions in Afghanistan and other war-torn countries.

The National Endowment for Democracy (NED) has been working to encourage both the development of these foundations and their collaboration in meeting common objectives. Since the NED has always taken a global and multisectoral approach to democracy promotion, it has been able to share with its new partners among the democracy foundations a comprehensive analysis of how best to strengthen democratic institutions, and it has welcomed learning about their own efforts to aid democratic movements. The NED's analysis has identified the principal barriers to the advance of democracy as well as new opportunities for democratic breakthroughs. And it has also set forth specific strategies for overcoming these barriers and taking advantage of the new opportunities. The reflections that follow draw heavily on the NED's analysis and experience.

A GLOBAL STRATEGY FOR AIDING DEMOCRACY

The countries where the barriers to democratic progress are greatest fall into three broad categories: dictatorships, semiauthoritarian systems, and war-torn countries. The problems and program needs differ from one category to the other, and there is also great variation within these sometimes overlapping categories. Dictatorships include both totalitarian and authoritarian systems, and semiauthoritarianism includes countries that are moving toward or away from full democracy, or are not moving perceptibly in either direction. War-torn countries include failed states, such as Afghanistan, that lack virtually any institutions of governance, democratic or otherwise. In addition, there is also a fourth category of transitional countries where there has been significant progress in democratization, but where democratic institutions remain weak. While programs must address the specific conditions and problems in each country, certain generalizations can be made about how to approach the group of countries that fall into each of these four categories. References to the NED's experience and goals are offered by way of illustrating the kind of role a democracy foundation can play and what can be done with relatively modest resources (the NED's current congressional appropriation is $33.5 million).

Opening Dictatorial Systems

Perhaps the most difficult challenge facing the democracy-promotion effort is to foster the opening of closed dictatorial systems. Often, these countries are ignored by democracy-assistance institutions, which require an in-country presence (and thus the permission of the host government) before they will conduct programs or provide support. The NED, as a nongovernmental organization with a policy of making direct grants to indigenous groups as well as to groups based in exile, has been able to play an effective role in these difficult situations, often at a relatively low financial cost. Its objective has been to create internal and external pressures for liberalization by aiding internal pockets of activity and linking them to like-minded groups in other countries, thereby strengthening their resolve and impact and also their international support.

NED programs in dictatorial countries place special emphasis on the defense of human rights and the provision of access to independent information, activities that are necessary first steps in opening closed societies. The principle governing such programs is feasibility. The NED presses the limits of what is possible to aid groups working to create new openings, to defend democracy activists, to develop alternative channels for the flow of information, and to promote capacity development and democratic education within the democracy movement itself as well as the wider society. If space opens up to make it possible to conduct democracy programs inside dictatorial countries with the acquiescence of the government, NED readily takes advantage of this opportunity, in accordance with its pragmatic approach. If access to the Internet is available, even if it is highly restricted, the endowment will seek to take advantage of that channel, too. The NED and its affiliated institutes also seek to build international pressure for democratic openings, as in the case of Burma, where American labor has defended the rights of Burmese workers in the International Labor Organization, and the National Democratic Institute has recruited more than 3,000 parliamentarians in a campaign of international solidarity.

NED programs in dictatorial countries thus vary along a spectrum of possibility. For example, in North Korea, which is the most closed country in the world, the NED has provided support to groups in South Korea that document the repressive conditions in North Korea and are working to build an international campaign for the defense of human rights there. In Burma, it has supported cross-border efforts from Thailand and India that provide training, education, and information to Burmese groups to help them develop their institutional capacity and their ability to communicate internally and with the international community. In Cuba, where it has become possible to support internal democratic groups, the NED has provided assistance to journalists, independent workers organizations, and cooperatives, all the while maintaining exile-based programs that defend human rights, provide uncensored information, and encourage dialogue within Cuba and in the diaspora about the political future of the country. And in China the NED has conducted an even more diversified effort, aiding both internal programs to promote democratization, worker rights, and market reform and external programs that defend human rights and provide access to independent ideas and information.

In these and other dictatorial countries, the strategy is to take advantage of any opening, however limited it may be, and to find ways to strengthen independent enclaves of democratic thought and activity. Because the struggle for democracy in such countries is especially difficult, Congress now provides special funding to expand programs in Burma, North Korea, China, and elsewhere, including programs that support the rights of Tibetans and dialogue about Tibet's political future. In all cases, a diverse, integrated, and flexible approach is taken that involves both support for internal programs, where this is possible, and to exile-based groups; and that builds international solidarity networks and campaigns in defense of human rights.

Democratizing Semiauthoritarian Countries

By far the largest and most diverse group of countries are what could be called semiauthoritarianism. This is one of many terms (including pseudo-democracy, hybrid regimes, and competitive authoritarianism) used to describe regimes that fall somewhere between dictatorship and the genuine political openness and competition of electoral democracy. A factor common to all such regimes is that the elections are not free and fair, because they are constrained and controlled by the ruling party or otherwise distorted by fraud and manipulation. In addition, such regimes tend to have an overwhelmingly dominant executive; formal democratic structures but authoritarian political culture and practices; serious human rights violations; residual authoritarian laws even where there is a new democratic constitution; and a very high level of corruption and inequality. The rule of law is extremely weak, as are the institutions of the state that are supposed to provide security and look after the social and economic needs of the people.

Ironically, these problems are the product of the democratic revolution of the past decades—or to be more precise, the *unfinished* democratic revolution. The fall of authoritarian regimes in Latin America, the Soviet bloc, and large parts of Asia and sub-Saharan Africa triggered major efforts to foster democratic transitions in scores of countries, involving the promotion of free elections, economic reform, civil society, good governance, and the rule of law. In central Europe and the Baltic countries, as well as in parts of Latin America and East Asia, these efforts produced significant results. But in the large majority of cases they came up against ingrained legacies of authoritarian culture and practice. As many transitions stalled, hopes for an inexorable forward movement toward democracy gave way to the realization that democratization is a slow and arduous process, subject to reversals, and that some variation of semiauthoritarianism, more or less harsh, is likely to persist in many former dictatorships for some time to come.

It is necessary to stay engaged in semiauthoritarian countries such as Russia, Ukraine, Kenya, Venezuela, and Morocco, whose success or failure will significantly affect the prospect for democratic development in their respective regions. The challenge is to craft a comprehensive multisectoral response that seeks not just the strengthening of civil society and independent media, but also political parties that can build effective governing coalitions, as well as business associations, trade unions, and policy institutes that can mediate between the state and the market and effect real economic reform.

In working to promote democratization in semiauthoritarian countries, it is important to bear in mind the need to:

- assist efforts to establish neutral, independent, and effective election administration and to assist civil society organizations and the mass media in monitoring the conduct of elections

- work to expand the constitutional, legal, and political space for civil society, Nongovernmental organizations, and opposition political party development
- establish linkages between civil society and political parties, and also promote collaboration between them and independent media, trade unions, business associations, and the grassroots informal sector
- develop practical strategies with feasible objectives, focusing on building up subcultures of democratic activism that try to achieve incremental gains, but that can also provide leadership if and when opportunities arise for more substantial breakthroughs
- encourage cross-border assistance within regions as a way of strengthening democratic cooperation and solidarity, sharing relevant experiences, building on local momentum for change, and promoting regional integration and the gradual enlargement of democratic practice
- develop independent and effective institutions—including the judiciary, the central bank, a public auditing agency to monitor government expenditures, and the electoral commission—that can provide "horizontal accountability," control corruption, and have the authority to resist political manipulation.

Consolidating New Democracies

In many countries, democratic institutions have been established only recently and are still very weak, and there is broad support within and outside the government in favor of deepening democratic consolidation. In such emerging democracies as Thailand, Mexico, Bulgaria, Ghana, or Bangladesh, democracy cannot be taken for granted and backsliding is an ever-present possibility (one need only remember the complacency about Venezuelan democracy just a decade ago). It is important, therefore, not to neglect such countries, even as resources and energies are concentrated primarily on countries where democracy is less advanced. In doing so, it is necessary to pay close attention to the problems of governance, working to make governments more accountable and transparent in their functioning; generating, supporting, and sharing innovative solutions to problems of consolidation; increasing broad-based participation in the political process; and strengthening the capacity and transparency of political parties.

The consolidation of these emerging and vulnerable democracies is especially important at a time when progress has stalled on so many other fronts. Models of successful transition help lift the spirit of those trying to break out of semiauthoritarianism. They also offer practical lessons in how to overcome the obstacles to making democratic institutions effective. No one is more capable of transmitting these lessons than the activists from newly consolidated democracies. Their contribution to those still struggling against the legacies of authoritarianism is one of the less appreciated by-products of successful transitions.

Healing War-Torn Societies

In many regions, the political uncertainties unleashed by the end of the Cold War and the pressures of globalization have led to the breakdown of old political structures and to heightened religious and ethnic conflict. While the wars in the Balkan region have attracted the most attention, many conflicts in such countries as Somalia, Sudan, Democratic Republic of Congo, and Afghanistan have been even more devastating.

Efforts by the international community to negotiate solutions to such conflicts are generally limited to holding talks among leaders of different ethnic, religious, or tribal factions. But peace agreements will not last unless civil society is brought into the process and becomes invested in negotiated solutions through an inclusive democratic process. Including civil society groups also has the effect of diluting the influence of the autocratic leaders of armed factions who would otherwise dominate the negotiations.

In many of these situations, the NED has been able to provide critically needed support to groups in civil society that defend human rights, educate about democracy, and provide training in conflict resolution. Often, these groups use innovative techniques, including popular theater and concerts as well as traditional media, to build trust and nurture a culture of tolerance. Regrettably, while such groups play a significant role in the Sudan and other war-torn countries, they are largely ignored by the international community and press, which focus exclusively on the warring parties. Nonetheless, these groups are able to establish enclaves of democratic values and interethnic dialogue and become centers of grassroots pressure for peace and reconciliation. They also help marshal international support for democracy assistance and the defense of human rights. If negotiations are started, they can then give voice and representation to civil society in the process of establishing peace. In a postwar setting, they can also help the process of healing and offer an alternative model and vision of democratic social and political organization.

AIDING DEMOCRACY IN THE MUSLIM WORLD

The Muslim world is a vast region that consists of more than 1 billion people and stretches some 10,000 miles from Morocco to Indonesia. It is an immensely diverse region politically, composed of countries that fall into all of the categories listed above—from dictatorships such as Iraq, Syria, Saudi Arabia, and Turkmenistan; to semiauthoritarian countries like Pakistan,

Egypt, or Tunisia; to electoral or emerging democracies such as Turkey, Mali, Indonesia, and Bangladesh; and to war-torn countries like Algeria, Sudan, Somalia, and Afghanistan. Fully one-eighth of the world's Muslim population lives as a minority in democratic India.

While recognizing this diversity, there are three principal reasons for highlighting the importance of aiding democracy in the Muslim world. First, there is a significant "democracy gap" between the Muslim world as a whole and the rest of the world. According to the latest Freedom House Survey of Freedom in the World, only 11 of the 47 countries (23 percent) with a Muslim majority have democratically elected governments, as compared with 110 of the 145 non-Muslim countries (76 percent); and none of the 16 Arab states is an electoral democracy. Second, it is also within the Muslim world that democracy is under political and ideological challenge from Islamic movements that preach intolerance and hatred. Such movements may not be broadly representative of the population in the countries where they exist, but their influence is considerable. Finally, since such movements often resort to violence to achieve their ends, it is within the Muslim world where the absence of democracy has provided fertile soil for the growth of terrorism that targets the world's democracies.

The crisis precipitated by the attacks of September 11, 2001, and the new war on terrorism have placed the issue of democracy in the Middle East and in other nondemocratic parts of the Muslim world on the agenda of the international community. Before the present crisis, democracy was often viewed as a Western system incompatible with Islamic culture and doctrine. The fear that Islamic fundamentalists might take advantage of democratic elections to impose a theocratic system, and the absence in the Middle East of discernible prodemocracy movements, discouraged efforts to support democratic development in authoritarian Muslim countries, especially those ruled by regimes ostensibly committed to protecting significant Western security and economic interests.

Not surprisingly, political repression has helped inflame religious extremism by forcing dissent into the mosque. The rise of terrorism and the widespread realization that such extremism is connected to the failure of political institutions in many Muslim countries have led to a growing recognition that efforts must be made to encourage political and economic modernization in the Arab Middle East and elsewhere in the Muslim world where it is lagging. Accompanying this new attitude is a sharpened clash within Muslim countries themselves between Islamic fundamentalists and moderate elements, both secular and religious, which are prepared to challenge the attempt by extremists to seize control of Muslim society and Islamic faith. For these moderates, democratization has become a matter of sheer survival.

They face four interrelated challenges. The first is to liberalize the political system, ending repression and human rights violations, permitting freedom of expression and association, and introducing genuine party contestation. The second is to modernize the state and the economy, so that meaningful steps can be taken to reduce poverty, ignorance, and inequality and to provide young people with opportunity and hope. The third is to control corruption and establish a genuine rule of law. And the fourth is to end the political abuse of religion and to reconcile Islam—the framework in much of the Muslim world for political and social activism—with modern concepts of pluralism, citizenship, and individual rights.

It cannot be emphasized too strongly that the precondition for progress on any of these fronts is a new birth of will and determination within the Middle East and other nondemocratic parts of the Muslim world to strive for human rights, free institutions, and responsible, elected government. But having said that, it is also true that international support can make a crucial difference. It is needed from a practical standpoint, and it also sends the message that democratic activists in Muslim countries are not alone.

The NED, with its multisectoral structure and the emphasis it has always placed on encouraging democratic values and ideas, has the capacity to provide help in all four areas. For example, the NED's affiliated party institutes work with moderate political leaders, legislators, and parties in Muslim countries, seeking new openings to improve party communications and outreach, to encourage women's participation in politics, and to promote contacts and exchange among Muslim parties and between them and the major international bodies representing parties from around the world. The NED's business institute promotes good governance and economic reform by strengthening private voluntary business associations and think tanks as advocates of open markets, legal and regulatory reform, transparency, sound corporate governance, and a stronger role for women in the economy. NED supports a wide array of grassroots organizations in the Middle East that defend human rights, train women to become leaders in politics and civil society, and promote civic education and women's rights in the context of Islamic texts and traditions. The NED's labor institute trains union organizers to defend the rights of workers and the poor.

The NED and its core institutes see the importance of involving in their programs liberal Muslims—individuals who work within the Islamic tradition and who are also in favor of liberal democracy—as a way of strengthening these elements and countering the political abuse of religion. Many NED country programs (and also regional and subregional programs) already involve devout Muslims who are committed to liberal values. Such programs can be expanded in the Middle East and, where appropriate, in parts of Asia and Africa to strengthen existing networks of liberal Islamic thinkers and develop new ones; to promote a public discourse on Islam and democratic politics; and to develop civic education programs that provide a modernist treatment of the role of Islam in public life.

It is also important that focus be given to the dissemination of firsthand accounts and systematic analyses of life in Iran, Sudan, and Afghanistan under the Taliban, the three contemporary examples of theocratic dictatorships. Conversely, there are positive lessons to be learned from the experiences of Turkey, Bangladesh, Mali, Senegal, Bahrain, and other contemporary examples of Muslim countries where democratization has progressed. Where appropriate, efforts should be made to include in these networks and discussions Muslims living in western Europe and North America, whose experience of democracy may significantly influence Islamic political thought.

Expanding women's leadership training programs is critically important for the promotion of democracy in Muslim countries. Empowering women at the grassroots level and promoting their enhanced participation in the political and cultural life of Muslim societies are preconditions for democratic progress. Programs are underway to develop women's leadership capabilities in the Arab Middle East, Africa, and Central Asia and, when feasible, in Iran and Afghanistan as well. Various types of media can be employed to reach larger numbers of women in Muslim countries.

BUILDING A NEW PARTNERSHIP FOR DEMOCRACY

Obviously, the agenda outlined here is extremely ambitious. The NED and its affiliated institutes can help advance this agenda, but the involvement of many other institutions and agencies from the United States and other countries will also be needed. A comprehensive strategy will require three different kinds of collaboration among those working to advance democracy.

The first is between democracy-support institutions in the advanced democracies and groups and individuals who are working for democracy in countries throughout the rest of the world that fall into the four categories mentioned above—authoritarian, semiauthoritarian, transitional, and wartorn countries. As already noted, this cooperation now exists in the form of a growing number of democracy-assistance programs that the established democracies fund in Asia, Africa, Latin America, central Europe, the former Soviet Union, and the Middle East. While these programs vary greatly in their scope, focus, and effectiveness, together they constitute what amounts to a new field of international assistance, one that has developed only recently since the end of the Cold War.

As with any new field of activity, there are still many issues that need to be worked out. For example, there is a tendency to see democracy aid as just another form of development assistance. Yet, democracy aid cannot side-step sensitive issues of politics, values, and culture, nor can the established democracies seek to impose or export their own values and culture. Rather, they have to engage with democrats who are authentic representatives of the political cultures in the democratizing or nondemocratic countries. Moreover, they must do so in ways that do not compromise—but rather respect and strengthen—the independence and effectiveness of these democrats. Often, this means that the best programs are carried out through nongovernmental channels and support grassroots efforts to achieve change as opposed to funding top-down social-engineering projects or creating nongovernmental organizations that are more responsive to Western donors than to indigenous needs. Most of all, it is important to remember that democracy assistance works best as an equal partnership between people who share common values, not as a relationship between donors and beneficiaries. Such a partnership helps build not only democracy, but also enduring relations of friendship.

The second form of collaboration is within and among the regions where democracy is weak or nonexistent. The most important example of such collaboration is what has been called "cross-border assistance," whereby veterans of successful democracy struggles provide aid to movements working for democratic breakthroughs in neighboring countries. The origins of such assistance can be traced to surreptitious meetings along the border between Poland and Czechoslovakia that were organized in the 1980s by the Polish-Czechoslovak Solidarity Foundation. Following the breakthrough in Poland, the foundation continued to reach out to allies in Czechoslovakia and later in Ukraine, Belarus, the Balkans, and other areas farther east. The collaboration grew as other Polish groups joined in, as did groups in the Czech and Slovak Republics and other central European countries. During the run-up to the pivotal 2000 elections in Yugoslavia, which saw the defeat of Slobodan Milošević, these groups were joined by Croatian activists who spearheaded a breakthrough in their own country the previous year. And activists from Poland, Ukraine, Lithuania, and Russia provided training and other forms of assistance in Belarus during the September 2001 elections there.

While cross-border assistance is most developed in central Europe, it can also be found in other regions. For example, activists with the National Movement for Free Elections in the Philippines, whose successful battle for fair elections led to the defeat of Ferdinand Marcos in 1986, helped support free elections in other Asian countries. These and similar efforts by Asian democrats led to the creation of the Asian Network for Free Elections, a Thailand-based coalition of twenty-one organizations from eleven Asian countries that monitors elections and aids democrats throughout Asia. A similar coalition exists within the Southern Africa Development Community. There are also regional human rights coalitions, such as the Forum Democracy Asia that links human rights defenders from Vietnam, China, Burma, Laos, and Tibet with members of the European Parliament.

The World Movement for Democracy (WMD), an initiative the NED helped launch in 1999, is probably the most comprehensive effort to promote networking and collaboration within and across regions. The WMD promotes three different kinds of networks: regional, functional, and thematic. The regional networks link activists working in different fields (such as political parties, unions, NGOs, research centers, and business associations) within the major geographical regions of Africa, Asia, Latin America, the Middle East, central Europe, and Eurasia. The functional networks link activists from different regions who work in the same field, such as local government or research. And the thematic networks strengthen multiregional collaboration on particular problems or challenges, such as opening dictatorial systems, fighting corruption in party financing, resolving ethnic conflicts, and helping democracy activists make better use of the new communications technologies in their work. The WMD is not a new international organization as much as it is a network of networks, a loose association that facilitates communication and cooperation among the immensely diverse and highly decentralized groups working for democracy throughout the world.

Such collaboration reflects the natural desire among democracy groups to support each other and strengthen their overall impact, a tendency that has been reinforced by globalization and the increased availability of communications technologies that help democrats build linkages and share experiences and information. In part, this desire is an expression of the spirit of democratic solidarity, and of the obligation felt by those in movements that have achieved significant breakthroughs against authoritarian regimes to aid activists still battling authoritarianism. It also reflects the realization that the survival of fragile new democracies depends on the advance and strength of democracy in neighboring countries and beyond. Polish groups have come to this realization from their country's experience during the last century, when it was a victim of aggression carried out by neighboring totalitarian states. But it appears that even many democrats who have not had a similar historical experience nonetheless possess an instinctive grasp of the idea that a democracy cannot exist as an island in a sea of authoritarian and unstable regimes. Democracy's well-being depends on a supportive international climate and neighbors who respect human rights and the rule of law.

The third and final form of collaboration that needs to be strengthened is among the advanced democracies themselves, in particular the transatlantic cooperation between Europe and the United States. The division between Europeans and Americans has many causes, not the least of which is the end of the Cold War and the disappearance of the Soviet Union, which was a unifying common enemy. While the United States and Europe have cooperated in fighting the war on terrorism, this new war has also sharpened European criticism of what they regard as growing U.S. unilateralism in international affairs. The Europeans have particularly objected to President Bush's State of the Union Address in which he labeled Iraq, Iran, and North Korea as part of an "axis of evil," and also to administration statements that it might take preemptive military action to overthrow the regime of Saddam Hussein in Iraq. But the disagreements are actually more profound and pervasive.

In a provocative essay on the U.S.-European divide, Robert Kagan has written that Europeans and Americans no longer share "a common view of the world." The Europeans, he writes, "believe they are moving beyond power into a self-contained world of laws and rules and transnational negotiation and cooperation," whereas the United States believes that "security and the promotion of a liberal order still depend on the possession and use of military might." Kagan traces the division to the vast and growing discrepancy in military power between the United States and Europe and observes that whether the Europeans like it or not, their "Kantian order depends on the United States using power according to the old Hobbesian rules." Even if one feels that the U.S.-European divide derives from factors other than simply American strength and European weakness—there have been sharp disputes, for example, over trade and the Kyoto Treaty on the environment—Kagan is correct in concluding that today Americans and Europeans "agree on little and understand one another less and less."

It seems especially important, therefore, that the United States and Europe seek ways to moderate their disputes by finding areas where they can strengthen their cooperation. Kagan writes that the United States "should honor multilateralism and the rule of law where it can, and try to build some international political capital for those times when unilateral action is unavoidable." Beyond such gestures, the United States and Europe should seek to build on the fact that they share a common Western tradition, at the heart of which are such fundamental concepts as individual freedom, democratic self-government, and the rule of law. They also share a common interest in promoting these values in the world. Even if they disagree on the importance of military strength in the defense of democratic values, they do not differ on the need to aid democracy through programs that strengthen the institutions of self-government and the rule of law. Deepening cooperation in this area is an important way to prevent Europeans and Americans from drifting too far apart over contentious issues of security and trade.

Democracy is not a cure-all. The fact that democratic countries do not, as a rule, go to war with each other does not mean that they will always agree or that their relations will always be amicable. As the world becomes increasingly democratic, disagreements will also proliferate among the democracies which will inevitably have different priorities and interests on a variety of issues. Still, support for democracy itself will remain an enduring area of agreement, and working together to encourage its spread offers a twofold advantage: it will both magnify the support given to democratic movements and strengthen the friendship among democratic allies. As we embark on what will surely be a long and difficult struggle against terrorists who are the enemies of democracy, it is important not to forget who are our friends and what the values are that hold us together, despite our disagreements and occasionally strained relations. These are blessings that we would do well to count.

4

Fashioning a Bipartisan
Foreign Policy

Lee H. Hamilton

Few words in politics are bandied about, and paid lip service, as much as bipartisanship. All politicians recognize that, like freedom or prosperity, its approval ratings approach 100 percent. Yet, translating rhetorical support for bipartisanship into practice can be extremely difficult. Politicians usually define bipartisanship as members of the opposing party following their lead. Although Americans have consistently said that they want their elected officials to work across party lines, the nation's politics have been excessively partisan in recent years.

American foreign policy always has more force and punch to it when the nation speaks with one voice. When the president and members of Congress work with the opposing party and take its views into consideration, the policy that results is more likely to be well designed and to have strong public support. And foreign policy with strong domestic support makes the United States more respected and effective abroad.

Congress has a special responsibility to develop a bipartisan foreign policy because its primary task is to produce consensus out of the many views and concerns of the American people. In a nation of our vast size and remarkable diversity, making policy is a tough and tedious job. All of our nation's ethnicities, religions, regional interests, and political philosophies bring their often-conflicting perspectives to Congress. It is the job of the House and Senate to give the various sides a chance to be heard and to search for a broadly acceptable consensus. Developing consensus can be arduous and exasperating, but it is the only way to produce policies that advance America's national interests and reflect the many perspectives of our diverse citizenry.

The founders of the United States spent much time considering how to encourage government to pursue the national interest rather than personal or special interests. Thomas Jefferson, in his first inaugural address, urged Americans "to unite in common efforts for the common good," and John Adams once wrote that policymakers should maintain a "disinterested attachment to the public good, exclusive and independent of all private and selfish interest." Thinking about the good of the country is the job of Congress as much as it is the job of the president and the Supreme Court. The best members of Congress, like Senator Richard Lugar, ask themselves constantly not what is good for them, but what is good for the nation.

THE BIPARTISAN APPROACH OF SENATOR LUGAR

For a quarter-century, Senator Lugar has developed foreign policy in a constructive and bipartisan manner. I had the opportunity to work with him on many foreign policy and national security issues, and was always impressed that he approached policy challenges from the perspective of the American national interest and sought to forge bipartisan consensus wherever possible. Whether the issue is trade, economic sanctions, or safeguarding nuclear weapons, he considers issues in a dispassionate and thoughtful manner, and works with Democrats and Republicans to craft sound policies.

Three important issues illustrate Dick Lugar's bipartisan approach to foreign policy: (1) U.S. policy toward the Philippines following the 1986 presidential election in that country; (2) the enactment of economic sanctions on South Africa to oppose apartheid; and (3) the development of the Cooperative Threat Reduction Program, popularly known as the Nunn-Lugar Program. On each of these key issues, Senator Lugar reached out to Democrats and to the administration to formulate a policy that best advanced the interests of the nation.

In February 1986, Senator Lugar took a congressional delegation to the Philippines to observe the election pitting authoritarian President Ferdinand Marcos against the upstart challenger Corazon Aquino. Senator Lugar and others concluded that Marcos was trying to steal the election and had orchestrated widespread vote fraud. Concerned that the Reagan administration might recognize a Marcos victory, Senator Lugar worked with other members of Congress, including key Democrats, and members of the administration to develop a policy that would encourage President Marcos to give up the presidency. The administration subsequently conveyed to Marcos that the United States would no longer support him, and he left power peacefully, culminating the Philippines' remarkable democratic transition.

Senator Lugar also played a central role in the mid-1980s in the development of American economic sanctions against South Africa. Although he has generally been a strong supporter of free trade, he concluded then that the United States should not trade with South Africa because of its repressive and unjust apartheid system. Senator Lugar led congressional efforts to craft far-ranging sanctions on South Africa, which were opposed by President Reagan, by working with Democrats and Republicans in both houses of Congress. His leadership was instrumental in building congressional support for the sanctions, leading to their landmark passage in 1986. The sanctions dealt a serious blow to South Africa's white minority-ruled regime and helped to pave the way for a majority-backed government, led by Nelson Mandela, to take power a few years later.

More recently, Senator Lugar has worked with former Democratic Senator Sam Nunn to create the Cooperative Threat Reduction Program, which has provided critical assistance over the past decade for dismantling and safeguarding weapons of mass destruction in the former Soviet Union. Following the end of the Cold War, Senator Lugar recognized that the United States had a vital opportunity to protect America's national security by moving U.S. nuclear policy from a policy of deterrence and mutually assured destruction with the Soviet Union to a policy of nonproliferation cooperation with the Soviet successor states. Beginning with an initial appropriation of $400 million in 1991, the so-called Nunn-Lugar Program has provided critical assistance for the removal of all nuclear weapons from Ukraine, Kazakhstan, and Belarus, and for safeguarding thousands of Russian-controlled nuclear warheads. The program, which continues to garner bipartisan support, helps address the most urgent security threat facing the United States: the danger that nuclear weapons or materials in the former Soviet Union could be stolen or sold to terrorists or hostile nations and used against Americans at home or abroad.

OBSTACLES TO A BIPARTISAN FOREIGN POLICY

Senator Lugar's achievements in foreign policy are all the more impressive when one considers the many obstacles to the development of a bipartisan foreign policy. The obstacles include: the complex world environment; the partisan atmosphere in Washington; the diffusion of foreign policymaking power in Congress; and the impact of domestic concerns, special interest groups, and the media on the foreign policy process.

With the world changing at such a rapid pace, it can be difficult for the president and members of Congress to shape a national consensus about the purpose of American foreign policy. During the Cold War, developing consensus on foreign policy was relatively easy because the battle against communism clearly defined American national interests and priorities. Today, however, security threats are more diffuse, and economic issues have greater prominence. Instead of facing one superpower with thousands of nuclear weapons, we confront complex threats from states and nonstate actors, including terrorism, proliferating weapons of mass destruction, information warfare, and international drug trade and organized crime. Additionally, the American national interest in many countries or issues is frequently complex and difficult to define. In some nations, such as China, we have so many interests that some of them conflict with others. In such cases, there is often a lack of consensus on what U.S. policy should be, complicating the task of uniting the president and Congress behind American policy.

Increased polarization and partisanship in recent years have also made it more difficult for Congress to speak with one voice in foreign policy. In the 1950s and 1960s, there was a powerful bipartisan, centrist contingent of members of Congress that shared a similar internationalist outlook and often voted together on key foreign policy issues. Since then, there has been an ideological divergence between the Republican and Democratic caucuses, accompanied by decreasing bipartisan cooperation and more bickering. Many members now view foreign policy as nothing more than an extension of American domestic politics, and frequently use foreign policy issues to further their domestic political interests, sometimes by attacking their opponents, rather than to advance the national interest.

The media's often negative, cynical, and adversarial coverage of politics helps to fuel incivility and partisanship in Congress. The media encourage policymakers to take controversial stances by focusing on political conflict more than foreign policy analysis. A member of Congress does not get onto television by agreeing with, or explaining, American foreign policy. He or she gets attention by accusing the administration or opponents in Congress of selling us up the creek.

Additionally, the growing influence of special interest groups makes it difficult to develop bipartisan consensus. The halls of Congress are filled with representatives of countless interest groups everyday—from the business community and labor unions to ethnic constituencies and nonprofit organizations. Their overall impact has grown markedly in recent decades, leading more members of Congress to advance parochial concerns, sometimes at the expense of the national interest. Many members of Congress rely on interest groups for critical financial contributions and as a means to reach blocs of voters, and that reliance can complicate the challenge of developing a foreign policy that advances the common good.

Changes in the internal dynamics of Congress have further complicated the task of developing a bipartisan foreign policy. Power in Congress on foreign policy issues has become more diffuse in recent decades, as the main foreign policy committees have lost influence to a variety of other committees, from appropriations to government affairs, and to individual members advancing specific causes. Power is diffused even more through the growing tendency to form ad hoc congressional caucuses on issues such as trade, terrorism, or the environment. This fragmentation of power has made it all the more difficult for Congress to fashion foreign policy consensus.

HOW TO OVERCOME THE OBSTACLES

It is not easy to overcome these obstacles to the development of a bipartisan foreign policy, but, as Senator Lugar has often shown, it can be done. Some of the obstacles, of course, such as the behavior of the media, are beyond the control of an individual politician. But there are several steps the president and members of Congress can take to shape a strong foreign policy with broad, bipartisan support.

Presidential Leadership

First, the president must demonstrate strong presidential leadership in foreign policy. His leadership and direction is the most important ingredient for foreign policy success. The president is the most important foreign policymaker. Only he is accountable to, and speaks for, all Americans, and only he can rally public support to a foreign policy cause. Moreover, while Congress plays an important role in the formulation of foreign policy, the president is responsible for its implementation. So, the United States can achieve little internationally without strong presidential leadership.

What must the president do to be an effective leader in foreign policy? Above all, he must make foreign policy a priority, decide on which foreign policy issues to focus, and formulate a broad strategic vision. He must then explain his goals to Congress and the American people, articulate his policy proposals clearly, and specify what kinds of resources he wants to expend on them.

The president must work hard to rally Congress and the nation behind his foreign policy by educating the American people about the important international challenges that we face. He must begin the education process at the outset of his term and keep at it until his final day in office. This cannot be done solely in interviews and press conferences. Presidential speeches are essential.

The president must also work closely with Congress to develop bipartisan consensus. To foster that consensus, the president must reach out to Congress and consult with it regularly. Sustained consultation fosters mutual trust between the president and Congress and helps prevent them from taking U.S. foreign policy in different directions. Although consultation does not—and should not—ensure congressional support for the president's proposals, it does help remove some of the hard edges of disagreement, and it almost always strengthens and refines policy.

To consult effectively, the president must involve both parties in Congress in the policymaking process. Consultation should take place, to the greatest extent feasible, prior to administration decisions, not after they have already been made. Administration officials should take the perspectives of Congress seriously and respond to congressional concerns. Consultation works best when the president and other high-level officials are personally involved.

Congressional Partnership

A second critical ingredient for a bipartisan foreign policy is constructive congressional partnership. Members of Congress should be independent critics of the president, but that criticism should always aim to improve U.S. policy. Within the institution of Congress, members must work with representatives and senators of the other party to develop consensus on tough foreign policy issues.

Although Congress sometimes acts irresponsibly in foreign policy, it can—and often does—play a constructive role. Congress brings many strengths to the foreign policy process. As the most representative branch of government, it reflects like no other institution the diverse views of the American people. Congress can mediate the various perspectives of Americans and help to shape them into a consensus.

Congress is also the most accessible branch of government. Ordinary Americans cannot easily reach policymakers in the executive branch, but they can contact their representative or senator, and expect at least to be listened to. That accessibility keeps Congress in touch with the American people and helps ensure that foreign policy reflects their concerns.

Additionally, Congress can usually help to refine policy. The president may not always appreciate having 535 national security advisors, but congressional advice is often constructive and helpful. Since members of Congress do not serve at the president's pleasure, they are in a better position than his aides to offer unvarnished criticism of his policies. Congress can also play a useful role by forcing the president and top administration officials to articulate and explain policy, and by helping the president educate the American people about foreign policy challenges.

Just as it is critical for the president to reach out to members of Congress and consult with them regularly, members of Congress must be receptive to consultation from the executive branch. They must strike the right balance between responsible criticism, based on measured oversight of the executive, and responsible cooperation. Members of Congress should encourage consultation by attending administration briefings and displaying consistent interest in foreign policy.

Mechanisms should be put in place to ensure that good consultation and bipartisan policymaking occurs. In 1993, I joined several other members of the House in introducing a bill to establish a consultative group of congressional leaders that would meet regularly with the administration's top foreign policy officials. Such a group—made up of the leaders of the House and Senate and the chairmen and ranking members of the main foreign policy committees—would provide a forum for foreign policy discussion and for dissemination of appropriate information to other members. It would help Congress to develop a consensus approach to foreign policy issues that gains bipartisan support.

Build on Areas of Agreement

The third key ingredient of a bipartisan foreign policy is for Congress and the president to build on the broad areas of agreement in American foreign policy. Despite significant disagreements over tactics and specifics, there is a great deal of consensus around several central foreign policy principles and objectives. The president and Congress should work to solidify and expand public support and congressional coalitions around these core ideals and goals. From that solid base, they can branch out to develop consensus on more specific or controversial issues.

The fundamental principle that should guide American foreign policy is that U.S. engagement and leadership are essential to promote American national interests. Most Americans recognize that the United States has a special responsibility and a special opportunity to make the world a better and safer place—by marshaling the forces of peace and progress, combating international terrorism, extending the benefits of the global economy, and strengthening democratic ideals and practices. At the same time, the president and members of Congress must be sensitive to the limits of our involvement. Our engagement must be selective, closely tied to our interests and opportunities.

Congress and the president should also recognize that we must strike the right balance between leadership and partnership. If we attempt to impose our policies on other nations, we run the risk of encouraging a backlash against us. So the challenge for U.S. leadership is to use America's power to develop an international consensus that is consistent with American values and objectives. National political leaders should follow the sound instincts of Americans, who generally prefer multilateral efforts to unilateral ones by overwhelming margins.

While we must be willing to act alone when our interests demand it, we should strongly support allies and international institutions that help us bear the burdens of leadership. If we do not consistently engage our friends and allies, we may be blissfully free, but we will also be alone and ineffective. America's genius over the past half-century has been in building international institutions—such as the United Nations, the International Monetary Fund, and NATO—that advance U.S. interests through multilateral cooperation. We must lead multilaterally whenever we can, and unilaterally only when we must.

The president and Congress should focus on America's four most important relationships—those with Europe, Japan, China, and Russia. This is exceedingly hard to do because foreign policy crises constantly pop up and distract our political leaders' attention. Yet much of what we want to achieve in the world requires cooperation with other major powers.

The president and Congress should keep our alliances in Europe and Asia—our most important international partnerships—at the center of our foreign policy. In Europe, we should maintain our military leadership and commitments in NATO, while expanding that organization to take on new members and new tasks, and we should encourage European efforts to develop a common security and foreign policy. In Asia, we should reinvigorate our key alliance with Japan, deepen our ties with India and Pakistan, maintain our military and political commitments on the Korea Peninsula, and continue our support for a democratic Taiwan. We must work with our friends and allies in Europe and Asia to root out terrorist networks, in places ranging from Central Asia to the Balkans.

The United States should also continue to build more constructive relations with our former adversaries, Russia and China. One of the big questions that will shape the international environment in the twenty-first century is: How will Russia and China define their roles in the world? Will they seek to control their people and dominate their neighbors? Or will they seek to build more democratic and open societies that compete successfully in the global economy? Our goal should be to encourage positive change in Russia and China by integrating them more deeply into the international community.

There is strong support among Americans for modernizing and strengthening the world's preeminent military. We should also adapt it to take on new challenges, such as the war on terrorism, homeland defense, and international peacekeeping. In a world where America may be attacked at home or overseas in a variety of ways, our conception of national security should be expanded to include the dangers of conventional or unconventional terrorism, organized crime, drug trade, and environmental degradation. As more threats to our security go online or into the stratosphere, we should devote more resources to maintaining our superiority in information technology and our leadership in space.

In the economic sphere, the president and Congress should build on the broad support for American leadership in promoting international prosperity. The United States should pursue open trade in conjunction with policies that reflect a compassion for those left behind. The United States should advance, with its allies and international institutions, policies of targeted debt relief and foreign assistance designed to spread the benefits of globalization to the world's poor. American political leaders should also tackle the central goal of developing a more stable and resilient global economic system—for instance, by making the international financial institutions more transparent and accountable.

The president should also use his political influence to prevent and resolve conflicts overseas, from South Asia and the Korea Peninsula to Colombia and the Middle East. Americans are justifiably proud of U.S. efforts to prevent and resolve these and other conflicts. Americans have learned dearly—for instance, on September 11, 2001—that overseas conflicts and instability can have devastating consequences that affect us. The United States can pursue peace making by diplomacy or, if need be, by force—in order to resolve conflicts before they escalate and harm American national interests. In some cases, only the United States has the standing and influence to serve as an effective facilitator of peace talks. Helping to prevent conflicts can also save the United States the much greater resources that might be necessary to intervene militarily to stop them later.

While pursuing these broad objectives, the president and Congress should keep American foreign policy firmly embedded in the values that are a great source of U.S. strength: freedom, equality of opportunity, tolerance, pluralism, the rule of law, and shared responsibility. Americans believe deeply in these fundamental ideals, and people around the world look to the United States to protect them when they are under threat. We have a responsibility and an important interest in ensuring that they continue to spread, rather than recede. Democracies and nations that respect human rights are less likely to go to war, less likely to traffic in terrorism, and more likely to stand against the forces of hatred, intolerance, and destruction.

If the president and Congress build on these areas of broad agreement, they will give themselves the best opportunity to craft a bipartisan foreign policy that gains public and international support.

Reduce Friction on Contentious Issues and Hot Spots

The fourth requirement for a successful, bipartisan foreign policy is to reduce the friction on contentious issues and hot spots. Many of the most heated foreign policy debates center around several long-standing disputed policy questions and countries of concern. The president and members of Congress must work hard to manage these difficult issues and must be prepared to deal with unstable situations that have the potential to explode into crises.

The question of when and how to intervene militarily is the toughest foreign policy problem that any president and Congress can face—and it is likely to come up again and again in the years to come. There will be pressures for the United States to intervene in many areas of the world—sometimes for humanitarian, and sometimes for national security reasons—but domestic or international opinion may be divided or opposed to intervention in many cases. To prepare for tough intervention decisions, the president should articulate a clear position on intervention and seek to build congressional and public support for it. Congress, for its part, should live up to its constitutional responsibility, which it often neglects, to share in the decision to deploy the armed forces. Congress and the president must recognize that while the United States should not be the world's peacekeeper, we have to intervene sometimes when our values or interests are at stake.

Few foreign policy issues stir up partisanship more than international institutions. The great challenge for the United States is to manage the tension between our unilateral instincts and our multinational commitments. The president should take the lead in explaining the importance of international institutions and strengthening public and congressional support for them. The president and members of Congress can bolster the case for key institutions, such as the UN and the IMF, by working to improve their capacity to deal with transnational challenges, such as terrorism, proliferation, the global environment, disease, money laundering, illegal drug trade, and computer fraud. Additionally, the United States should spearhead a renewed effort to strengthen the UN peacekeeping capacity and adapt the IMF, World Bank, and WTO to meet the challenges of globalization.

The U.S. foreign aid budget has long been a source of heated dispute that has served our national interests poorly. The president and Congress should renew American support for foreign aid by revamping our programs to make them more selective, better coordinated, and marked by strict standards of accountability and conditionality. They should also seek to build a broader consensus in support of substantially increased overall levels of foreign aid, as a means to combat poverty, promote peace and democracy, and spur economic development in poor nations across the world. Greater and wiser use of foreign aid is a critical tool in the war on terrorism because it can decrease the hardship and despair that often fuel support for radical and violent movements.

The president and Congress must also strive to develop a consensus on the U.S. approach to a number of hot spots and countries of concern. For instance, in the Middle East America faces the difficult challenges of reducing conflict between Israel and the Palestinians, dealing effectively with Saddam Hussein, and promoting U.S. interests in Iran. One of the main goals of the United States must be to prevent Iraq and Iran from developing weapons of mass destruction that could threaten stability in the region—but there is little consensus on how to do that. The president and Congress must work together to formulate policies toward these countries of concern that can protect American interests and gain bipartisan support.

Other hot spots will certainly pop up from time to time; there are invariably issues and conflicts that occupy far more of Washington's attention than anyone could have predicted. The key for the president and Congress is to develop greater consensus on approaches to difficult issues before crises develop. That way U.S. policy has a stronger foundation when America is forced to deal with an issue that was previously out of the public eye. Congress and the president should take a hard look at what U.S. policy toward each potential hot spot can best advance U.S. interests and gain bipartisan support

CONCLUSION

Developing a bipartisan foreign policy is a difficult, but critical, task. Many obstacles—from the complexity of world affairs and the pressure of special interest groups to the diffusion of power in Congress—stand in the way of policymakers that seek to build consensus on important foreign policy issues. But it is the responsibility of the policymaker to pursue the national interest—or, in the words of the founders, the "common good"—in any foreign policy challenge. This responsibility applies to members of Congress as much as to the president. Indeed, Congress's chief responsibility as our most representative body is to develop consensus out of the many views and concerns of the American people.

As Senator Lugar has demonstrated time and time again with his bipartisan approach to foreign policy, a determined policymaker can overcome the obstacles and build consensus that advances the national interest. To establish an overall foreign policy that gains broad bipartisan support, we need strong presidential leadership, constructive congressional partnership, an emphasis on the main areas of agreement in foreign policy, and reduction of friction on contentious issues and hot spots. A foreign policy of greater national unity is essential if the United States is to promote effectively its values and interests, and help build a safer, freer, and more prosperous world.

II

CHALLENGES
AND OPPORTUNITIES

5

Living with a New Europe

Zbigniew Brzezinski

The transatlantic alliance is America's most important global relationship. It is the springboard for U.S. global involvement, enabling America to play the decisive role of arbiter in Eurasia—the world's central arena of power—and it creates a coalition that is globally dominant in all the key dimensions of power and influence. America and Europe together serve as the axis of global stability, the locomotive of the world's economy, and the nexus of global intellectual capital as well as technological innovation. Just as important, they are both home to the world's most successful democracies. How the U.S.-European relationship is managed, therefore, must be Washington's highest priority.

In the longer run, the appearance of a truly politically united Europe would entail a basic shift in the distribution of global power, with consequences as far-reaching as those generated by the collapse of the Soviet empire and by the subsequent emergence of America's global preponderance. The impact of such a Europe on America's own position in the world and on the Eurasian power balance would be enormous (see table 5.1 for an indication of how a united Europe would dwarf the United States), inevitably generating severe two-way transatlantic tensions. Presently, neither side is well equipped to handle such potentially significant change.

Americans generally do not fully comprehend the European desire for an upgraded status in the relationship and they lack a clear appreciation of the diversity of European views concerning the United States. Europeans often fail to grasp both the spontaneity and the sincerity of America's commitment to Europe, infusing into their perception of America's desire to sustain the Euro-Atlantic alliance a European penchant for Machiavellian duplicity.

Table 5.1.

	United States	EU 15	EU 27ᵃ	EU 27+Turkey
Population	272,639,608	374,324,512	479,779,201	545,378,407
GDP (purchasing power parity)	$8.511 trillion	$8.053 trillion	$8.747 trillion	$9.172 trillion
GDP per Capita	$31,500	$20,927	$15,061	$14,759
Military Expenditures	$267.2 billion	$166.3 billion	$221.6 billion	$228.4 billion
Military Expenditures As % of GDP	3.4%	1.84%	1.97%	2.06%
Total Exports	$0.905 trillion	$2.032 trillion	$2.189 trillion	$2.233 trillion
Exports As of World Total	16.5%	37.0%	39.9%	40.7%
Total Imports	$0.757 trillion	$2.028 trillion	$2.146 trillion	$2.174 trillion
Imports As of World Total	13.5%	36.0%	38.1%	38.9%

Sources: The World Factbook, 1999 (Washington, D.C.: Central Intelligence Agency, 1999). Export and import estimates are calculated from 1998 trade figures in *Direction of Trade Statistics Quarterly* (Washington, D.C.: International Monetary Fund, December 1999), 2–5.
ᵃEU 27 consists of current members and all potential candidates for membership in central and eastern Europe.

It should be noted, however, that the operative words in the preceding paragraph regarding the significance of a truly united Europe are "would be." A European Union with genuine political weight and unity is not fore-ordained. The emergence of such a Europe depends on the depth of its political integration, on the scope of Europe's external expansion, and on the degree to which Europe develops its own military as well as political identity. The decisive steps in these regards have yet to be taken.

Currently, Europe—despite its economic strength, significant economic and financial integration, and the enduring authenticity of the transatlantic friendship—is a de facto military protectorate of the United States. This situation necessarily generates tensions and resentments, especially since the direct threat to Europe that made such dependence somewhat palatable has obviously waned. Nonetheless, it is not only a fact that the alliance between America and Europe is unequal, but it is also true that the existing asymmetry in power between the two is likely to widen even further in America's favor.

This asymmetry is due both to the unprecedented strength of America's economic expansion and to the technological innovation that America pioneers in such complex and diverse fields as biotechnology and information technology. What is more, the American-led technological revolution in military affairs enhances not only the scope of the military reach of the United States, but also transforms the very nature and uses of military power itself. Regardless of any collective action on the part of the European states, it is highly unlikely that Europe will be able to close the military gap with America at any point in the near future.

As a result, the United States is likely to remain the only truly global power for at least another generation. And that in turn means that America in all likelihood will also remain the dominant partner in the transatlantic alliance for the first quarter of the twenty-first century. It follows, therefore, that transatlantic debate will not be about fundamental alterations in the nature of the relationship, but rather about the implications of anticipated trends and the corresponding yet somewhat more marginal adjustments. That said, it hardly needs to be added that even incremental adaptations can breed conflicts which should be avoided if the U.S.-European relationship is to remain constructive and truly cooperative.

HISTORICAL DIFFERENCES

A basic historical mystification both inspires and complicates the ongoing dialogue between America and Europe. Both sides instinctively think of America when they dream of a united Europe. The Europeans crave America's continental scale and global standing and, in their more effervescent moments, they even envisage a future Europe as a global superpower coequal to America. The Americans, when welcoming—occasionally somewhat skeptically—Europe's future unity, instinctively draw on their own historical experience. That vision renders some U.S. foreign policymakers uneasy, for the inescapable presumption is that Europe—when it "unites"—will become America's peer, and potentially its rival.

The American experience is often invoked by European statesmen in Europe's march to unity (one such figure recently declared to me that the European Union today is somewhere between 1776 and 1789). Yet, most European political leaders realize that the European Union lacks both the ideological passion and the civic loyalty that inspired not only the framers of America's Constitution but—and this is the crucial test of political commitment—those prepared to make the ultimate sacrifice for the independence of the American colonies. As of now, and for the foreseeable future, it is simply the case that no "European" is willing to die for "Europe."

It follows that Europe, as it integrates, will be something altogether novel in the history of political entities, both in form and in substance. It will doubtless be a polity, in addition to being globally a most significant single economy. As a polity, however, it will lack the emotional and idealistic commitment that the United States evoked when it took shape. That commitment was expressed in a transcendental concept of political liberty, proclaimed to enjoy universal validity, that provided both the philosophical foundation and a politically attractive beacon for a new nation-state. The commitment of those who founded that state, and of those who later flocked to it and became assimilated by it, was almost religious. In short, the American Revolution created a new kind of nationalism, one that was open to all, a nationalism with a universal face.

The Preamble to the U.S. Constitution conveys the singular character of that American commitment to national unity and liberty:

> We, the people of the United States, in order to form a more perfect Union, establish justice, insure domestic tranquility, provide for the common defense, promote the general welfare, and secure the blessings of liberty to ourselves and our posterity, do ordain and establish . . .

Nothing quite like it characterizes the drumbeat of the European nations' march toward a common Europe. It is striking that the Treaty of Rome, the historic 1957 pledge of six European nations "to lay the foundations of an ever closer union," places emphasis in its very opening on ensuring "economic and social progress," on "constant improvements of the living and working conditions," on "the removal of existing obstacles" to "balanced trade and competition," on "the progressive abolition of restrictions on international trade," and so on. It is an admirably pragmatic, but also pedestrian, document.

To emphasize this essential difference between America and Europe is not to denigrate the historical significance of Europe's undertaking. Nor is it to question the good faith of those Europeans engaged in creating a new architecture. It is to note that the defining motivation of the European enterprise has, over time, become one of convenience and practicality. The initial impulse for European unity was more idealistic. Europe's "founding fathers" of the late 1940s and early 1950s were inspired by a transnational political conviction and very much motivated by the determination to end, once and for all, the nationalistic conflicts that twice in the twentieth century came close to destroying European civilization. They were also fearful that America, disenchanted by European feuds, might simply abandon the European nations to the other great historical option—also "unifying" in its own ugly way—the one east of the Cold War's new dividing line "from Stettin to Trieste."

Today's Europeans are serious about Europe in a more pragmatic way, though some—as noted earlier—do dream of an entity that will match America. French statesmen, at times unable to conceal their hyperenvy of America's global standing, see in Europe the recovery of France's past grandeur. The Germans have sought in Europe their own redemption. The British, more skeptical, have finally concluded that there will be a Europe of sorts and that they must be in it if they are to infuse some genuine significance into their own special relationship with America. Other peoples on the Continent—including the recently liberated peoples of central Europe—also wish to be European, because they share the view that to be part of Europe is to be more secure, more prosperous and free. None of these motivations is base, all are historically justified, and they deserve America's respect.

Nonetheless, pragmatism differs in substance as well as in its effects from patriotism. A polity construed on convenience is bound to be different from a polity derived from conviction. The former can still generate loyalty. It can create a shared community. But it is also likely to be less ambitious, politically less assertive, and, above all, less inclined toward idealism and personal sacrifice. Despite some similarities in scale, the "Europe" that is actually emerging is thus likely to be politically quite different from America: a hybrid of a huge transnational corporation, to which it is prudent and convenient and even gratifying to belong, and of a confederated state that over time may also gain the genuine loyalty of its hitherto distinctive communities. In short, the European polity of convenience will be less than a United States of Europe, though more than just a European Union Incorporated.

Indeed, it is no aspersion on anyone or any state to suggest that on the global scene the emerging Europe is likely to be more similar to a Switzerland writ large than to the United States. The Swiss constitution—which ended intercommunal strife—stresses that the ethnically differentiated Swiss Cantons resolved, "to renew [their] alliance," that they were "determined to live [their] diversity in unity respecting one another," and went on to identify the practical purposes of the confederation. Abroad, the main emphasis of Switzerland's international engagement has been in the important areas of international finance and trade, while avoiding engagement in global political-philosophical conflicts.

Integration, Not Unification

In any case, it seems reasonable to conclude that "Europe," in the foreseeable future, will not be—indeed, cannot be—"America." Once the implications of that reality are digested on both sides of the Atlantic, the U.S.-European dialogue should become more relaxed, even as the Europeans address the dilemmas connected with their simultaneous quest for integration, expansion, and some militarization; and even as the Americans adjust to the inevitable emergence of a novel European polity.

Unification of several peoples normally occurs as a result of external necessity, shared ideological commitment, domination by the most powerful, or some combination thereof. In the initial phase of the European quest for unity, all three factors were at play, though in varying degrees: the Soviet Union was a real threat; European idealism was nurtured by the still fresh memories of World War II; and France, exploiting West Germany's sense of moral vulnerability, was able to harness Germany's rising economic potential in support of its own political ambitions. By the end of the century, these impulses have perceptibly waned. As a result, European "integration"—largely a process of regulatory standardization—has become the alternative definition of unification. Yet while integration is a perfectly sensible way of achieving an operationally effective merger, a merger still falls quite short of an emotionally meaningful marriage.

The plain fact is that bureaucratically spearheaded integration simply cannot generate the political will needed for genuine unity. It can neither stir the imagination (despite the occasional rhetoric about Europe becoming America's peer), nor develop the mortal passion that can sustain a nation-state in a time of adversity. The 80,000 page-long acquis communautaire (organized into 31 policy sectors)—which a new member of the European Union must ratify—is not likely to provide the average European with the needed nourishment for politically energizing loyalty. However, it should be reiterated that by now, given the absence of the other three more traditional ways of seeking unity, integration is not only necessary but is the only way that Europe can move forward toward "unity."

That gap between "unification" and "integration," in turn, explains why integration is bound to be slow; and why, were it somehow accelerated too sharply, could even divide Europe once again. Indeed, any attempt to accelerate political unification would probably intensify internal tensions between the leading states within the union, since each of them still insists on preserving its sovereignty in the critical area of foreign policymaking. At this stage, anti-Americanism as the impetus for unity—even when disguised by talk of "multipolarity"—cannot be a unifying force as anti-Sovietism once was, because most Europeans do not subscribe to it. Moreover, with Germany reunited, no one in Europe, outside of Paris, still regards France as the putative leader of the new Europe—but also no one in Europe desires Germany to become Europe's dominant leader.

Integration, however, is not only a slow process, but each successful step increases the very complexity of the undertaking. Integration inherently means an incremental and highly balanced progression toward deepening interdependence among constituent units, but their growing interdependence is not infused with the unifying political passion required for the assertion of genuine global independence. That may happen eventually, when Europeans come to view themselves politically as Europeans while remaining, for example, German or French as a matter of linguistic and cultural peculiarity.

Horizontal Expansion

In the meantime, because of Europe's slow progression, external expansion is likely to become a partial compensation for the crawling pace of internal integration. Europe will grow, but more horizontally than vertically since, as a practical matter, the two cannot significantly advance at the same time. This painful reality is a sensitive point among Europe's true believers. When Jacques Delors dared to declare flatly in early 2000 that "the pace [of enlargement] is unquestionably being forced . . . we thus risk diluting the blueprint" for European integration, with the result that "we will inevitably move away from a political Europe as defined by Europe's founding fathers," he was almost immediately and publicly taken to task by a compatriot European Union commissioner, Michel Barnier.

The commissioners in Brussels hope that bureaucratic streamlining and institutional renewal will invigorate the process of integration. Buoyed by the modest success of the euro—despite some apocalyptic predictions from its largely American and British detractors—Brussels has moved forward, in anticipation of significant expansion, with the long-standing intergovernmental conference on the renewal of the European institutions. Key institutional decisions are to be made by the end of the year. But even the most forceful proponents of expansion concede that, at best, politically significant integration will have to be confined for a while to the smaller inner core of the EU, thus perhaps creating a so-called multispeed and variable geometry Europe (see table 5.2).[1]

Yet, even if that were to happen, it is doubtful that this formula would resolve the basic tension between integration and expansion insofar as the development of a common foreign policy is concerned. Such a Europe would mean division into first- and second-class members, with the latter objecting to any major foreign policy decisions taken on their behalf by a directorate of allegedly more truly European states.

Table 5.2. A Decalogue Regarding European Developments and Prospects

1. For most Europeans, "Europe" is not an object of personal affection. It is more convenience than conviction.
2. On the global scene, the EU will not be like America but more like a Switzerland writ large.
3. Most Europeans do not partake of anti-Americanism as the impulse for unity.
4. Integration is essentially a bureaucratic process and not the same as unification.
5. The EU's expansion inevitably collides with deepening integration.
6. The EU needs to expand for demographic and economic reasons.
7. A federated inner core of foreign policymaking states within a larger EU of twenty-one or more states is not politically workable.
8. Slow expansion plus bureaucratic integration is likely to produce a Europe united economically but only confederated politically.
9. The EU is unlikely to acquire an autonomous military capability.
10. The EU will thus be a novel type of polity, with its global influence primarily economic and financial.

In any case, enlargement, too, is bound to become an increasingly absorbing and complicated task. With some 200 EU teams about to begin the tedious process of negotiating the modalities of accession with the dozen or so new aspirant nations, expansion will probably slow down, both because of its inherent complexity and because of a lack of will on the part of EU member states. In fact, the admission of any central European state by 2004 is becoming increasingly problematic. In the long run, however, expansion cannot be avoided. An amputated Europe cannot be a true Europe. A geopolitical void between Europe and Russia would be dangerous. Moreover, an aging western Europe would begin to stagnate economically and socially.[2]

No wonder, then, that some leading European planners have begun to advocate a Europe of as many as thirty-five to forty members by the year 2020—a Europe that would be geographically and culturally whole, but almost certainly politically diluted.[3]

A Question of Muscle

Thus, neither integration nor expansion is likely to create the truly European Europe that some Europeans crave and some Americans fear. Indeed, an increasing number of Europeans do sense that the combination of the euro and integration with slow expansion can only create economic sovereignty. Political awareness that more is needed prompted the three leading European states—France, Great Britain, and Germany—to join in 1999 in an effort to create a credible European military capability, and to do so even before an integrated Europe with a defining foreign policy of its own emerges. The projected European military force is meant to put some muscle behind a common foreign and security policy (CFSP), which is to be shaped by the newly created post of Europe's High Representative for External Relations and Common Security.

The proposed joint European rapid reaction force, which is to be operational by 2003, will be the first tangible manifestation of a political Europe. In contrast to the already existing, but largely symbolic, "Eurocorps"—composed primarily of French, German, Spanish, and other draftees and possessing neither mobility nor real military capability—the planned force would be assembled when needed from prededicated combat units, would number up to 60,000 men deployable within 60 days, and would be sustainable in a theater of deployment "in or around Europe" for at least a year. In effect, according to various European estimates, such a force would be equivalent to a full corps, supported by some 150 to 300 aircraft, 15 large combat vessels, a strategic air transport capability, and the requisite C3I (command, control, communications, and intelligence). European military experts are to conduct an accelerated audit of the inventory of the available European assets so that the force can engage in peacekeeping or even in some (otherwise unspecified) limited combat operations. Its appearance would mark the emergence of a genuine European Security and Defense Identity (ESDI), capable of military action outside of NATO.

However, the European defense initiative—driven by the genuinely felt sense of Europe's military inadequacy revealed by the Kosovo war, fueled by French ambitions, but tempered by British and German inclinations to reassure the Americans—has yet to pass three basic tests: will the force be rapidly deployable, will it be militarily capable, and will it be logistically sustainable? Europe has the means to create such a force; the question is whether it has the will.

At this stage, skepticism is very much in order. European defense leaders have stated that the force can be assembled without additional expenditures through a very deliberate reallocation of existing defense budget items, a proposition that defies common sense. It is evident to serious European commentators that the planned force will require improvements in central logistics control, joint military depots, and presumably some joint exercises. That would entail additional costs, not to mention the more basic need for adequate reconnaissance and intelligence as well as for a more competitive and more consolidated European defense industry. Yet, in recent years the overall percentage of the European budgets allocated to defense as well as to defense-related R&D has actually been declining, with European defense expenditures having fallen in real terms by about 22 percent since 1992.

The critical fact is that political parsimony undermines the military seriousness of the venture. As Daniel Vernet wrote in *Le Monde* in September 1999, for the European force to come into being, the Europeans "must know exactly what they want, define defense restructuring programs (politically sensitive and financially costly), and, finally, allocate the budgetary resources to match their ambitions." In addition, to sustain a force of 60,000 men in the field for more than a year, a rotational pool of about 180,000 combat-ready European soldiers must be available. It is not.

A further complication, casting additional doubt on the credibility of the proposed enterprise, is that some European states are members of the EU but not of NATO (the "neutrals"), and others of NATO but not of the EU (America's "Trojan horses," according to some Europeanists). Their prospective relationship to ESDI is thus unclear and, in any case, it inevitably complicates the picture. Finally, but perhaps most important of all, the meshing of the proposed force with existing NATO arrangements could become disruptive operationally and divisive politically.

Ultimately, the most probable outcome for ESDI is that the proposed force will produce neither a rival to NATO, nor the long-missing second European "pillar" for a more equal alliance. Although the Europeans will probably somewhat enhance their own military planning and joint command structures, especially after the expected absorption of the Western European Union by the EU itself, more likely is the piecemeal emergence over the next five or so years of a somewhat improved European capability to provide for non-NATO peacekeeping in some not overly violent European trouble spot (most likely in the Balkans). In effect, the so-called European pillar will be made less out of steel and concrete and more out of papier-mâché. As a result, Europe will fall short of becoming a comprehensive global power. Painful as it may be for those who would like to see a politically vital Europe, most Europeans still remain unwilling not only to die but even to pay for Europe's security.

FOR STRATEGIC DIRECTION

U.S. policymakers should keep in mind a simple injunction when shaping American policy toward Europe: do not make the ideal the enemy of the good. The ideal from Washington's point of view would be a politically united Europe that is a dedicated member of NATO—one spending as much on defense as the United States but committing the funds almost entirely to the upgrading of NATO's capabilities; willing to have NATO act "out of area" in order to reduce America's global burdens; and remaining compliant to American geopolitical preferences regarding adjacent regions, especially Russia and the Middle East, and accommodating on such matters as international trade and finance. The good is a Europe that is more of a rival economically, that steadily enlarges the scope of European interdependence while lagging in real political-military independence, that recognizes its self-interest in keeping America deployed on the European periphery of Eurasia, even while it chafes at its relative dependence and halfheartedly seeks gradual emancipation.

U.S. policymakers should recognize that "the good" actually serves vital American interests. They should consider that initiatives such as ESDI reflect the European quest for self-respect, and that carping injunctions—a series of "do nots" emanating both from the State and Defense Departments—merely intensify European resentments and have the potential to drive the Germans and the British into the arms of the French. Moreover, American opposition to the effort can only serve to convince some Europeans—wrongly—that NATO is more important to U.S. security than it is to Europe's. Last but not least, given the realities of the European scene, what ESDI poses for NATO are problems of process not ones of principle, and problems of process are not likely to be constructively managed by elevating them into issues of principle.

Hence, dramatic warnings of "decoupling" are counterproductive. They have a theological ring to them, and as such, they threaten to transform differences that can be accommodated into ones involving doctrinal debates. They are reminiscent of earlier NATO collisions that accomplished nothing good—whether over the abortive Multilateral Nuclear Force initiative of the early 1960s, which accelerated the French nuclear program, or, more recently, the brief spasm in 1999 of American-pushed efforts to revamp NATO into some sort of a global ("out of area") alliance, which quickly came down to earth with the outbreak of the Kosovo war. Such disputes detract and distract from a fundamental reality: NATO, a truly remarkable success, may be far from perfect but it does not require a dramatic overhaul.

One should pause here and ask: Even assuming that the new European force were to come into being by 2003, where and how could it act on its own? What credible scenario can one envisage in which it could act decisively, without advance guarantees of NATO support and without some actual dependence on NATO assets? Let us assume a conflict in Estonia, with the Kremlin stirring up the Russian minority and then threatening to intervene; Europe would not lift a finger without direct NATO involvement. Suppose Montenegro secedes and Serbia invades; without U.S. participation, the planned European force would probably be defeated. While social unrest in some European province—say, Transylvania, or even Corsica!—might prove more susceptible to a deployment of European peacekeepers (much as has been the case in Bosnia), such an intervention is hardly an example of Europe becoming "an independent actor on the international stage," to quote French defense minister Alain Richard.

In a genuinely serious mission, the planned European force still would have to rely heavily on NATO assets in the key areas of reconnaissance, intelligence, and airlift. These assets are primarily American, though dedicated to NATO. Thus, NATO would be de facto involved, even if initially it had exercised its option of first refusal. In brief, if the crisis is serious, the European reaction will not be independent; if the reaction is independent, the crisis will not be serious.

To be sure, adjustments within NATO will be unavoidable as Europe slowly evolves into a more defined polity. ESDI will make NATO's decision-making processes somewhat more cumbersome, and European contributions to NATO's own military enhancement may even marginally suffer as the EU seeks some sort of force of its own. ESDI, especially after the Europeans organize within the EU some sort of a European defense organism, will also have the effect of stimulating a shared European strategic perspective, which America will have to take into account. But a shared European security posture is more likely to emerge through the gradual consolidation of the European defense industry[4] and intensified European military planning than through any precipitous leap—especially by 2003—into an autonomous European combat capability.

Indeed, of greater consequence to NATO's future than the European underperformance revealed during the Kosovo war is Europe's nonperformance after the Kosovo war. The staggering fact is that "Europe" not only cannot protect itself, but also it cannot even police itself. The inability of the

European states to engage entirely on their own in effective peacekeeping in a small and weak region—and their reluctance to provide the needed financing for its economic recovery—poses a more serious long-term challenge to NATO's cohesion than does ESDI. It is likely to breed growing American uneasiness regarding the proper role for U.S. forces committed to Europe's defense.

In the nearer term, an even more divisive issue—one of greater strategic import—may be generated by U.S. plans to deploy a missile defense system. The ongoing debate in the United States over missile defense has been driven primarily by domestic political considerations, and a unilateral American decision, made in the heat of a U.S. presidential race, would doubtless be badly received in Europe. Indeed, American unilateralism on this matter could have far graver consequences than even the most intense U.S. concerns regarding ESDI's alleged "decoupling" effect on American and European security. If transatlantic security ties are to be sustained as America's central strategic priority, it is clearly better at this stage to engage in comprehensive discussions with America's allies regarding the feasibility, the costs, the defense trade-offs, and the political as well as strategic effects of a missile defense deployment. In any case, it is too early to make a prudent judgment as to how urgently needed and how practicable such a defensive shield may be. That is a decision for the next U.S. president to make.

In the meantime, a basic strategic priority of the United States should be the continued expansion of NATO. NATO enlargement offers the best possible guarantee of continued transatlantic security ties. It serves to create a more secure Europe, with fewer areas of geopolitical ambiguity, while increasing the European stake in a vital and credible alliance. Indeed, the case can be made that the 1999 NATO decision to return to the issue of enlargement no earlier than 2002 should be revised, and that a serious effort to decide on new members should be made in 2001, once a new U.S. president is in office. Several countries appear to be ready for inclusion, meeting not only the standards set recently for Poland, the Czech Republic, and Hungary, but even previously for Spain. An earlier resumption of the process of enlargement would provide a clear signal that not only does the transatlantic security link remain vital, but also that America and Europe are both serious about shaping a secure Europe that is truly European in scope.

American support for the resumption of NATO enlargement is consistent with the American stake in expansion of the EU. The larger Europe becomes, the less likely it is that either external or internal threats will pose a serious challenge to international peace. Moreover, in the long run the more overlap there is in membership between NATO and the EU, the greater will be the cohesion of the transatlantic community and the more compelling the complementarity of the Atlanticist and Europeanist visions. It is a felicitous fact that some of the candidates currently qualified for either NATO or EU membership happen to be the same countries. The United States can argue persuasively that Slovenia, Slovakia, and Lithuania already meet, or are close to meeting, the criteria for NATO membership. According to a comparative study prepared by PricewaterhouseCoopers, several central European states (including Slovenia and Estonia) are more qualified—in terms of macroeconomic stability, Gross National Product, economic interaction with the EU, and economic infrastructure—for EU membership than was Greece. Poland and the Czech Republic—both already NATO members—were recently listed in *The Economist* as being more qualified than Italy! Which makes it all the more egregious that "the present accession requirements are more numerous and stringent than those that were faced by the South European countries that joined the EU earlier."[5]

That some countries merit entry into the EU and NATO should facilitate and encourage stronger U.S. support for the enlargement of both. High-level NATO-EU consultations regarding a staged, progressive, and continuing expansion therefore would be very much in order. But it is premature at this stage even to speculate as to what might be the eventual outer boundaries of the two, hopefully overlapping, entities.

Much will depend on the evolution of Russia, for whom the doors to an Atlanticist Europe should be kept open. An expanded EU overlapping with NATO can encourage Russia's positive evolution by dampening old imperial temptations. Russia may then recognize its own interest in accommodating and becoming associated with NATO. If it does not, then a larger NATO will provide the needed security for a larger Europe. But in any case, the a priori exclusion of any qualified European state either from NATO or the EU would be unwise (see table 5.3).

Table 5.3.   A Decalogue of Basic U.S. Policy Premises and Guidelines

1. Europe remains America's natural and preeminent ally.
2. An Atlanticist Europe is essential to a stable Eurasian equilibrium.
3. An autonomous European defense capability, in any case unlikely in the near future, should not be opposed by the United States.
4. Allied political unity is more important than the enhancement of NATO's capabilities.
5. The United States should defer any deployment decision regarding a ballistic missile defense system until consensus is reached with NATO allies.
6. The United States should seek an enlarged NATO in Europe but not an "out of area" NATO.
7. The United States has a bigger stake in Europe's enlargement than in Europe's integration.
8. NATO and the EU should work together on joint plans for further expansion.
9. Eventually, Turkey, Cyprus, and Israel might be included in both entities.
10. There should be no a priori limitations or exclusions on NATO and EU memberships.

Moreover, from a geopolitical as well as economic point of view, it is not too early to note that once both NATO and the EU have expanded to include the Baltic and some southeastern European states, the subsequent inclusion not only of Turkey but of Cyprus (following a Turkish-Greek accommodation) and of Israel (following a comprehensive peace with all its neighbors) may also become desirable. In addition, as Europe expands, the transatlantic community at some point will have to respond to signals from countries such as Ukraine, Georgia, and even Azerbaijan, that their long-term objective is to qualify for participation in the great historical undertaking occurring within the EU and under NATO's security umbrella.

In promoting this great project, the United States should remain supportive of the EU's quest for deeper integration, even though that support will be mainly rhetorical. The United States has wisely avoided identifying itself with the conservative British opposition to Europe's political as well as monetary unity, and it should likewise avoid the occasional temptation to display Schadenfreude when Europe stumbles. Precisely because European integration will be slow and because the European polity will not be like America, America need not fear the emergence of a rival. The transatlantic relationship is more like a marriage that blends together mutually respected differences—including some division of labor—as well as commonalties, and both in fact serve to consolidate the partnership. That has been the case over the last half century, and it will remain so for some time to come.

In fact, the evolving character of the international system should reinforce the transatlantic bond. Europe and the United States account jointly for less than 15 percent of the world's population and are highly visible as islands of prosperity and privilege in a seething and restless global environment. In this age of instant communications, an awareness of inequality can be rapidly translated into political hostility targeted at those who are envied. Hence, both self-interest and a sense of potential vulnerability should continue to provide the underpinning for a durable U.S.-European alliance.

The European polity, situated on the western edge of Eurasia and in the immediate proximity of Africa, is more exposed to the risks inherent in rising global tumult than the politically more cohesive, militarily more powerful, and geographically more isolated America. The Europeans will be more immediately at risk if a chauvinistic imperialism should again motivate Russian foreign policy, or if Africa and/or Southcentral Asia suffer worsening social failures. The proliferation of nuclear or other weapons of mass destruction also will endanger Europe more, given Europe's limited military capabilities and the proximity of potentially threatening states. For as far as one can see, Europe will continue to need America to be truly secure.

At the same time, a close relationship with Europe philosophically legitimates and gives focus to America's global role. It creates a community of democratic states without which the United States would be lonely in the world. Preserving, enhancing, and especially enlarging that community—in order to "secure the blessings of liberty to ourselves and our posterity"— must therefore remain America's historically vital task.

NOTES

The article is reprinted from *The National Interest,* no. 60 (Summer 2000): 17–29.

1. Variable geometry implies that the willing and able will be permitted to deepen the level of their integration in specific policy areas, while the unwilling will not be obliged to follow suit. A multispeed approach implies that, while the willing and able proceed with integration in a given policy area, the willing but unable will have a clear road map of how they can join at a later date. See Robin Niblett, "The European Disunion," *The Washington Quarterly* (Winter 1997): 104-5.

2. The OECD estimates that the EU will need 35 million immigrants in the next 25 years to keep the population at 1995 levels, and an additional 150 million by 2025 if it wishes to keep the current ratio of retirees to workers. Moreover, it is estimated that by 2030, state pensions will absorb 5.5 percent of the GDP in Britain, 13.5 in France, 16.5 in Germany, and 20.3 in Italy. (The equivalent estimate for the United States is 6.6.)

3. According to a report prepared by Jacques Attali at the request of the French foreign minister, France—"combining continental generosity and strategic coherence"— should deliberately "promote what it can no longer avoid," namely, a Europe that embraces thirty-five or even forty members, including among others Ukraine and Georgia, thereby opting for "pluralism" over federalism. Contrarily, Werner Weidenfeld has warned recently in *Frankfurter Allgemeine Zeitung* that "this clear abandoning of any attempt to deepen the European identity will turn out to be Europe's Achilles' Heel."

4. A significant step in that direction was taken during 1999 through the merger of Aerospatiale Matra SA and DaimlerChrysler Aerospace AG to create the European Aeronautic, Defense and Space Co., with resources and capabilities that are competitive by American standards.

5. Eva Ehrlich and Gabor Revesz, *The State of the Economy in Central and Eastern Europe Compared with the EU's Requirements* (Budapest: The Hungarian Academy of Sciences, 1999), 4.

6

The United States and Asia in the Twenty-First Century

Casimir A. Yost

In the 1990s, the United States gained power and lost influence. In the first decade of the twenty-first century, it must, to secure its global interests, not only seek to retain its military and economic power, but to improve its ability to affect favorably the actions of governments and others in the regions critical to American interests. Nowhere is this twin responsibility greater than in the Asia-Pacific region stretching from South to Southeast to Northeast Asia.

BACKGROUND

The United States became the world's sole superpower in the 1990s with the collapse of the Soviet Union. It is unchallenged militarily by any individual state or combination of states. Moreover, with the decade-long stagnation of the Japanese economy, the United States also lost its primary economic competitor. However, overwhelming U.S. power did not translate into overwhelming U.S. influence in the 1990s.

True, American foreign policy registered successes after the Gulf War. Trade liberalization expanded under American leadership. NATO enlarged its membership at U.S. initiative. But, on issue after issue from India and Pakistan's decisions to "go nuclear," to loosening Iraqi sanctions, to Israeli and Arab refusal to settle differences, America's wishes did not prevail. Why? The obvious answer is that in a post-Soviet threat world, others cared more about "their" issues than we did. Somewhat less obvious was the inability of the United States to translate power into influence or, more precisely, to use its power effectively. The results are all too evident—two newly minted nuclear states, a Palestinian/Israeli conflict in free fall, a weakening of sanctions on

Iraq, and terrorism left underattended to in the 1990s now dominating our foreign policy agenda after September 11, 2001.

Our most troubling constraints on the exercise of influence were at home. Our government had no comprehensive strategy for the pursuit of interest. At best, we sought ad hoc objectives, frittering away influence. Our indecision was all too evident in years of vacillation with respect to China and the tentative manner with which we utilized force in Kosovo, relying on air power alone. In fairness to executive branch policymakers, the Congress acted in the 1990s, as if U.S. power automatically translated into influence and that our government's tools of influence—diplomacy, foreign assistance, intelligence, force—could be underfunded or micromanaged without cost to our international objectives. Domestic interest groups wreaked havoc on U.S. foreign policy in the 1990s demanding that our leaders focus on the "micro" at the expense of the "macro." Members of Congress were too prone to play to these special interests on issues ranging from payment of U.S. dues to the United Nations to U.S. policy toward China.

Nowhere was American lack of strategic purpose more evident than in Asia. This region is home to two-thirds of the world's population and responsible for one-third of global economic output. It is a region filled with contrast and complexity defying easy categorization. It contains several of the world's few remaining communist states as well as mature democracies in Japan, Australia, and New Zealand. The 1990s saw a number of new democracies emerge in the region. The growth of the nongovernmental organization (NGO) sector in Asia has been tremendous, contributing to political vibrancy throughout the region. It is America's most important regional economic partner and yet our attention to it, over more than a decade, has been woefully inadequate. This essay will argue that the American tendency either to ignore the region or to try to impose our priorities on it flies in the face of a region undergoing dramatic change. The gap between Asian realities and American preferences is widening. We are challenged in Asia less by crisis—though crisis is present in South Asia, and certainly possible elsewhere in the region. The real challenge we face is the gradual erosion of the U.S. position in this critical part of the world. We very much risk losing both power and influence as a result of poor decisions and neglect. Alternatively, if we act decisively, we cannot only solidify our position in Asia, but can also contribute to building a stable region in which the risk of war is diminished and in which prosperity and good governance become new norms.

U.S. INTERESTS, INFLUENCE, AND IMPEDIMENTS

Interests

U.S. interests in Asia remain broadly constant. We do not want the region or subregions dominated by a hostile state or coalition of states. We seek expanding commercial and financial access to the region. We, in turn, are a major market for Asian exports. Over one-third of total U.S. trade is conducted with Asian nations. Our citizens benefit from low-cost imports and our exporters need Asian markets. Finally, we value an Asia which is becoming broadly more democratic and where individual rights are respected. The major debates in U.S. policy and political circles about the region relate less to these broad objectives than to the means to achieve them, the relative priority to be attached to each, and the energy and resources we should devote to the region. We debate constantly among ourselves about how best to pursue our interests. We discuss what reliance to place on allies, where sanctions are appropriate, and how to relate to militaries in the region. We remain fundamentally undecided over whether a rising China poses a threat to our interests and what our responsibility should be toward regional hot spots and states in trouble. More generally, we remain ambivalent about Asia's place among our broader relationships. Squeaky wheels in Europe and the Middle East capture our attention more easily than those in Asia.

Influence

U.S. influence in the region rests on two major pillars: the security that our military presence in the region offers and the importance of U.S. markets and investment for Asia's economic well-being.

Asia is a region of historic animosities centered most particularly around Japan in Northeast Asia. The U.S. alliance system has permitted the states of the region to largely avoid major conflict in the contemporary period. It is notable that in that region of Asia where the United States has not been present militarily—South Asia—India and Pakistan have engaged in periodic wars. It is, however, also notable that Asia lacks a regional security organization comparable to NATO. This means that excessive weight is placed on U.S. bilateral treaties and bases in Japan and Korea to maintain stability in the region.

The importance of the U.S. market to the region cannot be overstated. The Asian economic miracle was in large part a function of access to U.S. markets. The United States, of course, also has other features that commend it to foreigners. Our education system is widely utilized by Asian elites. Our concern for individual liberties is broadly admired. Our NGOs operate throughout the region despite cutbacks in U.S. aid levels to Asia.

Impediments

What then are the impediments to our exercise of influence in Asia? They come in two broad categories: domestic, which I will treat here, and changing Asian realities, which the next section of this essay will explore.

The 1990s, as was noted earlier, was a period in which the United States tried—unsuccessfully—to define a global role for itself. Broadly, we said that our objective was to expand the community of free market democracies. But this effort lacked consistency and constancy. The executive branch engaged in a constant struggle with the Congress in the 1990s over foreign policy objectives and the means to achieve them.

In practice, this struggle translated into erratic, unfocused policies on the ground, confusing to all concerned. When American officials turned their attention to Asia, it was too frequently to lecture Asians either on their political shortcomings or on the need to open their markets. Our style was all wrong—we spoke without listening. Our priorities in the region frequently seemed to be generated by narrow U.S. interest groups rather than from a broad sense of strategic purpose.

This pattern did not improve at the beginning of the Bush administration. Early administration moves seemed guided more by a desire to change past policies than to map out a positive new course. It fast became clear that on the Peoples Republic of China (PRC), North Korea, and Taiwan the new administration was unwilling to pick up where the last administration had left off. At one level—logically—it should not. If the previous administration was thought to be too solicitous of China and North Korea, then change was appropriate. However, actions were taken by the incoming administration without the benefit of a strategic rationale, and they came across in the region as petulant rather than reasoned.

Then came September 11 and the Bush administration focused on the war on terrorism. This focus offers both an opportunity and risks. The opportunity is to provide strategic direction to an American policy that had been drifting. The dangers are first, to impose on U.S.-Asian relations priorities made in Washington and not central to Asian concerns; and second, to give inadequate attention to other crucial issues.

CHANGE IN ASIA

It is to these risks that this essay now turns. The National Intelligence Council's December 2000 Report "Global Trends 2015," forecasts "that East Asia over the next 15 years will be characterized by uneven economic dynamism—both between and within states—political and national assertiveness rather than ideology and potential for strategic tensions if not outright conflict."[1] Asia's very diversity should be a warning against facile assumptions. It is, of course, a region of many religions, ethnicities, and historical traditions. Long dominated by authoritarian rulers, many Asian states now have more pluralistic systems. Ideology is of declining importance, but nationalism is rising.

This is a region of enormous economic accomplishment. Despite its troubles, Japan is still the world's second largest economy. China is a rising economic powerhouse with a vast domestic market and expanding exporting clout. This is a region that has benefited from globalization with the high tech boom of the 1990s and significant flows of foreign investment. But, the region has also suffered from its economic dependence on the rest of the world. A combination of structural rigidities, asset inflation, and corruption contributed to capital flight which sent regional economies into a tailspin in 1997–1998 from which they have not fully recovered.

This is a region undergoing significant and underappreciated changes. Its politics are becoming more pluralistic in every country but North Korea. A recent internal report of the San Francisco-based Asia Foundation argued that "formidable domestic and global forces are placing heavy strains on all highly centralized forms of governance (in Asia)—the rise of a prosperous and demanding middle class, the globalization of trade and investment, extraordinarily rapid advances in technology and an exponential increase in the flow of ideas and information on a global scale."[2]

At the same time, Asians are turning inward, focusing their energies on their own countries and on their own region. A rising factor in this phenomenon is that intra-Asian trade is growing with China. With the stagnation of the Japanese and U.S. economies, Asians are looking increasingly toward China to place their investments and to send their exports. This will have political consequences. Just as a source of U.S. influence in Asia has been its market, so too will China's economic growth be a source of the PRC's influence over its neighbors.

China is emerging as the region's low-cost production base. One estimate is that China's share of total East Asian exports rose from 16 percent in 1997 to 22 percent in 2002.[3] In 2001 China received $50 billion in foreign direct investment (FDI), five times the amount going to the Association of Southeast Asian Nations region. China's neighbors are the beneficiaries of China's market; but they are also hurt by the PRC's expanding export markets and receipt of FDI.

The "Asian" agenda, to the extent that one can generalize, focuses on two broad challenges: economic growth with domestic stability and the national fragilities inherent in each of the three regional subsystems. These include underlying tensions between China, South Korea, and Japan; uncertainty surrounding Taiwan's and North Korea's futures; ASEAN weakness; and dangerous tensions in Kashmir. Increasingly, Asians are looking to themselves for solutions. Examples include the formation of Asian-only forums such as ASEAN Plus Three or regional dialogues that do not include the United States, such as the Shanghai Cooperation Group. Asian attitudes toward the United States are ambivalent. One study found, "Taken as a whole, the countries of Asia welcome American engagement in the region, and are probably more concerned about potential American inattention than potential American dominance."[4]

But this statement masks a more complex reality. Asians are less certain today than in the past that the U.S. agenda is their agenda. The region still depends on the American security presence to maintain stability and the U.S. market to bolster prosperity. But elites in the region are becoming more assertive. Many reacted negatively to what they viewed as the preaching style of the Clinton administration on human rights and open markets even as Asian markets and politics were both becoming more open.

Today, all of China's neighbors are mindful of the growing impact of China on the region. There is widespread concern that the Bush administration is needlessly baiting North Korea with talk of its membership in the axis of evil and unnecessarily challenging China with more explicit support of Taiwan. Some, but not all Asians, view the Bush administration's search for a national missile defense capability as destabilizing. Many, though not all, find the administration's litmus test on the war on terrorism objectionable even as they recognize that terrorist cells can and do operate in the region.

In the short term, the reaction of many Asian leaders to ambivalence about the United States is a sophisticated form of hedging: building intra-Asian ties, opening lines to Europe, being receptive to Russian visits, and carefully engaging with China.

What could shift the balance of opinion in Asia against the United States? Certainly, new strains in economic ties would have a negative influence. The growing U.S. current account deficit is putting pressure on the dollar. A weakening dollar will make Asian exports less attractive to American consumers. A sharp drop in the value of the dollar could have serious negative consequences for Asian economies and therefore on America's position in the region.

A second factor that could erode Asian ties with America would be deterioration in U.S. bilateral security agreements with either Japan or South Korea. We can only speculate how long popular opinion in these countries will continue to welcome U.S. bases and force presence, but it will not be forever, and the erosion could come more quickly if adjustments are not made to reduce their impact on local citizens.

Third, the U.S. agenda may simply not command interest in an Asia focused on economic progress and political evolution. In the long run, the United States may be proved right to focus attention on the nexus of weapons of mass destruction (WMD) and terrorism but, at present, these issues are far higher on Washington's agenda than they are on the agendas of most Asian capitals.

FIVE KEY COUNTRIES

Five countries in Asia deserve special comment: Japan, South Korea, China, Indonesia, and India (Russia, for the foreseeable future, will be a relatively minor player in Asia, except, perhaps, as a supplier of military hardware).

Each offers special challenges and lessons for American foreign policy. These are relationships the United States must get right if its policies toward the region are to succeed.

Japan

At the beginning of the 1990s we feared Japan's economic strength. Now we worry about an economy which cannot reform and grow and a leadership that cannot lead. Properly, the Bush administration came into office determined to refocus American attention toward working with allies. However, Japan remains so mired in domestic difficulties that it cannot play the political role its economic weight suggests. Nonetheless, Japan is inching toward a changed role. Japanese leaders are pushing constitutional limits on the projection of its military forces abroad, and some Japanese are raising questions about the character and durability of the U.S. military presence on Japanese soil.

Japan's ability to play a larger role is affected negatively by fundamental economic problems: banks overburdened by bad loans, a dangerous national debt-to-GDP ratio, a rigid labor market and highly regulated economy, and a shrinking labor force as Japan's population ages. Japan's role, as an engine of broader Asian economic growth has eroded. Moreover, Japan has never fully come to terms with its past, and this too is a weight on progress in the eyes of neighbors. Japan's future role in Asia, in short, is a question mark and, therefore, it is a central issue for U.S. policy.

South Korea

There are important changes occurring on the Korean Peninsula as well. The United States is linked by alliance to a democratizing and modernizing South Korea and by necessity to a Stalinist autocracy in the North capable either of aggression or collapse. President Kim Dae Jung reordered priorities on the Korea Peninsula with his Sunshine Policy of opening to the north, but his failure to build solid support for it and the political transition in the south leaves in doubt the commitment of his successors to this policy.

There are few other places in the world where the possibility of dramatic change with severe impact on U.S. interests are so present as on the Korean Peninsula. Positive evolution is likely to come slowly, given the nature of the DPRK regime in the north, but the negative implications of a collapse of that regime or a military deterioration are significant.

U.S. policymakers exhibit considerable ambivalence about whether engaging or isolating the north makes the most sense. Since these represent profoundly different choices, this ambivalence has policy consequences. The Bush administration's skepticism about North Korea is justified; its challenge is to move from skepticism to policies that effectively diminish the threat posed by the DPRK regime.

China

China is, by definition, an experiment in process. Never in human history has there been a polity of 1.3 billion people. The United States has roughly the same size landmass as China but less than a quarter of China's population. Consider, if California had four times its present population, it would have 120 million people with unknown—but presumably profound—consequences for its governance, environment, and economy. China is an economic powerhouse with severe economic vulnerabilities: a banking sector overburdened by debt, inefficient and money-losing state-owned industries, and a labor force lacking a social safety net and feeling restive. The political authority presiding over this country remains deeply authoritarian and repressive. But China has evolved economically and politically in dramatic ways since the late 1970s. It has moved decisively in the direction of a market economy and power is now more evenly distributed between the center and provinces and public and private sectors (state revenue has fallen from over 30 percent of GNP in the 1970s to roughly 12 percent in the late 1990s). The Communist Party has lost its ideological legitimacy in the eyes of large segments of its people, so its ability to maintain support depends on performance, especially with respect to the economy.

In recent years Chinese foreign policy has focused on, among other things, improving relations with nations on its periphery. Active Chinese diplomacy has scored many successes. Relations with most states in the region have improved.

There is in the United States both consensus and ambivalence about how to deal with China. Across the American political spectrum there is agreement that China's political system must change for its good and ours. Liberals and conservatives share this view (by way of contrast Chinese have no interest in affecting our political system). The disagreement comes over how to encourage this change. The ambivalence comes over whether the China we will face will be a threat or a partner.

For now, the "test" for the relationship increasingly seems to be focused on Taiwan. The Bush administration appears bent on clarifying what has been kept ambiguous. The PRC views unification as the essential unfinished business of the revolution. Meanwhile, as Nancy Bernkopf Tucker points out, "A growing tide of Taiwan investment in China has raised questions about its political consequence, suggesting some version of unification could materialize—not immediately, but not too far off either."[5] Growing economic interdependence does not, of course, remove the very large political gap across the straits or the danger that unanticipated, undesired, and unintended incidents could lead to war, not reunification.

There is temporary respite in Sino-U.S. tensions as the United States focuses on its war on terrorism and China focuses on its economic needs and leadership transition. This respite is reinforced by China's entry into the World Trade Organization and China's prospect of hosting the 2008 Olympics. Fundamentally, however, the United States will still need to deal with the place of a rising China in a region of vital interest. The PRC, in turn, will need to focus on the implications for its security of an expanded U.S. military presence on its South and Central Asian periphery and what a robust U.S. missile defense program means for the credibility of China's strategic nuclear arsenal.

Indonesia

Indonesia is a shining example of both the rewards and pitfalls of the Asian financial miracle. It is the fourth largest country in the world. Its economy and regional leadership role grew in the 1980s and 1990s. It was ASEAN's bulwark. But, while it grew over time, the collapse came suddenly—first its economy and then its political structure. The downsides of authoritarian rule became evident in the collapse—the lack of transparency and the incredible corruption. But democracy has brought weak and ineffectual rulers, a rise in sectarian violence, and ambivalence among many Indonesians about Indonesia's future.

The United States shares in this ambivalence. U.S. policymakers have been unwilling, since the end of the Vietnam War, to accord Southeast Asia the same importance attached to Northeast Asia. Similarly, the United States is uncertain about how to deal with the newly impoverished Indonesia whose problems seem to crowd out the opportunities.

Indonesia captures America's contemporary dilemma. If the Cold War was about confronting state strength, then the contemporary period is very much about managing state weakness—particularly when that weakness is in a state as important as Indonesia.

The fact that Southeast Asia has a large Muslim population (Asia has over half a billion Muslims) adds complexity to U.S. relations with the region. Its growing economic ties to China compound this complexity (ASEAN-China trade has grown at about 20 percent per annum in recent years).

South Asia

For too long South Asia was the forgotten backwater of American foreign policy, exciting our interest only with its periodic wars or the incursion of Soviet troops into Afghanistan. Nuclear tests in India and Pakistan in 1998 challenged this American indifference. The Clinton administration and then the Bush administration (particularly after September 11) successively defined South Asia as critically important to the United States.

At one level this is logical. India is the world's largest democracy, and Pakistan is vital to the success of the war on terrorism. Remarkably, for a brief period of time the United States has had good relations with both countries. But the region's problems are sucking America into a morass. To succeed in rebuilding a stable Afghanistan, for example, the United States must make a commitment that will stretch for years. This is an incredibly unstable region, prone to serious conflict and seemingly incapable of resolving fundamental disputes. India remains a central part of the problem, but also a central part of the solution.

The Indian reality is large and complex. Indian politics are so divisive and factionalized that an enlightened leadership has not emerged. The results are one-dimensional policies toward a weak and fragile neighbor (Pakistan is, like Indonesia, a classic weak state). India has refused to pursue an essential need: prudent management of Kashmir, which would mean confronting directly the Kashmiri people's unhappiness with Indian rule. For the United States, South Asia represents the classic case of a region long neglected that is becoming a central factor in American foreign policy.

CONCLUSION

No region in the world offers greater opportunities and more difficult challenges to American foreign policy in the years ahead than does Asia. The opportunities include the possibility of participating fully in Asia's prosperity and being a partner in building a stable security environment in the region, which may or may not include American bases in Japan and Korea.

Central challenges include accommodating the rise of China and India, the evolution of Japan to a more "normal" status, and the strengthening of the economies and governance of weak states throughout the region.

The interplay of three factors will be critical to America's role in Asia in the decade ahead: rising Asian nationalism and assertiveness, diminishing support for an indefinite U.S. base presence in the region, and a general diminution in the authority of the public sector in a region experiencing the effects of a globalized world. Taken together, these factors contribute to a fluid, unpredictable regional environment requiring that Americans combine strategic purpose with a heightened awareness of instinctive Asian wariness of our preponderant power.

Americans' descriptions of our contemporary reality dwell on America's strength and authority—we are the "sole superpower," the "indispensable nation." In the 1990s we ran helter-skelter responding to emergency calls, driven more by domestic imperatives than strategic vision. Now our organizing principle is focusing American energies on the war on terrorism and responding to the threats of WMD. American audiences appreciate this clarity of objective, as we argue about means to achieve a world of diminished risk.

But in the meantime, much of Asia is operating on an agenda that has little to do with issues that the United States defines as essential. Little, of course, is not the same as nothing. Japan recognizes the risks posed by a nuclear weapons-capable North Korea with the means to deliver those weapons. Southeast Asia knows that terrorist cells operate in their countries. South Asia is all too mindful of the risks of WMD and terrorism.

But these are not the leading issues on Asia's agenda. Their main issues are those of governance, of economics, and of resolution of several intraregion security issues. It is on these issues that the United States must effectively assert its involvement or watch the steady erosion of our position in the region.

The United States must come to grips with the following questions about its role in the region:

1. How will the United States position itself in a region when permanent bases are not possible and Chinese influence has expanded?

2. How, in particular, do we react to three significant challenges: the "emergence" of India and China; the fragility of North Korea, Indonesia, and Pakistan; and the divisions of the Korean Peninsula, PRC/Taiwan, and Kashmir?

3. What sort of roles do we imagine Japan and maybe India might play as counterweights to the rise of China, should such counterweights prove necessary?

4. Should we accept or resist direct mediating roles on the Korean Peninsula, Taiwan, and Kashmir when any of these conflicts could be catastrophic for U.S. interests?

5. Can we wrap our minds around the true challenge that the rise of China poses—not military (except over Taiwan and perhaps the South China Sea) but political/economic as the region reorients itself toward the reality of Chinese power?

6. Are we capable of playing for the long haul in Southeast Asia by staying engaged throughout the region's current period of economic troubles?

NOTES

1. "Global Trends 2015: A Dialogue about the Future with Nongovernment Experts," National Intelligence Council, Report NIC 2000-02, December 2000, Washington, D.C., 61.

2. Internal document of The Asia Foundation, San Francisco, California.

3. Clay Chandler, "China's Rivals Slow to Grasp Export Might," *Washington Post,* 25 May 2002, E1.

4. The Asia Foundation, *America's Role in Asia: Asian Views* (San Francisco: The Asia Foundation, 2001), 9.

5. Nancy Bernkopf Tucker, "If Taiwan Chooses Unification, Should the United States Care?" *Washington Quarterly* (Summer 2002): 15.

7

Defeating the Oil Weapon

James Woolsey

The wealth produced by oil underlies—almost exclusively—the strength of the three major groups in the Middle East who have chosen to be at war with us. The World Bank pointed out in the mid-1990s that, excluding oil, the exports of the 260 million people of the Middle East and North Africa (the Arab states plus Iran) totaled less than those of the 5 million people of Finland.[1] Moreover, with 25 percent of the world's oil consumption and 3 percent of the world's remaining proven oil reserves, the gap between our gluttony and our reserves is fundamental to the Middle East's, and especially the Saudis', leverage over us. As Edward Morse and James Richard have put it: "The hope of Saudi Arabia and OPEC for an increased market and for greater market share is uniquely dependent on growth in U.S. demand."[2]

Our oil dependence, and the demonstrated effect it has had on our conduct over the last quarter-century, has helped encourage each of these three groups—extremist Shia, extremist Sunni, and fascists (Baathists)—to believe that we are vulnerable. Each group is anchored in a leading oil-producing state.

In Iran, Khomeini and his successors were originally emboldened by their success in seizing our embassy hostages in 1979, holding them for over a year, and seeing us respond with an ineffective rescue attempt and yellow ribbons. After driving us from Lebanon in 1983, their affiliate Hezbollah and other Shi'ite extremists have continued to conduct numerous terrorist attacks against us. The Iranian regime continues to paint us as a threat in order to justify its repression of Iranian moderates and its increasingly hated rule.

Also in 1979 in Saudi Arabia—in the aftermath of the Iranian Revolution and a massive attack by fanatics on the Holy Mosque in Mecca—the Saudi royal family decided to subordinate important aspects of their rule to the wishes of their long-standing partners, the Wahhabi sect. Their approach for over two decades has been to forestall Wahhabi criticism and to reduce the likelihood of further terrorist incidents in the kingdom by accommodating the sect's fundamental hatred of the modern world and of infidels. Under bin Laden's influence, the target of Wahhabi- and Islamist-inspired terror shifted in the mid-1990s from governments in the region such as that of Egypt ("the near enemy") to us ("the Crusaders and the Jews").

In Iraq the Baathists—modeled after the fascist parties of the 1930s—came to regard us with clear enmity at the beginning of the 1990s. They were surprised to learn that, although they had been able to use us for intelligence and other assistance in their war with Iran, we would not permit their conquest of Kuwait to stand. Spared in 1991, Saddam has been the opposite of grateful. He has violated the terms of the 1991 cease-fire by developing weapons of mass destruction and ballistic missiles, tried to assassinate former President Bush, and explicitly, publicly, and continuously characterizes the United States as the enemy; recently the government of Syria, historically close to Iran, has on some matters begun to work closely with its fellow Baathists in Iraq.

Over the years in dealing with these three groups and other assorted pathological Middle East predators, we have occasionally acted forcefully: Ronald Reagan's strike against Tripoli in 1986 and George H. W. Bush's 1991 conduct of the Gulf War, up until the cease-fire, serve as examples. But generally for over two decades until we deposed the Taliban in 2001, the Middle East has seen us as inclined to respond to attacks by temporizing, retreating, or at most launching a few air strikes from afar.

The region's assessment of our likely behavior has enhanced our vulnerability. We have given evidence on a number of occasions that we shrink from force or even confrontation because we care only about reliable access to oil. Our behavior in 1991 in Iraq at the end of the Gulf War is the most frequently cited example of our valuation of oil above human beings. In the course of the war, we had encouraged the Kurds and Shia to rise against Saddam. Once our access to Kuwaiti and Saudi oil was secure, we signed a cease-fire, stood aside, and permitted hundreds of thousands of these rebels to be slaughtered by Saddam's Republican Guard.

OUR SAUDI PROBLEM

Although the use of oil to produce electricity has nearly disappeared in the United States (it now accounts for 2 percent of production) oil's dominance of our transportation fuel market (97 percent) continues. As we drive more and as more vehicles also crowd the world's roads in Asia and elsewhere, the demand for oil is growing rapidly and is highly inelastic. We cannot switch from one transportation fuel to another nearly as easily as we have in the case of fuel for electricity generation.

The Middle East, including the Caspian Basin, is the home of some three-quarters of the world's proven oil reserves and about the same share of the world's surge capacity for oil production. The former establishes our underlying dependence, but the latter is what creates tactical power, largely in the hands of the Saudis. The nearly 3 million barrels/day of reserve production capacity that is under Saudi control is termed by Morse and Richard "the energy equivalent of nuclear weapons" and indeed the "one clear weapon" the Saudis possess. Because it gives them great leverage over spot oil prices, it enables them to threaten Western economic stability whenever the mood strikes them.

We had a working partnership with the Saudis for much of the Cold War: We offered protection against the Soviets and their client states in exchange for a reliable supply of cheap oil. But this relationship has frayed badly over time, in spite of our defense of the kingdom in the 1991 Gulf War. The deterioration began with the Saudi royal family's reaction to the tumultuous year of 1979, when it chose to strike what Judith Yaphe of National Defense University calls a Faustian bargain with the Wahhabi sect. Not only did the royal family accommodate Wahhabi views about Islamic law, it effectively turned over education in the kingdom to the Wahhabis and began to enable their expansion into the rest of the world.

The Wahhabis' extreme, hostile, antimodern, and anti-infidel form of Islam has unfortunately now become familiar to many nations. As Faust in the drama, the Saudi elite has received a more-or-less free pass from the Wahhabis who have kept their side of the bargain by being willing to overlook the Saudi elite's corruption and lifestyle. The other two players have assigned us the role of the dependent and exploited party—Margaret—in this long-running production. Former Secretary of State George Shultz calls this redirection of Wahhabi anger away from the royal family and toward us while we still provide strategic protection for the kingdom "a grotesque protection racket."

As a consequence of this arrangement, as Adam Garfinkle puts it in "Weak Realpolitik,"[3] the Wahhabi sect, which would have been regarded by a large majority of Muslims as recently as fifty years ago as "exotic, marginal and austere to the point of neurotic," is extremely powerful and influential in the Muslim world.

The increasing influence of the Wahhabis and of Islamist ideology in the last few decades has been highly inimical to political freedom in the Middle East and elsewhere. The Faustian bargain has given the Wahhabis growing leverage in the world's Sunni Muslim communities. It is well known that the religious schools of Pakistan that educated a large share of the Taliban and al Qaeda are Wahhabi. But Pakistan is not the sole target. The Wahhabis' reach has spread as far as Malaysia and Indonesia and indeed into a substantial number of nongovernmental organizations, lobbies, mosques, and Muslim schools in Europe, Britain, and the United States.

The bargain between the Saudi royal family and the Wahhabis has had a sharp negative effect on opinion in the kingdom about the West. Bernard Lewis points out that until relatively recent times in most parts of the Muslim world, Muslims have been *more* tolerant than most other religions. Muslims treated Jews and Christians, as "People of the Book," especially tolerantly. Today in the kingdom, however, young people are systematically infused by the Wahhabis with hostility for all infidels. Moreover, as a result of the type of education they receive, most young Saudis are not equipped on graduation to perform the work necessary in a modern economy. The vast majority of private-sector jobs in the kingdom that require any skills are filled by non-Saudis. The Saudis themselves are employed (if that is the right word) as, for example, religious police—performing such tasks as ensuring that women wear their veils properly.

Based on their indoctrination and their lack of useful work, young Saudis' anger is palpable. It is not an accident that fifteen of the nineteen terrorists who attacked us September 11, 2001, were Saudis. Much of young Saudis' hatred of us clearly derives from U.S. support of the ruling regime that serves them so poorly. The *New York Times* (January 27, 2002) cites a poll conducted by Saudi intelligence and shared with the U.S. government that over 95 percent of Saudis between the ages of twenty-five and forty-one have sympathy for Osama bin Laden. Whether this official Saudi report to us of their young adults' views is accurate or exaggerated, it makes an important point about the degree of hostility to us, either by the people, by the government, or both.

Because of the First Amendment and our cultural values, most Americans are reluctant to make judgments about others' religions. But the Wahhabis and the Islamists whom they work with and support are not religious movements as most Americans ordinarily understand the term. Their behavior is not focused on spiritual or ethical matters in any sense we would recognize. The essence of their views is hatred, and not of our flaws—as most Americans would define them. As a District of Columbia taxi driver quipped to me a few months after September 11: "These people don't hate us for what we've done wrong—they hate us for what we do *right*."

One analogue for Wahhabism's role in the world today might be the part played during the period after World War I by that era's extremely angry form of German nationalism. Not all German nationalists, not even all the angry and extreme ones (or their sympathizers in the United States), became Nazis. But just as the angry and extreme German nationalism of that era was the fertile soil in which Nazism grew, Wahhabi and Islamist extremism today is the soil in which al Qaeda and its sister terrorist organizations are flourishing.

Some of the consequences of the partnership between the Wahhabis and the Saudi government have been quite lethal, even before September 11. It has produced American deaths and a failure to apprehend the killers. Garfinkle chronicles some of the history: The Saudis impeded the investigations into the Riyadh and Khobar Towers bombings that killed twenty-three Americans in 1995 and 1996. The Saudis refused to participate in an FAA-run airplane manifest agreement that lets U.S. officials know who is arriving in the United States from abroad. The Saudis refused to take bin Laden into custody in 1996 when the Sudanese offered to deliver him there. They also refused to let the United States take Hezbollah's Imad Mughniyah (responsible for the bombing of our Marine barracks in Beirut in 1983 and the murder of a U.S. Navy diver in 1985) into custody when he had planned to stop over in Jeddah in 1995.

This hostility to helping us fight terrorism is matched by officially sponsored Saudi verbal hostility. The canards about the United States and especially about American Jews that are spread by the Saudi Ministry of Religious Affairs and government-controlled media are extensive and grotesque. The Saudi ambassador in London specializes in particularly puerile and nasty jibes about President Bush, presumably with the approval of Riyadh.

There are obviously issues on which we must continue to work with the Saudi government and matters on which it is in our interest to do our best to maintain cordial official relations. But in light of the direction the Saudis have taken for nearly a quarter of a century, we have no reason whatsoever to refrain from taking steps to reduce their leverage over us. If by reducing our dependence on their oil we cause them to have to explore some alternative ways of supporting themselves, then so be it. The world does not owe them a living for being lucky enough to sit on top of a quarter of its oil.

A STRATEGY FOR DEALING WITH THE OIL WEAPON

In order to parry the Saudis' use of the oil weapon and to demonstrate to the entire region that the United States has the will to pursue our long-run interest instead of only our short-term appetites, we must take some decisive steps. These must reinforce one another and form a coherent strategy.

Two Old Political Sidetracks

There are two approaches to reducing dependence on the Middle East for oil that historically have had substantial political support in the United States but that would have, at best, a negligible effect on the problem.

First, we will not come anywhere near being able to break this dependence by producing more oil domestically. We now hold only 3 percent of the world's proven reserves. Of the more than 4 million oil wells that have been drilled in the world since the mid-nineteenth century, 3 million have been drilled in the lower forty-eight states. We thus will not find much more here. Even exploiting

Alaska's National Wildlife Refuge would increase our share of world reserves only to 3.3 percent. Our appetite for 25 percent of the world's oil would still be essentially eight times as gluttonous as we can satisfy from our own resources. Offshore exploration may yield something, but it is unlikely to be enough to dent our problem substantially.

It will also do us no good to increase our domestic production of transportation fuels using exotic and expensive processes with costs substantially above the equivalent of $30/barrel oil. The Saudis will just undercut these technologies by using their swing production capacity to increase supply and lower oil prices. They will watch as our thirst forces us to buy their cheaper oil and close down these expensive domestic facilities. Then they will smile and raise the price of oil again.

Oil is fungible. It is also a key part of both our economy and the rest of the world's. Since our economy can't exist in isolation, it is the world's supply and the world's demand that will determine the market, and our strategy must work within that context.

The Basic Characteristics of a Strategy

Not only must the U.S. strategy for blocking the Middle East's use of the oil weapon be sound for the long run, it must begin to show some results promptly. Otherwise it will not be able to build political support in this country and will not convince the rest of the world that we are serious.

This strategy must counter the Saudis' "energy equivalent of nuclear weapons": their spare production capacity of nearly 3 million barrels/day. Although the Saudis have been unable for twenty years to increase their basic production capacity, this spare capacity (which is over and above Saudi Arabia's daily production, in mid-2002, of around 7.4 million barrels/day) exceeds the total exports of all other oil-exporting countries except Russia. It is what gives the Saudis the leverage over our and others' behavior. If a crisis in the Middle East produces a spike in the oil spot market, the only way today for the world to increase supply quickly and to keep prices stable is for the Saudis to increase production from their spare capacity. Thus it is only they who can assuage Western fears of another oil crisis.

The Saudis use this leverage deftly. One tactic is for a "senior Saudi official" to make subtle threats in the press to cut production and cause price increases if, for example, we fail to please them on some aspect of our approach to the disputes between Israel and the Palestinians. If another producer seeks to take market share from them, they can also use increases in production from this spare capacity to lower prices and punish the competitor.

A strategy to counter the oil weapon can work only if it reduces the overall demand for oil, brings major new production from outside the Middle

East into the market, moves toward alternative transportation fuels, and makes these underlying changes while we protect ourselves against the Saudis' use of their spare production capacity. The approach thus has four elements: improving efficiency, increasing oil supplies from Russia, moving toward the use of inexpensive ethanol and other fuels derived from cellulosic biomass and waste, and adopting aggressive management of an expanded Strategic Petroleum Reserve (SPR). These four elements are complementary. Each has some independent merit, but undertaking any one alone would be insufficient and in some cases would involve high risk. If implemented together, each can augment the effectiveness of the others and also serve as a hedge against delays or problems with the others.

Improving Efficiency

Any serious effort to block the use of the oil weapon must reduce the demand for oil generally. We should start with improving efficiency—a better term than "conservation," since we are talking about doing more with less, not just using less. Efficiency improvements can be dramatic because technology has moved some distance since we were last serious about this subject over two decades ago. Much has been developed that is ready for implementation.

The last time we used this tool we did quite well. In the six years after the 1979 oil shock, Hunter Lovins and Amory Lovins point out, Americans cut oil use 15 percent and Persian Gulf imports 87 percent while the economy grew 16 percent.[4] For a time in the early and mid-1980s, we were improving new domestic-car gas mileage by more than 1 mpg a year (7 mpg improvement in 6 years). During this period, the world's oil market dropped by 10 percent, of which the United States accounted for one-quarter of the cut. As Lovins and Lovins stress, only 4 percent of our automotive fuel savings came from making cars smaller. In eight years we showed a stunning 52 percent increase in oil productivity and OPEC's share of the world market dropped from 52 percent to 30 percent. Those who contend that we are essentially helpless against the oil weapon have to contend with the fact that, two decades ago, we showed that we were not.

In spite of the fact that fifteen of the nineteen suicide killers of September 11 came from the world's premier oil producer, we don't seem to have gotten the message nearly as well as we did at the end of the 1970s. Since much of the public has a preference for large cars, trucks, and SUVs and is quite averse to increased gasoline taxes, the most politically plausible approach toward efficiency is to encourage the use of hybrid-electric vehicles and other fuel efficiency improvements without pushing for smaller vehicles per se. Whether our concerns are environmental, strategic, or both, we do not have any substantial reason to want people to drive small cars rather than large ones—we just care about gasoline consumption. The first hybrid SUVs that are now coming on the market should get about 30 mpg, with improvements to come. Substantial improvements in mileage have been demonstrated via the use of lighter materials, lower aerodynamic drag, better tires, and other modifications. We do not need to drive tiny cars to make a huge dent in our oil consumption.

There is a whole range of complementary steps available to encourage efficiency if we are prepared to use them. For example, twelve years ago the California legislature passed (it was later pocket-vetoed) financial incentives to reward purchases of efficient cars and discourage inefficient ones. We should be able to devise Detroit-friendly incentives such as tax credits and rebates to encourage scrapping older inefficient vehicles, promote new-car purchases of hybrids, and foster other fuel-saving features. Hybrid technology is here today and thus has much to commend it over very long-range solutions that may be more ideal but that show essentially no prospect of reducing oil use without substantial changes in the transportation infrastructure, many years of development, or both.

In this context, take most automotive fuel cells. Please.

Kenneth Stroh, who heads fuel cell research at Los Alamos National Laboratory, points out that even mass production economies will not permit fuel cell efficiency to come within range of that of internal combustion engines any time soon. According to one expert, assessment of internal combustion beats automotive fuel cells in cost per unit of produced power by a factor of a hundred.[5] Other analysts, such as Lovins and Lovins, stress that the promise of lighter, aerodynamic vehicles will make it possible for fuel cells to be small enough to afford, and for hydrogen tanks to be small enough to fit.

The basic problem of automotive fuel cells is that if we want to remain with the existing infrastructure and be able to pump gasoline at stations, then we must reform gasoline into hydrogen on board the automobile. We would need to make fewer changes in the transportation infrastructure, but the problem of fuel cell design and cost is much more demanding. If, on the other hand, we are willing to have filling stations pump hydrogen (say by reforming natural gas at the station), the fuel cell problems are considerably smaller but the need to change the infrastructure is much more substantial. And then there is the "Alfonse and Gaston" problem: who makes the investments first, the car manufacturers or those who own various parts of the infrastructure?

Among fuel cell advocates, Lovins and Lovins' answer to this conundrum is the most ingenious. They would lower costs by intertwining the electric power generation and automotive hydrogen fuel cell markets: pump hydrogen into your fuel tank, plug your car in when you park it, and sell power to the grid. Their approach would require major infrastructure changes but ultimately would more than pay for these with efficiencies. For now, it would be reasonable to use financial incentives to encourage consumers to move quickly toward light aerodynamic vehicles powered by the already-available hybrid engines. Then we could move toward Lovins-style dual-use hydrogen fuel cells when feasible.

Bringing Russian Oil into the Market

A second component of our strategy should be to help Russia substantially improve its share of the world's oil market. In light of Russia's overall behavior since September 11, this has come to be a reasonable course.

President Putin seems now to have cast Russia's lot in important ways with the West. He has shown this by his response to September 11, his acceptance of U.S. military deployments (over his advisors' objections) in Central Asia and, even more surprisingly, in Georgia, his reasonable response to President Bush's announcement of the U.S. withdrawal from the 1972 ABM Treaty, and his spurning of OPEC. The Russian level of oil production capacity is high and could be substantially higher: Jeffrey E. Garten, dean of the Yale School of Management, has estimated it could expand its current production of 6.9 million barrels per day by at least 50 percent.[6]

Russia's main problem is the deplorable state of its existing pipelines, most of which (unlike the Russian oil companies themselves) are still government owned. It also lacks pipelines in many places where they are needed. We should urge Russia to take steps to obtain Western investment to modernize and expand its pipeline network, urge Europe to take more Russian oil, and give American oil companies incentives to cooperate with Russian companies in the Middle East and elsewhere.

There are certain aspects of Russian oil production, including Russia's climate, that will restrict Russia's ability to move as far as we might like to provide Saudi-style reserve production capacity that could be surged as needed. So from the point of view of countering Saudi Arabia's spare production capacity weapon we will need to rely on the SPR, as discussed below, as well as enhanced reserves in other parts of the world. But Russia is likely to be a much more reliable supplier than the chaotic Middle East, so a steady shift toward Russia of as much of the world's oil purchases as is practical would generally be a stabilizing step. It would also be a nicely bracing development for the Saudis and other OPEC members. Such a shift would have the added effect of providing a tangible quid pro quo for some of the steps President Putin has taken.

Another reason to take this step is to give Russia time to diversify its economy as it prospers from added oil sales. For some years to come until other industries are successfully developed, Russian prosperity will depend heavily on its oil exports. We have a real interest in encouraging Russian prosperity, since it is the only way we can help foster the growth of a middle class and the kind of stability that can give solid roots to Russian political liberalization and the development of the rule of law. Russia has serious problems: corruption and criminality, loose nukes, suppression of free media, and brutal behavior in Chechnya. But at this point it looks far more likely that Russia will be able to develop a stable and diversified economy and become an increasingly democratic member of the family of nations than will Saudi Arabia.

Using Cellulosic Biomass and Wastes to Produce Transportation Fuels

Third, we should shift decisively toward the replacement of petroleum-based transportation fuels with domestically produced alternative fuels, especially those derived from wastes and cellulosic biomass. This latter comprises about three-quarters of most plant material and two-thirds of urban garbage. Over three years ago Senator Richard Lugar and I assessed the case for exploiting the development of genetically modified biocatalysts that can process agricultural and forest wastes, grasses, and garbage cheaply into transportation fuel.[7] We looked at the issue from the point of view of national security, the environment, reduced greenhouse gas emissions, U.S. economic security, and rural development around the world. We concluded that if we do not take advantage of these breakthroughs, future generations "will look back in angry wonder at the remarkable opportunity that we missed."

The case for making this shift is considerably stronger today than in 1999, due to the further development both of these biocatalysts and of other promising waste-to-fuel technologies such as thermal depolymerization that, unlike incineration, create no pollution and leave no secondary waste streams.

With cellulosic biomass as a feedstock, this is not your father's ethanol. We should *not* be moving toward increased reliance on ethanol derived from corn or other starches. Corn-derived ethanol will never provide more than a tiny share of our transportation fuel needs and requires substantial energy to produce. Ethanol derived from cellulosic biomass is superior by orders of magnitude on both counts. If we turn toward using wastes of various sorts and cellulosic biomass as feedstocks to produce fuel, we can sharply reduce costs. This cost reduction can make biomass and waste-derived fuels competitive with gasoline, as our earlier study points out, even if the price of petroleum should move down as far as $10 to $13/barrel.

Large-scale production of ethanol from cellulosic biomass can readily be achieved without introducing marginal land into cultivation and even without replacing existing crops on existing farmland. For example, Professor Lee Lynd of Dartmouth's Biochemical Engineering Program estimates that by taking only a little over half of the 60 million acres of cropland now idled by federal programs for conservation and other purposes, and using for ethanol production the mown grasses with which much of this acreage is ordinarily planted, we could produce enough ethanol to fulfill around 25 percent of our annual gasoline needs. This is at today's average vehicle mileage. At hybrid mileages the share of gasoline thus replaced could be over half of our annual usage, from this source of biomass alone.

Ethanol and other waste-derived fuels can be used in the existing transportation infrastructure. This means that we can make substantial reductions in oil use while driving the vehicles most of us own today and even larger reductions using vehicles that are already in production and readily available. Further, we can use the existing infrastructure for fuel transport and storage—with only very modest modifications.

If this transition to biomass- and waste-derived fuels is combined with encouraging the use of higher-mileage vehicles such as hybrids, we could make truly remarkable oil savings. For example, if a full-sized hybrid passenger car that achieves around 40 mpg in *fuel* efficiency uses E-85 (85 percent ethanol), it would thereby achieve approximately 200 mpg of *gasoline* mileage, since only 15 percent of what it burns is gasoline. Although most current vehicles can use only up to 10 percent ethanol, there are already millions of Flexible Fuel Vehicles (FFVs) on the road that can burn up to 85 percent ethanol. It would be a simple matter for all new cars, including hybrids, to be FFVs—it requires only a different kind of plastic in the fuel line and a differently programmed computer chip in the fuel system. If you buy, say, an FFV Ford Taurus today instead of the non-FFV model, there is no added charge. All cars in Brazil, except those that run on pure ethanol, are FFVs. As cellulosic ethanol comes on the market in volume, there could easily be available a rapidly growing fleet of vehicles that would be able to use as much of it as can be produced.

As an added benefit, any mixture of gasoline and ethanol above 22 percent ethanol burns more cleanly in all regards than gasoline. And in its life cycle of production and use cellulosic ethanol adds essentially no new carbon to the atmosphere. Even very demanding global warming gas emission reductions could thus be easily attained.

Using the Strategic Petroleum Reserve to Counter the Saudi Oil Weapon

Fourth, we need to use the SPR aggressively. This is plausible because Saudi Arabia does not have infinite flexibility in wielding its oil weapon. The Saudis cannot tolerate lengthy cutbacks or reductions in their basic production. There are several reasons for this. The kingdom has been living well beyond even its substantial means for many years. The Saudi government has run deficits since 1983, and its domestic debt exceeds its gross domestic product. In spite of this runaway spending, its per capita standard of living has dropped by half since 1980. The government realistically fears severe social dissatisfaction if there are further cuts in its generous welfare programs. And it has logistical problems in cutting off oil production: much of the

Saudis' infrastructure such as electricity production and desalination plants require the natural gas that is produced in association with oil production.

These Saudi problems in making substantial long-term cuts in production enhance our ability to use the SPR. By selling from it and replenishing it in a timely fashion, we can limit the Saudis' ability to use their reserve capacity to manipulate the market. We could, for example, sell SPR oil on the spot market to counter any Saudi refusal to increase production in a crisis when the spot price typically rises (or to counter, of course, their actually cutting production). It is possible to draw as much as 4 million barrels/day from the SPR, thus more than matching the amount of reserve capacity the Saudis can readily manipulate. Even if more than 4 million barrels/day in Middle East production were cut due to a war in the region or some other severe cause, we should be able to mitigate the reductions for some time and hold down much of the spot price increase that would otherwise occur.

John McCormack, an energy industry expert, has pointed out an important feature of the oil market of which we can take advantage in managing the SPR. The curve of oil futures prices exhibits a characteristic which is called in the trade "backwardation," namely, future prices are almost always below current spot prices. Moreover, future prices typically do not rise nearly as much as spot prices even in a severe crisis, such as a war in the Middle East.

Thus, if we sell oil drawn from the SPR in the spot market to counter Saudi production cutbacks, we can use the funds we receive to buy forward and thus more than replenish the amounts we have drawn from the SPR. To take one example, if a crisis caused the spot price to rise to $39/barrel, the future price two years out might rise modestly, but could still reasonably be at, say, $26/barrel. If we sold 10 million barrels to bring the spot price down, we could use the proceeds to purchase 15 million barrels for the $390 million we had received, for delivery two years later. Alternatively, we could merely replace what we have sold and use the extra proceeds for some other purpose. Such management of the SPR—even though spot oil prices could not be kept completely stable—holds out the possibility of denying to the Saudis the ability to cause severe recessions here as they did in 1973–1974 and 1978–1980.

We could have even greater leverage if we added several hundred million barrels to the SPR. Jeff Garten suggests doubling the SPR to 1 billion barrels, perhaps giving Russia a preference in selling us the oil to fill it, and proposing to other energy importers such as China, India, and Brazil (and presumably the EU) that they hold substantially larger reserves as well. A total reserve in oil consuming countries that approaches 2 billion barrels would constitute about two years of Saudi swing production. The existence and proper management of such a reserve would effectively deprive the Saudis of their principal oil weapon.

Major oil companies as well as, of course, the Saudis and their OPEC partners will oppose such use of the SPR or other reserves. Their argument will be that there is a danger of politicizing the oil market. Perhaps they plan to echo the character played by Claude Raines in *Casablanca* and tell us that they are "shocked, shocked" that anyone would consider letting politics affect oil prices.

First of all, we are at war.

Second, the oil market is not exactly the model of a classical free market now. OPEC has its mechanisms for administering its cartel, and the Saudis have their oil weapon. We should be able under the current circumstances to convince ourselves to do what is necessary to counter *their* continuing and egregious politicization of the oil market. To this end, we should try to come up with some reasonable international framework in which representatives of major oil importing nations can meet in a crisis and agree to manage their reserves according to certain criteria. Even if it proves too difficult to do this internationally— to manage an Organization of Petroleum *Importing* Countries—we can do much ourselves. The United States, especially with a billion-barrel reserve, could itself moderate the swings in the spot market, perhaps according to legislated criteria that set national security criteria for SPR use.

CODA

As we do our best to work with the Saudis on military matters, Middle East peace proposals, and the rest of business that we will have with them, we need to move to protect ourselves from the use of their oil weapon. We must show the entire Middle East as well that we are not helpless addicts unable to control our oil habit. We can do both by a program of improving fuel efficiency, working to bring Russia on line as an increasingly substantial supplier, moving to biofuels, and managing the SPR to counter the Saudis' use of their spare production capacity to set oil prices.

The consequence of not acting can best be envisioned by considering a hypothetical. Suppose Torquemada and the clique of Dominicans around him who managed the Spanish Inquisition had survived unreconstructed into our own time and had powerful influence within a twenty-first-century Spanish monarchy that, quite unlike the real one, was as unreceptive to democratic values as the Spanish monarchy of the fifteenth and sixteenth centuries. Suppose also that this imaginary reactionary Spanish monarchy controlled 25 percent of the world's oil. Oh, and to complete the analogy: further suppose that a portion of the rest of the Spanish-speaking world—in governments heavily influenced by Spain's power and by organizations reflecting Torquemada's attitude toward Jews, Muslims, and heretics—controlled an additional 40 percent of the world's oil reserves.

Torquemada and his Dominicans were more given to torture. The Wahhabis are more given to lopping off limbs and heads. Otherwise, in this hypothetical case Christians appalled by Torquemada's fanaticism, and everyone else, would have a similar problem to the one that non-Wahhabi Muslims, and the rest of us, have in the real world of today.

If we do not forge a strategy and act now, we leave major aspects of our fate in the hands of a regime that was once our friend and ally, but that has increasingly come to be in thrall to fanatics who hate us. The spread of this hatred and the perceived leverage of Middle Eastern oil sustain those who have chosen to make war on us.

It is time to break their sword.

NOTES

1. World Bank, *Claiming the Future: Choosing Prosperity in the Middle East and North Africa* (Washington, D.C.: World Bank, 1995).
2. Edward Morse and James Richard, "The Battle for Energy Dominance," *Foreign Affairs* (March–April 2002).
3. Adam Garfinkle, "Weak Realpolitik," *The National Interest* (Spring 2002).
4. "Mobilizing Energy Solutions," *American Prospect,* 28 January 2002.
5. David H. Freedman, *Technology Review* (January–February 2002).
6. "Economic Viewpoint," *Business Week,* 28 January 2002.
7. "The New Petroleum," *Foreign Affairs* (January–February 1999).

8

The Americas: The Stakes and Challenges

William Perry

Despite the desire of many Americans to lay down the heavy burdens attendant to the Cold War, it has become evident that the United States will have an even more extensive and onerous worldwide role in the new era we have now entered. This fact of our national life during the foreseeable future is undergirded by a rapidly globalizing international economy, as well as continuing advances in communication and an unprecedented movement of people across international borders. Moreover, American leadership is even more imperative because of an intensification of dangerous resentments and quarrels around the globe, from which it is painfully obvious that our homeland is no longer immune. Indeed, failure to appreciate and face these new realities on the part of our leadership and population can already be seen as the gravest error of the immediate post–Cold War period.

The tragic events of September 11, 2001, have now awakened our government and reanimated our people's traditional willingness to confront a clear challenge. But, alone, they do not provide us with the comprehensive course that must now be pursued in the hazardous world of the future. Indeed, it is far too easy for our foreign policy establishment to re-focus on the geographic priorities of the Cold War—Europe, the former Soviet Union, the Middle East, and Asia—for the purpose of a struggle against international terrorism and rogue states with disturbing new capabilities. While such an effort in these regions is certainly necessary, it is also insufficient. A substantial effort must also be made to incorporate fresh geopolitical factors that have become relevant over the past fifteen years into our foreign/security strategy. The most significant new element in this regard is the importance that the Western Hemisphere has assumed—in terms of both vital overseas interests and the makeup of our domestic society.

THE UNITED STATES AND THE WESTERN HEMISPHERE

The realities of our new interrelationship with diverse countries of the Latin American/Caribbean region and Canada are simply too powerful to be prudently ignored—even by those who have not traditionally paid much attention to this region. During the 1980s, the practice of democratic government expanded within the region to the point that it became almost universal—with the sole, lamentable exception of Cuba. At the same time, traditionally statist economic models were gradually replaced by more liberal, market-based approaches to national development. This politico-economic process was accompanied by an abatement of internal contention and regional rivalries—which gave rise to a stronger disposition toward cooperation among local countries and between them and the developed nations, most notably the United States. Consequently, older subregional integrative initiatives—such as the Andean Pact and the Central American and Caribbean Common Markets—experienced perceptible revival and new ones—most notably the Common Market of the South (Mercosur)—were launched. This phenomenon is closely linked with Washington's prompt reaction to transformed regional circumstances which came in the form of a farsighted proposal for an all-embracing Western Hemisphere free trade zone in June 1990. This component of President Bush's Enterprise for the Americas Initiative (EAI) later evolved into the Free Trade Area of the Americas (FTAA) process.

Over the course of the subsequent decade, U.S. trade with the remainder of this hemisphere soared by approximately 170 percent, considerably outpacing even the dynamic growth experienced worldwide. By the end of that period, two-way commerce with the other nations of the Americas constituted almost 40 percent of the United States' worldwide total (33 percent involving our NAFTA neighbors). In the process, Mexico surpassed Japan to become The United States' second largest trading partner after Canada. And export performance was even stronger (rising to 45 percent of the goods we send abroad)—giving the lie to fears that our economy would somehow be especially disadvantaged by increased inter-American trade. Indeed, this is the region where our productive sectors have run their very best commercial balances compared to other parts of the globe. Also, this region has risen to be an ever-larger locus of direct U.S. investment—some $366 billion, about 30 percent of the worldwide total by 2000—concentrated in Canada (one-third) and other key countries like Brazil and Mexico.

The nations of the Western Hemisphere now comprise a larger trading partner for the United States than the European Union or all the countries of Asia together. And continuation of 1990s' trends could make the Americas more important in this regard than Europe and Asia *combined* in the not-too-distant future. Moreover, Mexico and Venezuela are very important petroleum exporters to the United States and the Western Hemisphere remains

self-sufficient in terms of energy resources—a factor of considerable importance in view of recent unsettling developments in the Middle East. Moreover, all the countries of the hemisphere (except Cuba) have agreed to
attempt to complete negotiation of their historic FTAA by the end of 2004
and to put it into effect during the following year.

Perhaps even more profoundly, accelerating improvement of communication and transport have given rise to dramatic increases in both visitors and
migration between the United States and its neighbors in the Caribbean/Latin
American area. This trend has produced both positive and negative consequences. On the one hand, we have gained many hardworking new citizens,
enriched our culture, and seen our tourist industry greatly expand. Moreover,
this process of hemispheric social integration has made Miami a kind of informal capital of the Americas (a status that might well be recognized if the
FTAA secretariat is definitively located there). On the other hand, increased
drug trafficking, other forms of criminality, and the social costs of excessive,
illegal immigration present us with some very real problems. Whatever the
balance, this trend is rapidly transforming both the nature of the region's relationship with the United States and the very fabric of our society. Indeed,
the United States has already become the fifth largest Latin American country in terms of population (it may soon move to third place)—with increasingly obvious cultural effects, especially in the more dynamic southern and
western parts of our nation. This trend, in turn, is having predictable domestic political consequences. Like all immigrants before them, Americans
tracing origins to other parts of this hemisphere demand enhanced foreign
policy attention to their countries of origin, the existing political class seeks
their votes, and the number of ethnic Latin American/Caribbean-elected (and
appointed) officials grows at the local, state, and federal levels of government.

TROUBLE ALONG THE WAY

In recent years, however, the countries of Latin America and the Caribbean
have failed to live up to the unambiguously bright prospects that seemed to be
emerging in the early 1990s; indeed, they seem to be entering a period characterized by grave challenges even to the political and economic advances
previously registered. Buffeted by the peso crisis of 1994–1995, a worldwide
recession during 1998–2000, and adverse conditions since September 2001,
the region has had difficulty maintaining consistently high levels of economic
growth. Moreover, economic liberalization produced substantial social dislo-
cation, while the need for budgetary discipline impelled cuts in government
employment and traditional (admittedly often inadequate and wasteful) welfare programs. The ugly specter of corruption simultaneously appeared to be

on the rise—or at least was more frequently exposed under newly democratic conditions. As a result, new electorates often experienced hardships and had difficulty perceiving benefits for themselves from the substantial sacrifices being made. The sale of major assets to foreign interests and job losses resulting from privatization and/or the easier importation of goods from abroad fanned nationalism and antiglobalization sentiments, as well as social grievances. And these conditions were even harder to bear in environments where allegations of sweetheart deals and outright corruption filled the air—but rarely resulted in effective prosecution.

Politically, Latin America's newly redemocratized governments (as well as those with an uninterrupted record of free elections since the 1950s, such as Colombia and Venezuela) ran into increasing difficulty as the 1990s progressed. Each case, of course, was unique. But in general, rising rates of common crime (in some instances greatly aggravated by the activities of increasingly powerful drug trafficking organizations), the inefficiencies (and eccentricities) of leaders, and the inability of political parties and political systems to deliver reformed socioeconomic conditions for a majority of their populations, tended to undermine public support for liberalization and for democratic government.

The list here is somewhat depressingly long and diverse. The once seemingly discredited Sandinista Daniel Ortega nearly made a successful comeback in Nicaragua's November 2001 presidential elections—largely on the basis of widespread popular disappointment with the performance of democratically elected governments since 1990. After a pair of quite successful terms in office, Peru's Alberto Fujimori came to grief in a sea of corruption and an illegitimate attempt to prolong his tenure. Ecuador has seen two presidents reach political impasse and fall by means not precisely envisaged by its constitution. Venezuela's once stable, but increasingly corrupt, two-party democracy progressively disintegrated over the course of the 1990s. And it was succeeded by the neopopulist and potentially authoritarian regime of President Hugo Chávez, which has subsequently polarized local society to an obviously dangerous degree. Argentina's previously touted adaptation to the new world of the 1990s is now immersed in a politico-economic crisis so profound as to threaten its very governability. And Colombia—under escalating attack by Marxist insurgent groups, drug trafficking mafias, and paramilitary bands—faces the prospect of even more bloody internal warfare. Haiti remains in a potentially incendiary condition, despite the UN-backed restoration of elected government there. And Cuba's Marxist dictatorship continues to cling to power, even as Fidel Castro has reached an age that makes transition and fundamental change an increasingly obvious necessity.

Even among countries that have fared better, there are now grounds for concern. Mexico scored an enormous triumph during its historic 2000 elections—by bringing eight decades of one-party rule to an end in a peaceful and democratic manner. But making the institutions of democracy operate effectively with executive and legislative power divided among political parties is a challenge unprecedented in Mexican history. And, after eight years of stability and liberalization under President Fernando Henrique Cardoso, Brazil now faces a situation that may well render an unfavorable verdict on his still-uncompleted program of reforms.

Meanwhile, the drive toward closer inter-American economic integration has stalled and little has been done to prepare for the enhanced politico-security cooperation that is now necessary. The 1993 battle on Capitol Hill over Mexico's accession to NAFTA proved tough and traumatic, especially within the Democratic Party. As a consequence, not only have no other countries since been added to the United States' regional free trade network—but also "fast-track" (now denominated "trade promotion") authority for the president was allowed to lapse, precluding progress even on bilateral arrangements. Thus, the enormous regional enthusiasm evident during the early 1990s in favor of a comprehensive regional free trade area has waned considerably. Some countries like Chile have taken their own way on this course; others are beginning to evidence degrees of skepticism or even veiled opposition. In addition, more recent protectionist measures on the part of Washington have produced general criticism throughout the hemisphere and doubts are now routinely expressed as to whether the U.S. Congress would accept a comprehensive FTAA accord, even if one could still be successfully negotiated before the rapidly approaching target date of 2005. It is also worth noting that Argentina's grave crisis has placed the future of Mercosur into some doubt.

Even less has been done to complement economic developments with an effective politico-security counterpart. The venerable Organization of American States (OAS) failed to respond adequately to the first serious challenges of the post–Cold War era—Panama in 1989–1990 and Haiti in 1994. Despite subsequent attempts toward improvement within that institution and the convening of now regular hemispheric summits since the Miami meeting in December 1994 (Santiago, 1997; Quebec, 2001), progress has been painfully slow. Production of the Democratic Charter at the Quebec meeting—setting out clear standards of acceptable conduct for membership in the Western Hemisphere community—was a significant step forward. But inter-American deliberative mechanisms have not evolved to the point of being able to forge effective collective means of dealing with the kind of tough problems that the nations of this hemisphere now face in such places as Colombia and Venezuela—or which may soon emerge in venues like Haiti or Cuba.

GEORGE W. BUSH TAKES THE HELM

The Bush administration inherited a regional environment that had deteriorated to a dangerous degree since the hopeful days of the early 1990s. Initial efforts in this region were hampered by a disputed U.S. presidential election, a truncated transition, and ongoing difficulty securing Senate confirmation of its choice for assistant secretary of state for western hemisphere affairs. As a candidate, George W. Bush had evidenced extraordinary interest in the Americas—building on his experience with Mexico as governor of Texas and, in part, carrying on the family legacy provided by his father's trade initiatives and his brother's lifelong involvement with the region. In addition, he provided clear evidence of the desire to make serious attention to "our neighborhood" a personal hallmark of his presidency. In this regard, George W. Bush was the only presidential candidate in living memory to devote an entire campaign speech to Latin America. The new president's first trip abroad was an informal visit to the ranch of Mexico's Vicente Fox, his summit debut came at the gathering of hemispheric chiefs of state in Quebec, and the initial state visit to Washington under the new administration was accorded to President Fox.

But priorities are not always established by the personal preferences of presidents. The shocking events of September 11, 2001, focused public and political consciousness toward the imperative of dealing with that outrage. Nevertheless, President Bush has repeatedly made clear his commitment to Western Hemisphere affairs—with particular attention to forging an FTAA, supporting democracy, and defending its peoples against criminality and violence. Thus, serious efforts have been made to proceed as originally intended. Evidence of this includes the decision to grant Ambassador Otto Reich a recess appointment as assistant secretary of state for western hemisphere affairs in January 2002; an address to the OAS later that same month; and a presidential trip to Monterrey, Mexico (where significant new resources were committed to the region), San Salvador, and Lima. Simultaneously, the White House has sought a new accommodation with Mexico on the thorny immigration question, a task made more difficult by economic recession and increased public concern with border security. Also, the administration pressed hard to realize the campaign promise to restore trade promotion authority to the president. An initiative has been announced aimed at loosening restrictions on military assistance to Colombia—heretofore limited to counternarcotics operations—in clear anticipation of that country's intensifying struggle against insurgents often linked to the narcotics trade. And at the foreign ministers' meeting in Barbados a new treaty was announced for the purpose of helping to control terrorism (and illicit financial flows) throughout the hemisphere.

IMPERATIVES FOR THE FUTURE

Support for democracy, promotion of a Western Hemisphere economic community guided by market-based principles, protection of its peoples against criminality and violence, and efforts to upgrade the attention that the region receives from U.S. foreign policy—these provide an appropriate foundation for our approach to the Americas. But the trick is to translate these general objectives into timely and effective action in the face of increasingly serious local difficulties and the need to deal with other priorities at home and abroad.

Defense of Democracy

For at least two decades, there has been a consensus within U.S. foreign policy circles that the countries of Latin America and the Caribbean could and should be expected to maintain democratically elected governments. Democratic norms reflect the legitimate aspirations of these societies, especially growing middle classes that have emerged over the course of past decades. They also facilitate relationships within the region, with the United States, and with the remainder of the international community. We have learned from hard experience that authoritarian regimes tend to lead their countries into often bloody deadends. It simply must be our expectation that countries as closely kindred to Western values as those of this region will find a stable place in a growing global network of prosperous democratic nations.

Thus, the nations of this hemisphere need to be held to a high standard of democratic practice. This means not only free and fair balloting on a regular basis, but also that elected leaders govern with respect for constitutional norms and the basic requirements of political pluralism. Such requirements are the sine qua non for effective inclusion within this hemisphere's emerging community of nations. The hemisphere's goal should be clear criteria for membership, better consultative mechanisms to address hard cases, and, ultimately, the willingness to act together on cases of gross dysfunction and/or misconduct.

We also have learned over the course of the past decade that elections are not sufficient to maintain long-term democratic stability. Transparent, participatory processes and honesty are also fundamental requirements of government and of individual leaders. So-called second-generation reforms are imperative to improve the efficacy of institutions, ensure the effective rule of law (in government, business, and on the streets), foster accountability, guarantee genuine enjoyment of basic rights to the whole of society, end impunity for the privileged, improve levels of health care and education, and encourage the widest possible access to economic opportunity. The United States and other developed nations ought now to be shaping their traditional support programs to take these factors into full account.

Inter-American Economic Integration

Liberalizing reforms, greater fiscal responsibility, and more reliance on market forces in Latin America and the Caribbean over the past decade are important steps toward ensuring economic dynamism and competitiveness in the broader global marketplace. These steps permit the countries of the region to attract and retain investment, credit, technology, training, and management skills which are so necessary in today's world. They combat chronically high inflation, expand the range of high-quality products at affordable prices, and reinforce the positive cycle of lowered trade barriers.

Washington has been the prime exponent of greater liberalization and freer trade within this hemisphere on the basis of its own enlightened self-interest. The increasingly competitive nature of the international economic system requires us to keep open access to world markets and the Americas comprise an area of great potential, as well as obvious natural advantage. In addition, many of our productive sectors require investment or joint production in lower-wage areas to maintain their competitiveness in world markets. Latin America is also a region that is critical to our global transportation and communications networks and from which we draw many needed raw materials. Moreover, because of local consumption patterns, investment there produces higher import levels of U.S. goods than is the case in most other parts of the world. And fostering greater prosperity within this region over the long term can only help to stabilize uncomfortably high immigration levels.

It is well to briefly restate the case in favor of the mutually beneficial nature of continued movement toward inter-American economic integration because this process is coming under increasingly heavy attack both in Latin American countries and in the United States. The present government of Venezuela, for example, seems less than fully favorable to a hemispheric free trade zone including the United States, and in Brazil (where an antiglobalization summit is now held each year) elements which have expressed similar views drew strong support in October's general elections. Moreover, the difficulties getting TPA approved—as well as the conditions now attached to it and other protectionist measures emanating from Washington—show that there are serious obstacles to be overcome in the court of domestic opinion as well.

It is imperative to move forward energetically with the FTAA negotiations in the hope of completing them by the end of 2004. As a supplement or stimulus to the FTAA process (or interim substitute, if it cannot be brought to fruition on schedule), it is surely prudent to push ahead toward a long overdue bilateral free trade agreement with Chile, and to explore prospects for doing the same with Central America, the Caribbean, and other countries like Uruguay. Perhaps even Colombia should be considered, in the context of the increased political, economic, and security support it now so obviously needs. In addition, we should find new ways to give added depth to inter-American economic cooperation. One example among many would be to develop and maintain hemispheric self-sufficiency in the energy sector.

Updating the Inter-American Politico-Security System

The need for changes in the traditional mechanisms of inter-American security cooperation did not attract much attention within U.S. policy circles during the 1990s—despite a greatly altered local environment, the implications of a closer economic community, and the fact that the old OAS-centered institutions established in the 1940s had not been functioning effectively for over two decades. This matter can no longer be safely ignored.

In the decade of the 1990s, we had a nearly universal constellation of democratic governments in the Western Hemisphere. These governments were inclined toward cooperation among themselves and with other nations of the wider international community. National rivalries were correspondingly at a historically low ebb and many forms of past internal contention (military/civilian rivalry and Marxist insurgencies) generally abated (although there remained a few significant exceptions on both these scores).

But significant threats have emerged. As already mentioned, drug trafficking was never brought under control in Colombia and has progressively fueled both a renaissance of that country's long-standing Marxist insurgencies and of paramilitary resistance to them. This witches' brew now threatens Colombian society to the degree that intensification of the conflict on the part of the administration of Alvaro Uribe may well be the only way of saving the country from descent into criminal anarchy. Meanwhile, open contention between President Chávez and his growing opposition have divided neighboring Venezuela to the point that a military coup, the loss of democratic government, and even civil conflict are now genuine, indeed imminent, possibilities. There are also disquieting signs of instability in other Andean countries. Haiti could well be on the edge of fresh disorder. Even in Mexico, President Fox has been unable to resolve the Chiapas rebellion. Drug trafficking remains a very serious problem in that country. And illegal immigration, although down somewhat because of the U.S. recession and stronger border controls, still requires serious attention—particularly after September 11 and with respect to Mexico.

All these dangers argue for greater and more coordinated efforts be undertaken on the part of the democratic governments of this hemisphere. It is difficult to imagine a successful economic community in the Americas without more in the way of politico-security cooperation among its component parts.

Some progress has been made at the OAS and through mechanisms created to handle the now regular summits. These mechanisms go beyond the hemispheric chiefs of state to regular meetings of ministers, including those with defense portfolios. More remains to be done, however, in light of the magnitude of the politico-security challenges now crying out for common action. We must work to overcome strong traditional reluctance among certain currents of hemispheric opinion to face these difficulties on an open, concrete, and co-operative basis, a task made harder by a historical pattern of inattention to regional matters on the part of high-level U.S. defense policy officials.

Filling this void will require imaginative, persistent, and flexible leadership on the part of Washington—as well as a willingness by hemispheric partners to think (and act) in fresh ways to confront the new politico-security challenges that face us all. Given the enormity of the changes that have taken place over the past two decades and the impending 2005 target date for consummation of a comprehensive free trade zone, one would think that wholesale reform of the traditional organs of inter-American politico-security cooperation should already be well under way. Any comparison with the time, energy, and resources invested in post–Cold War retooling at the Pentagon or by NATO could only strengthen such an expectation. But the old and less than fully functional statutes and organs of the OAS continue to operate in Washington much as they always have (together with a generally ignored Inter-American Defense Board and somewhat isolated Inter-American Defense College). It is true that a changed attitude at the top of this venerable institution has produced modest forward movement; periodic summits have invigorated consultation at the highest levels of governmental leadership and there have even been preliminary calls for rewriting the long moribund Inter-American Reciprocal Assistance Treaty (more commonly known as the Rio Treaty). But not even a proposal for more general, top-to-bottom reassessment has been made as yet.

Serious thinking and effort along this line is now warranted. If existing OAS-centered institutions prove unreformable within some reasonable length of time, serious consideration ought to be given to a politico-security component to the free trade area/summit process. Alternatively, especially in the near term, the United States may be obliged to rely on fresh or newly invigorated subregional, functional, and/or bilateral accords to treat particularly pressing problems. The goal here is to secure necessary levels of real and effective cooperation in such critical areas as:

- common defense of democratic order and government
- conflict prevention/resolution and peacekeeping, regionally and elsewhere
- control of drug trafficking and other forms of organized criminal activity
- prevention of terrorism
- illegal immigration and refugee matters
- natural disaster relief, search, and rescue
- nonproliferation and the control of sensitive technologies
- standardization, weapons sales, and joint weapons production
- collaborative patrol, maneuvers, and other exercises
- enhanced military/law enforcement exchange, coordination, and cooperation

THE STAKES AND CHALLENGES

The age of globalization that we have entered requires a simultaneous spread of responsible government. Rogue states and regimes that cannot or will not control dangerous subnational actors have become a legitimate concern of the international community of nations, especially in the developing world. The events of September 11, 2001, and their aftermath naturally focus attention on South Asia, the Middle East, and other areas where Islamic fundamentalism and/or other grievances represent significant threats. But we must recognize that ensuring at least minimal levels of stability is now a *worldwide* challenge. Progressively incorporating societies into an international community of democratic nations is the most effective response to global threats over the long term. The countries of the Latin American/Caribbean region—already practicing democracy and scheduled for integration into a Free Trade Area of the Americas with the United States in 2005 are among the strongest candidates for inclusion. Conversely, the failure of Western Hemisphere nations to make this transition would threaten U.S. interests, as well as set a negative example for the remainder of the developing world. Local terrorist organizations (some with documented overseas connections) are active with horrific impunity in the region, and Middle East-based groups could well strike us directly from this quarter (as is evident from bombings against Israeli/Jewish targets in Buenos Aires during the 1990s). The consequences of failure are high.

A number of serious obstacles must be overcome if the United States is to ensure that its relationship with the rest of the Western Hemisphere is to become a decided asset, and not a debilitating liability, in the uncertain world of the future. Of these, the forces presently practicing violence and criminality or favoring authoritarian government on the basis of ideology or self-interest are only the most obvious. In addition, there are old habits and institutional patterns to be superceded which have long impeded democratic stability, the rule of law, and persistent pursuit of sound economic policies. Globalization and the need to maintain market-oriented approaches to development in a democratic setting impose special burdens on countries where large sectors of the electorate are poor. Frustrated aspirations can easily lead to irresponsible populism, extremist ideologies, and excessive nationalism—which in this hemisphere usually translate themselves promptly into anti-Americanism. Moreover, in some countries of the region, the situation is further complicated by sharp class divisions (not infrequently associated with racial factors) and/or the historic grievances of (usually native) ethnic minorities.

In addition to these difficulties of circumstance there also exist significant conceptual obstacles to achieving progress. Democratic thinking in Latin America has tended to be rather formalistic in nature. It is heavily focused on the form of elections and elaboration of ambitious ideals—as evidenced in the production and frequent amendment of constitutional documents. But real, day-to-day performance of institutions to the benefit of the average citizen and the common weal have often been comparatively neglected, with disappointing, and occasionally disastrous, consequences. When pervasive frustration sets in, publics often ask what concrete benefits democracy has brought them and opponents propose radical change of the "model" or political system. This tendency has contributed to a cyclical pattern of Latin American political history—the much-touted "twilight of the tyrants" in the late 1950s and early 1960s, followed by another period of authoritarian government and ideological contention, with a return to the democratic renaissance in the mid/late 1980s. This cycle must be broken if long-term integration into the modern world is to be ensured.

The current Latin American political elite is, naturally enough, a product of the period during which it came of age. Even under the favorable circumstances that appeared to be dawning in the late 1980s, there existed a considerable reservoir of mental reservations about free market economic policies and an organically closer relationship with the United States. Intervening difficulties have now raised fresh doubts and fueled adverse political pressures. Moreover, the corporatist traditions of many regional societies have isolated their intellectual and political elites from involvement in security affairs— which were historically an almost exclusive preserve of the armed forces. And it will be particularly difficult to deal with the new constellation of emerging threats for local politicians, many of whom grew up believing "security" to be a code word for military predominance and overbearing influence on the part of Washington. Thus, making democracy actually work, staying the course with sensible economic policies, and dealing effectively with security issues— as well as maintaining solid links to the wider international system—comprise the key challenges to the region's present leadership at this critical juncture.

U.S. policy faces a similar need for considerably updated patterns of thought. The fact is that this country's foreign policy establishment was trained almost exclusively in the geopolitical realities of the Cold War, as even the briefest glance at the regional specialties of the great majority of its members clearly indicates. In this scheme of things, the Americas were deserving of attention only as an occasional arena in that global struggle. No brilliant careers were to be made in this region after the beginning of World War II. The powerhouses of the field rarely mentioned Latin America or the Caribbean in their great works and never traveled there, except perhaps on vacation. Indeed, the old claim that American experts were unwilling to read about the region came uncomfortably near the mark. The societies to our south were generally looked down on and regarded as a somewhat undifferentiated mass, the governments of which could function poorly without much danger to the United States unless communists were involved or the financial interests of U.S. companies were jeopardized. This situation was not aided by a

Latin Americanist community in this country which, despite its academic accomplishments and social good works, became progressively alienated from our mainline foreign policy establishment. This community has been largely inclined toward left-of-center politics, addicted to apologizing for its local clients, no matter their views or performance (except the military regimes it abhorred), and critical of U.S. involvement in the region.

To be sure, this situation has improved somewhat over the course of the past two decades. Increasing involvement of Latin American countries in periodic worldwide financial crises, the national debate over NAFTA and the great spurt of trade and investment during the 1990s have had the effect of highlighting the escalating interrelationship of our economy with the region. This nation's mushrooming Latin American/Caribbean population has both provided it with political weight and stimulated opposition to illegal immigration. Our Latin Americanists have had more democratic governments and sounder economic policies (and even closer relations with the United States) to defend. And shafts of light have more frequently fallen on the U.S. foreign policy establishment and governmental apparatus—especially during the tenures of presidents who hail from states where the rest of the Americas has come to comprise an unmistakably relevant part of the world. Indeed, the NAFTA and broader FTAA efforts were launched from the White House, without demand or discussion on the part of high-level foreign policy generalists, and even in the face of their indifference or opposition.

The underlying attitudes and habits of present-generation elites (as well as the general public) and governmental institutions have still clearly not evolved to full appreciation of the new realities of our altered relationship with the Western Hemisphere. Moreover, the horror inspired by the terrorist attacks of September 11, 2001, could produce a regression to Cold War–era geographic priorities. In the face of these challenges, we need to ensure that the Western Hemisphere is elevated to the front rank of this country's diplomatic, economic, and security concerns. This would simply reflect a broader, deeper understanding of the fundamental importance that this region has acquired to the well-being of our society.

A change of this magnitude will require real leadership—first and foremost at the presidential level—to recognize and to articulate the need for such a realignment. The effort to bring the countries of Latin America and the Caribbean together with the United States and Canada in a more prosperous and democratically stable community of nations at the immediate end of the Cold War showed great strategic vision. Since that time, every U.S. president has rhetorically supported this effort. But, frankly, this critical task was not pushed forward with sufficient vigor when circumstances were most favorable. And it now must be completed under the pressure of more adverse conditions if today's challenges are not to overwhelm the hopes and needs of all Americans on both sides of the Rio Grande.

9

Africa: Growth and Opportunity

Charles B. Rangel

I came here to say simply this: Let us work with each other, let us learn from each other, to turn the hope we now share into a history that all of us can be proud of.

—President William Clinton in South Africa, March 26, 1998

Africa is one of the last frontiers of untapped markets and an incubator for democratic institutional development. . . . A stable and more prosperous Africa will be better equipped to cooperate on a range of global issues, including weapons proliferation, narcotics trafficking, terrorism, the environment, contagious diseases, and much more.

—Senator Richard Lugar to the Senate Finance Committee, June 17, 1998

In May 2000, President Clinton signed into law the African Growth and Opportunity Act (AGOA), launching a new era in relations between the United States and sub-Saharan Africa. Africa was now on the map for the first time as a potential trade and investment partner.

The story of AGOA's enactment is unusual because it was driven by good trade policy rather than partisan politics. Beginning more than half a decade earlier, a number of members of Congress with strong commitments to sub-Saharan Africa began to make the case that the region deserved more attention—and a more active and enlightened policy posture—from Washington. For the first time, Africa was seen not merely as a charity case, but as a potential economic partner. Americans such as the late Commerce Secretary Ron Brown visited Africa and came back with a vision of how trade between Africa and the United States could benefit both economies. African ambassadors, representing emerging African democracies, were relentless in their advocacy of a "partnership" between Africa and the United States.

The sense that we could and should be doing more to help markets flourish in the world's poorest region eventually took shape as a law which for the first time creates a trade and investment framework for a relationship with sub-Saharan Africa. AGOA lowered U.S. tariff barriers to virtually all African exports, promoted investment in the region, and built new commercial and diplomatic bridges between America and the governments and people of sub-Saharan Africa.

American businesses stood to benefit from growing commerce with Africa, and they ultimately became strong supporters of the new approach. AGOA would have gone nowhere, however, were it not for its champions in the U.S. House and U.S. Senate. That is where the distinguished senior Senator from Indiana played such a vital role. Richard Lugar understood exactly why an African Growth and Opportunity Act was needed and summed it up perfectly in his statement introducing the Senate version of AGOA: "Our bill signals the start of a new era in U.S.-African relations based less on bilateral aid ties and more on business relationships, less on paternalism and more on partnerships, and one that builds upon the long-term prospects of African societies rather than on short-term, reactive policies."

Being from Lenox Avenue, New York, in one of the nation's long-established African-American communities, I knew that it made no sense for America to build trade relationships with every populated continent in the world except Africa. What amazed me was that a man with a totally different life experience and roots in Indiana would come to the same conclusion. I concluded that Senator Lugar is a man of principle and a foreign policy visionary; he understands that in the twenty-first century, America could not afford to leave Africa out of its foreign and trade policies.

During the struggle to enact AGOA—and at times it was a struggle—Dick Lugar remained a steadfast advocate for creating a framework to build strong economic ties between the United States and Africa. When it looked as if AGOA would never see the light of day in the Senate, Senator Lugar neither became mean-spirited nor did he give up. His persistence was eventually rewarded with an overwhelming seventy-six to nineteen vote in the Senate. Dick Lugar's steadfast leadership in the Senate was critical to AGOA's enactment.

DECADES OF MISSED OPPORTUNITIES

When President Clinton stepped off Air Force One to greet an enthusiastic crowd in Accra, Ghana, in March 1998, he became the first sitting American president in twenty years to visit sub-Saharan Africa. Until Ron Brown's mission to Senegal in 1995, no U.S. cabinet member had set foot in sub-Saharan

Africa in nearly as long. The absence of senior U.S. officials from sub-Saharan Africa reflected a more general pattern of neglect. Our major diplomatic, commercial, and military partnerships have been forged elsewhere.

To the extent that America has engaged sub-Saharan Africa at all, we have too often treated it as a pawn in a larger geopolitical game. During the Cold War, both the United States and the Soviet Union meddled in Africa's affairs to prop up regimes friendly to their respective causes—often without much regard for the African people themselves. As President Clinton acknowledged during his 1998 visit, "Very often we dealt with countries in Africa and in other parts of the world based more on how they stood in the struggle between the United States and the Soviet Union than how they stood in the struggle for their own people's aspirations to live up to the fullest of their God-given abilities."[1]

The U.S. record in sub-Saharan Africa has not been uniformly poor. From time to time, the region's problems received heightened attention from Washington: sanctions against apartheid South Africa, episodic food aid to combat famine, and participation in international peacekeeping or elections-monitoring efforts are examples of U.S. actions toward Africa. These initiatives, however, have largely been sporadic. Before the mid-1990s, America neither developed a comprehensive set of long-range policy objectives in Africa nor consistently committed to helping the African people respond to crises.

This neglect stemmed in part from a gloomy view of the continent's prospects. For the better part of four decades, American policymakers dismissed sub-Saharan Africa as a political quagmire and an economic nonentity. Even today, and against a mounting body of evidence to the contrary, this "Afro-pessimism" remains all too common a point of view.

This dismissive approach has in part become a self-fulfilling prophecy, as even a passing look at the region's major economic, health, and social indicators reveals. Living standards in many countries have declined over the past several decades, and 40 percent of sub-Saharan Africa's 700 million people subsist on less than $1 per day.[2] The region also suffers from severe health crises. One in ten children will die in infancy,[3] and one in three is malnourished.[4] In many countries, an entire generation has been decimated by the scourge of HIV/AIDS. These problems have been accompanied—and exacerbated—by massive political instability such as genocide in Rwanda, civil war in the Congo and Sierra Leone, and racial violence in Zimbabwe.

THE VIEW FROM AFRICA: ECONOMIC REFORM AND GLOBAL INTEGRATION

As globalization has accelerated, many African leaders have come to view foreign trade and investment as central to a successful development strategy.

The rationale for increasing economic openness, under the proper framework of trade and investment laws and policies, has long been clear: rules-based trade allows each country to specialize in the goods that it produces best, increasing standards of living. Investment from abroad can help to ensure that each country's growing industries have money they need to expand.

The economic logic of a rules-based trading and investment system has been reinforced by clear historical examples. Since World War II, those regions that have joined the world trading system and lowered barriers among neighbors—Europe, Southeast Asia, and Latin America—have, in general, grown more prosperous. Those that have not—the Middle East and Africa—have largely suffered stagnation.

In recent years, Africa too has begun to embrace the process of globalization. Thirty-eight African nations have joined the World Trade Organization, and in recent years, African negotiators have played a more active role in shaping the organization's future. New regional economic associations have also sprung up. The fourteen-member Southern African Development Community promotes regional economic cooperation, while the Common Market of Eastern and Southern Africa has worked to speed the cross-border transit of goods.

In many countries, international integration has been accompanied and supported by domestic macroeconomic reforms. More than thirty African nations undertook significant market-oriented economic reforms in the 1990s, such as liberalizing trade and investment regimes, rationalizing tariffs and exchange rates, ending subsidies, and reducing barriers to private-sector development and stock market development.[5]

This progress toward the establishment of functioning market economies, integrated into regional and global trade networks, has both reflected and reinforced a rising tide of democracy in sub-Saharan Africa. South Africa made the transition from apartheid without the bloodshed that many feared, holding multiparty elections for the first time in 1989. Nigeria, long under the thumb of authoritarianism, moved determinedly toward democracy. Overall, more than twenty-five African states held free and fair elections between 1990 and 1997, with the total climbing to forty-two by 2002.[6]

Those countries that have made a commitment to reform and liberalization have begun to reap its rewards. Several nations which undertook bold reforms—Botswana, Mauritius, Mozambique, and Namibia—each experienced economic growth of more than 50 percent over the course of the 1990s.[7] Uganda has performed even more impressively, doubling the size of its economy in those ten years.[8] Living standards in these half-dozen countries have increased dramatically.

The good news is not limited to these countries, however; countries across the region are putting their economic houses in order. By 1997, average economic growth in the region topped 4 percent, while inflation had been tamed to 13 percent and budget deficits were halved to 4.5 percent.[9] This rediscovered dynamism and macroeconomic discipline has given rise to what South African president Thabo Mbeki has repeatedly called an "African renaissance."[10] President Clinton's commerce secretary, William Daley, speaking before the House Ways and Means Committee, summed up Africa's new reality: "Certainly Africa faces enormous challenges, which cannot and must not be ignored. But the region also presents a wealth of opportunities."[11]

THE VIEW FROM WASHINGTON: ENVISIONING A NEW PARTNERSHIP

Reducing poverty in the developing world is a two-way street, requiring both developing and developed countries to do their part. "There is a new global deal on the table," declared United Nations secretary general Kofi Annan in the *New York Times* on March 19, 2002. "When developing countries fight corruption, strengthen their institutions, adopt market-oriented policies, respect human rights and the rule of law, and spend more on the needs of the poor, rich countries can support them with trade, aid, investment and debt relief."[12]

During the 1990s, the countries of sub-Saharan Africa began to follow this path in larger numbers. But the developed world, including the United States, had not moved beyond the old formulas based almost entirely on providing relatively small amounts of aid. Foreign assistance is a critical component of successful development in sub-Saharan Africa; however, it had become clear by the mid-1990s that aid alone would not be enough to help Africa pull itself out of poverty. In the last two decades, official American assistance to Africa has fallen by almost half on a per capita basis; by 1997, U.S. aid amounted to barely enough to buy each African a cup of coffee.[13]

In contrast, the trade and investment engine in recent years has been far more powerful. U.S. private investment in sub-Saharan Africa totaled about $7 billion in 1997, seven times more than U.S. aid.[14] Trade played an even bigger role: the United States alone did more than $22 billion in trade with sub-Saharan Africa in 1997, dwarfing our trade with eastern Europe or the countries of the former Soviet Union.[15]

These trade and investment figures, however, reflect only a fraction of Africa's potential. The last decade saw global trade and investment flows to developing countries increase severalfold, but the money is increasingly concentrated in the largest and fastest-growing countries. Sub-Saharan Africa participates in barely 2 percent of global trade and receives less than 1 percent of global foreign direct investment.[16] While several countries in sub-Saharan Africa were able to participate successfully in the global trade and investment booms of the 1990s, the region's overall share in both areas has fallen precipitously since the 1960s. Recapturing part of the lost share would boost export earnings and investment flows by tens of billions of dollars.

The United States in particular has too often overlooked the economic opportunities in sub-Saharan Africa. Economic preeminence in the region has belonged to Europe, which exported about five times as much to Africa during the 1990s as the United States did.[17] Europe's success is owed largely to the maintenance of strong relationships with former colonies, particularly through economic agreements such as the Lome Convention and its successors. France especially has built on these relationships, obtaining favorable trade and investment status from its former colonies in return for economic and military assistance. Europe's strong engagement with Africa has highlighted America's relative detachment. While we had extended the benefits of increased American trade to every other region of the world—Europe, Asia, Australia, and the Americas—we had left Africa behind.

By the mid-1990s, it had become apparent that our neglect of this growing region, rich with potential, worked against both African interests and our own interests. The American interest in building peace and prosperity in Africa is compelling, as it is in other major regions of the world. Increased economic integration with the region serves both purposes, by promoting stable, democratic governance and raising incomes.

THE ROAD TO AGOA

From 1974 to 1994, the Generalized System of Preferences (GSP) had operated as the United States' de facto trade policy toward Africa. GSP extends duty-free access to imports entering the U.S. market from developing countries, generating more than $15 billion in export earnings for developing countries in 1997.

Sub-Saharan Africa has benefited relatively little from the program, however. The region's countries participated in less than 10 percent of GSP-facilitated trade in 1997.[18] The program also excludes from duty-free status key products, such as apparel and textiles, that hold the greatest promise for the least-developed countries of sub-Saharan Africa. Imperfectly suited to Africa's particular development needs, GSP made a poor substitute for an Africa-specific U.S. trade and investment policy. As Representative Jim McDermott (D-Washington) commented during a congressional hearing in 1996, "The first and most important thing that one must say about U.S. trade policy toward sub-Saharan Africa is that there is no U.S. trade policy toward sub-Saharan Africa."[19]

Representative McDermott, whose long-standing interest in sub-Saharan Africa stemmed from his experience as a Foreign Service medical officer in Zaire in the 1980s, was among a small group of legislators who began to build the case for a new policy. In 1994, following the recent round of global talks on lowering trade barriers, Congress passed and the president signed into law the Uruguay Round Agreements Act. The legislation required the president to take several steps in regard to sub-Saharan Africa: to examine U.S. trade and investment policy toward the region, to develop proposals for change, and to submit five annual reports to Congress.

In 1996, the administration delivered its first report. Those of us in Congress interested in African policy found little objectionable in the report; however, it lacked the innovative and creative proposals for which we had hoped. In response, I joined with Representative McDermott and other key congressional leaders to convene a bipartisan group, the Africa Trade and Investment Caucus, with the goal of developing new legislation and spurring executive branch action. "Some may think that this is naïve, overly optimistic, or just completely unrealistic," commented Representative McDermott. "Well, it is time that someone was optimistic about Africa, that someone was willing to challenge the status quo. This is what we intend to do here."[20] This early work of the caucus formed the seed of a dramatic policy shift.

The first version of AGOA was introduced in 1996 in the 104th Congress. But the initiative had not yet ripened politically; its ideas were ahead of their time. It would require more work with members of Congress, policymakers, and the private sector to reshape and overcome outmoded ways of thinking about Africa. In this first attempt, the bill died in the House Ways and Means Committee.

The formation of the Africa Trade and Investment Caucus, its commitment to developing a new policy framework for trade and investment in sub-Saharan Africa, and the introduction of AGOA spurred the Clinton administration to focus more attention on U.S. trade and investment policy toward the region. In the summer of 1997, the president announced an approach new in name, scope, and spirit: the Partnership for Economic Growth and Opportunity in Africa. The proposal entailed four central aspirations:

- increasing trade flows between the United States and sub-Saharan Africa
- improving the investment climate in sub-Saharan Africa
- promoting economic reform, the development of the private sector, and infrastructure in sub-Saharan Africa
- strengthening moves toward democratic governance in sub-Saharan Africa

The administration's new vision was entirely consistent with AGOA—indeed it seemed to require AGOA's passage in order for the new policy to succeed.

Congressional and public support for African trade legislation began to solidify in part due to two official visits to the continent. In December 1997, I led a congressional delegation to six sub-Saharan African countries: Côte d'Ivoire, Uganda, Ethiopia, Botswana, Mauritius, and Eritrea. The trip gave us the chance to communicate our determination to increase trade and investment between the United States and Africa, and to describe the concrete steps we were taking in that direction.

In January 1998, the president, in his State of the Union address, urged the Congress to "pass the new African Trade Act."[21] This and subsequent presidential statements of support for AGOA helped substantially to expand congressional backing for the bill. But the president's actions spoke even more loudly than his words. In March 1998, he embarked on a much-anticipated eleven-day trip to sub-Saharan Africa. Several then members of the Congressional Black Caucus and I joined him on this trip. The president spoke before a crowd of more than 200,000 in Ghana, danced and sang with schoolchildren in Uganda, spoke with genocide survivors in Rwanda, toured a park in Botswana, addressed South Africa's Parliament, and visited a rural village in Senegal. The president's visit was punctuated by outpourings of support from African people almost everywhere he appeared. Along the way, he acknowledged America's past mistakes in dealing with Africa, but focused on new realities and emerging possibilities. "Yes, Africa still needs the world," Mr. Clinton told an audience in South Africa, "but more than ever it is equally true that the world needs Africa."[22]

The president's trip served several purposes critical to the furtherance of the new policy and AGOA's enactment. First, the trip cast a positive light on Africa and its impressive progress in recent years. The president's aspiration, as he put it, was to "introduce the people of the United States to a new Africa: an Africa whose political and economic accomplishments grow more impressive each month."[23] For those of us who accompanied the president—and, I imagine, for all of those who watched the evening news—the experience drove home images of both the region's massive challenges and of its equally great unrealized economic opportunities. The visits also opened lines of communication with the African people and their leaders, through a series of one-on-one meetings, a regional summit, and a variety of public appearances. Finally, the visits served notice that the United States would no longer commit the "sin of neglect and ignorance" toward sub-Saharan Africa, as President Clinton termed it, but would finally give this promising region the attention that it demanded.

AGOA began to build momentum. In April 1997, we had reintroduced an augmented version of the bill in the House of Representatives. It was reported successfully out of committee in the fall, and passed the House by a 233-186 vote in March 1998. But once again, the bill ran aground. In the summer of 1998, despite the efforts of Senator Lugar, who sponsored the Senate version of the bill, AGOA stalled in the Senate.

Those of us working on the bill, however, were not discouraged. To the contrary, we had become convinced not only of AGOA's merits, but also of its political viability. The small group of original supporters had succeeded in building a coalition stretching across two branches of government and both parties. The president had thrown his weight behind the effort. In the House, Democrats such as Representatives McDermott, Ed Royce (R-California), William Jefferson (D-Louisiana), and I were joined by the chairman of the trade subcommittee of the Ways and Means Committee, Philip Crane (R-Illinois), who became the legislation's lead sponsor. In the Senate, the leadership of Senator Lugar, along with Senators Frist (R-Tennessee) and Moynihan (D-New York), among others, rallied support from members of both parties.

The bill's bipartisan appeal, however, did not reflect unanimous support. One alternative to the bill downplayed the opportunities for trade while emphasizing the need for aid and debt relief. (AGOA both increases trade and calls for higher levels of aid and debt relief.) Other opponents voiced concern about the impact on certain American industries and their workers. By proposing to allow greater opportunities for African clothing to enter America's textile and apparel markets, AGOA brought a flood of letters and lobbyists into congressional offices and hearing rooms. Some in the domestic textile and apparel industry, including the major union and manufacturers' organizations, vigorously argued that providing substantial but limited duty-free opportunities to African-made clothing would lead to American job losses. The industry was concerned not only about African producers, but also about illegal "transshipments" of Asian textiles routed through Africa to benefit from duty-free status. The legislation ultimately accommodated some of these concerns by placing caps on textile imports from Africa and imposing tough safeguards against transshipment.

For the time being, however, the small African textile and apparel industry appears to pose little threat to American jobs. Before AGOA, textile and apparel imports from all of sub-Saharan Africa comprised less than 1 percent of the total U.S. imports (tiny Honduras by itself exports more).[24] A study completed by the U.S. International Trade Commission found that even with AGOA's duty-free benefits, African imports are unlikely to exceed 2 percent of the U.S. total, and most of the gains will be won at the expense of low-cost Asian producers rather than more highly-skilled American workers.[25] Given the small current base of African industry, exports can grow rapidly—delivering substantial benefits to Africa—without having a significant impact on American jobs.

On the whole, American businesses, workers, and consumers—as well as African businesses, workers, and farmers—were positioned to benefit significantly from AGOA. The new policy would create new job opportunities in Africa; strengthen core labor standards, the rule of law, and the key elements of a responsible framework of globalization; and generate greater export and foreign investment opportunities throughout Africa.

Before 1999, however, American businesses were not especially vocal advocates for liberalizing trade with Africa. The contrast with NAFTA, enacted several years earlier, was striking. American industry, which had enjoyed important successes in the Mexican market prior to the conclusion of a free-trade agreement, was a major force for establishing NAFTA. Opportunities in Africa, however, were perceived as smaller, riskier, and less familiar. AGOA's initial introduction, and subsequent legislative activity in the period 1996 to 1999, thus reflected the initiative of Africa's advocates in Congress, not the efforts of American businesses. The bill's growing momentum, however, alerted the American business community to the possibilities opening up in a market of nearly 700 million people. Soon enough, key elements of the business community began to work more actively to support it.

AGOA would have lacked credibility without the involvement and support of Africa's leaders, many of whom joined with us in formulating AGOA and backed it actively and enthusiastically. From the beginning, AGOA had the strong support of each of the forty-eight sub-Saharan African ambassadors in Washington. President Yoweri Museveni of Uganda was one of the bill's earliest and strongest proponents. President Museveni's comments on a recent trip to Washington echo his long-standing commitment to AGOA and opportunities it creates. "The biggest request we are making of Western countries is to open their markets," he said. "Give us the opportunities, and we will compete."[26] With more than a decade of impressive economic growth under its belt, Uganda has already seen many of the benefits of foreign investment and trade. Uganda's foreign affairs minister, Amama Mbabazi, pointed to one multinational company whose Ugandan operations contribute thousands of jobs to the economy and more than $50 million in tax revenue. "If we had a thousand of such companies," Mbabazi said before a House committee in February of 1999, "we would join the donor's club."[27]

In February 1999, we reintroduced in the House a virtually identical version of AGOA. Five months later, the bill again won passage from the House. The Senate then began a protracted struggle over the bill. Several Senators from textile-producing states, concerned about the effect on jobs in their districts, were able to insert an amendment requiring that African garments receiving duty-free entry into the U.S. market use U.S.-made cloth. With this and other changes, the Senate agreed to AGOA on a seventy-six to nineteen vote.

To me and many of the bill's other supporters, however, the rules-of-origin provision negated the impact of the new policy. If burdened by a requirement that cloth be shipped across the Atlantic before being sewn, African producers would be unable to compete fairly. In May 2000, House and Senate conference committee members agreed on a deal that placed caps on the import of garments that use local African cloth, but exempted the least-developed countries. President Clinton signed the bill into law on May 18, 2000.

THE NEW POLICY

Consistent with the "global new deal" that UN secretary general Kofi Annan and others have described, the philosophy that underlies AGOA places the onus for progress on both the United States and the countries of sub-Saharan Africa. The bill's nine statements of policy set forth an ambitious and wide-ranging agenda, including the expansion of economic and diplomatic ties and the promotion of civil society and political freedom. As I have mentioned, many of these elements are reflective of reforms that African countries had already undertaken or began to undertake.

The centerpiece of the new policy is the reduction of barriers to trade and investment. Eighteen hundred goods not covered by the Generalized System of Preferences program are given duty-free access to American markets under AGOA.[28] The expansion of trade is also a key mechanism for helping to build a flourishing private sector and encouraging economic and political reform—two other aims of the new policy.

Among the most important products to many of our African trading partners are textiles and apparel, which had been excluded from GSP. For two centuries, countries have built their capabilities in manufacturing by starting in textiles and apparel. Many of the economies that have grown by leaps and bounds in recent decades—from China and Taiwan to Mexico and Costa Rica—have relied heavily on their textile and apparel industries. A few African countries, notably Mauritius, Lesotho, South Africa, and Madagascar, already do a substantial and growing business in this sector. Encouraged by more open access to the huge U.S. market, other sub-Saharan African countries are likely to follow in their footsteps in the coming years.

Moreover, AGOA provides a model for fulfilling the secretary general's vision of a "global new deal" on trade and investment. For example, AGOA recognizes the important links between trade and human rights and between trade and labor standards. In order to reward sound economic management and ensure that the benefits of increased trade go to countries that can use them effectively, AGOA's eligibility criteria reflect the fact that the United States has certain expectations of its trading partners. An eligible country must "have established, or be making continual progress toward establishing" a market-based economy; the rule of law and basic political rights; the elimination of barriers to U.S. trade and investment; economic policies to reduce poverty, increase the availability of health care, and build physical and economic infrastructure; a system to combat corruption and bribery; and protection of basic, internationally recognized worker rights. To be eligible for AGOA's benefits, eligible countries must also refrain from engaging in activities that are contrary to U.S. national security or foreign policy interests, and from committing gross violations of human rights.[29]

Our insistence on extending AGOA's benefits to countries that are playing by the rules of today's global economy has led some critics to charge that this new approach imposes "IMF-style conditions" that threaten African nations' sovereignty and self-determination. But AGOA does not prescribe specific macroeconomic policies or require governments to curtail spending on social services or education. In fact, it requires beneficiary countries to make progress toward reducing poverty, improving health care, and protecting human and workers' rights. These are goals already central to the policies of most of Africa's governments.

AGOA also reflects a recognition that growing trade in goods requires growing investment in both businesses and workers. Both Africa and the United States will benefit most from AGOA if Africa receives a steady stream of capital, enabling its businesses to invest and grow. The World Bank estimated that to achieve 6 percent economic growth and significantly raise living standards, sub-Saharan Africa will require at least $100 billion in investment each year.[30] To reach this goal, Africa's governments must continue to develop favorable investment climates, including the enforcement of property rights, the establishment of predictable and fair tax systems, and the liberalization of capital flows.

U.S. and international financial institutions also have a part to play in ensuring increased foreign investment in sub-Saharan Africa. To that end, AGOA directs the Overseas Private Investment Corporation (OPIC), an agency charged with promoting private investment in developing countries, to provide an additional $500 million in long-term equity to finance critical infrastructure development projects. This OPIC capital will, we hope, bring in its wake a growing stream of private investment dollars.

The new American consensus on expanding trade and investment in Africa does not diminish the value or importance of continued development aid. Both sources of income will be critical to Africa's ability to address the problems it faces. Some of Africa's most serious challenges—providing clean water, managing the AIDS crisis, and building the rule of law—can be met only through the combined resources of African governments and international donors. The United States now dedicates barely one-tenth of 1 percent of its GDP to aid, its lowest level in decades.[31] U.S. aid to Africa ought to be increased substantially and updated continually to ensure that it is meeting real needs on the ground and serving those who need it most. AGOA strongly supports this aim.

One particularly important source of aid is debt relief. Many African governments groan under the weight of debt burdens incurred by previous regimes. In some countries, debt service payments drain 20 percent or more of GDP. In recent years, and in response to insistent calls by African governments, the international community has responded with the Highly Indebted Poor Countries (HIPC) initiative. By the spring of 2002, HIPC had delivered more than $35 billion in debt relief to twenty-two sub-Saharan African countries.[32] The architects of AGOA continued this work by helping to secure almost $500 million in unilateral debt relief by the United States in the past two years.[33]

The success of this new partnership with Africa will depend not only on removing barriers to trade and investment, but also on better communication and knowledge sharing. AGOA specified the creation of an Africa Trade and Economic Cooperation Forum to help surface and resolve trade issues and promote closer diplomatic ties. To ensure that trade with Africa receives heightened attention, and in response to an AGOA provision, President Clinton created a senior position in the Office of the United States Trade Representative dedicated to African trade affairs, and expanded the number of field officers in sub-Saharan Africa working on commerce. Going forward, the U.S. secretaries of state, commerce, and the treasury will meet with their African counterparts annually in order to raise issues and work toward fuller economic cooperation.

SHOWING IMMEDIATE IMPACT

In the two years since AGOA's enactment, the new U.S.-African partnership is off to a fast start. Thirty-five countries are eligible for AGOA benefits, and almost half (seventeen) have qualified for textile and apparel benefits.[34] More than $8 billion in African exports entered the United States duty-free under AGOA in 2001, representing almost 40 percent of total African exports to the United States.[35] America has become Sub-Saharan Africa's biggest export customer.

Excluding oil, which saw a precipitous drop in prices in 2001, total imports from sub-Saharan Africa increased by 11 percent in the year following AGOA's passage.[36] As expected, apparel has played a central role, with exports to the United States jumping 28 percent in 2001.[37] Success stories abound. In Lesotho, 11 new factories were opened and 8 expanded, creating 15,000 new jobs. Investors have channeled more than $78 million into the textile and apparel industry in Mauritius. Plans to sink $250 million into the nascent Namibian industry have been finalized.[38]

U.S. and African officials have also successfully launched new forums to improve dialogue on trade and investment issues. The Africa Trade and Economic Cooperation Forum, kicked off in 2001, annually brings together the president and senior cabinet officials with their counterparts from our African partners. From 1999 to 2001, the United States provided almost $200 million in trade capacity-building assistance to sub-Saharan Africa.[39] These cooperative efforts have led to the first steps toward free trade agreements between the United States and the countries of sub-Saharan Africa.

Our work is not done. AGOA's opponents have shifted their fight to the regulatory process, aiming to convince the Department of Commerce (which oversees AGOA's implementation) that the bill's provisions ought to be construed as narrowly as possible. The new policy's supporters, meanwhile, will continue to press for administrative decisions that reflect AGOA's broad legislative intent. We have also introduced "AGOA II," which seeks to expand and build on the success of its predecessor.

LOOKING AHEAD

For all the good that increased access to American markets can do for Africa, trade is not the beginning and end of the continent's concerns. Both our national interest and our sense of basic human decency tell us that we must do more to help avert humanitarian disasters and build lasting economic security in sub-Saharan Africa. We have already taken some steps. The Africa: Seeds of Hope Act, signed into law in 1998, aims at stimulating food production in sub-Saharan Africa. The Global AIDS and Tuberculosis Act of 2000 authorizes $600 million in new funding to combat the HIV/AIDS epidemic.[40] President Clinton's Leland Initiative has helped to increase Internet access in the region.[41]

But we must do more, in terms of both trade and aid. As Africans tell us time and again, our domestic agricultural subsidies continue to pose a trade barrier to African food products. We must find a way to safeguard the survival of farmers in America without impoverishing farmers in Africa.

We must also seek to diversify trade across the entire region. Today, U.S. trade with Africa is highly concentrated on particular countries and particular goods: almost 80 percent of U.S. trade involves just four of the region's forty-eight countries (Nigeria, South Africa, Angola, and Gabon) and oil and precious metals comprise more than 70 percent of the total value.[42] In the long run, AGOA's success will be measured not just on whether it increases overall trade levels, but on the extent to which it encourages development throughout sub-Saharan Africa.

Notwithstanding these ongoing challenges, AGOA's enactment is a landmark in U.S.-African relations. It represents a new spirit and commitment in American policy toward sub-Saharan Africa, rooted in a new optimism about its future. As Senator Lugar declared, "AGOA is a modest bill which, if adopted, could have immodest results in Africa. It takes a long-term view and provides a policy road map for achieving economic growth and opportunity. . . . If we are successful, Africa will provide new trade and investment opportunities for the United States. It will also improve the quality of life for a broader segment of the people of Africa, a goal we must all support and applaud."[43]

I have long been convinced that the path forward for U.S.-African relations lies in transcending the old inequalities in order to establish a genuine partnership based on open dialogue and the mutual benefits of foreign trade and investment. Thanks to Dick Lugar and his work on behalf of the enactment of AGOA, we have taken the vital first step on that path to a brighter future.

NOTES

1. Cited in "What Road to Democracy?" *Foreign Policy in Focus,* at www. foreignpolicy infocus.org/papers/africa/democracy_body.html.

2. World Bank, *Global Economic Prospects and the Developing Countries, 2001* (Washington, D.C.: World Bank, 2001).

3. World Bank, *World Development Report, 2001* (Washington, D.C.: World Bank, 2001).

4. UN Children's Fund, *State of the World's Children, 1998* (UN Children's Fund, 1998).

5. Rangel talking points before Ways and Means Subcommittee on Trade bill markup, 1998.

6. World Bank, "Can Africa Claim the 21st Century?" Press release.

7. World Bank, *World Development Indicators, 2002* (Washington, D.C.: World Bank, 2002).

8. World Bank, *World Development Indicators, 2002.*

9. Office of the United States Trade Representative, "Comprehensive U.S. Trade and Development Policy for Toward Sub-Saharan Africa," Report to Congress, 1998.

10. Victory speech following national election in South Africa, June 2, 1999, at news.bbc.co.uk/hi/english/world/monitoring/newsid_360000/360349.stm.

11. Secretary Daley, testimony before House Ways and Means Committee, February 3, 1999.

12. Kofi Annan, "Trade and Aid in a Changed World," *New York Times,* 19 March 2002, 23.

13. Raymond W. Copson, "Africa: Foreign Assistance Issues," Congressional Research Service, June 13, 2002.

14. U.S. Department of Commerce, Bureau of Economic Analysis, "International Accounts Data," at www.bea.doc.gov/bea/di/dia-ctry.htm.

15. Office of the United States Trade Representative, "2002 Comprehensive Report," 24.

16. World Trade Organization, "International Trade Statistics 2001," at www.wto.org/english/res_e/statis_e/its2001_e/stats2001_e.pdf.

17. World Trade Organization, "International Trade Statistics 2001."

18. World Trade Organization, "International Trade Statistics 2001."

19. Representative Jim McDermott, testimony before House of Representatives Ways and Means Subcommittee on Trade, 1 August 1996.

20. McDermott, testimony before House of Representatives Ways and Means Subcommittee on Trade.

21. President Clinton, 1998 State of the Union Address.

22. President Clinton speech before the South African Parliament, 26 March 1998, at www.polity.org.za/govdocs/speeches/foreign/sp0326-98.html.

23. President Clinton, 20 March 1998, at clinton4.nara.gov/WH/Work/032398.html.

24. U.S. International Trade Commission, "Likely Impact of Providing Quota-Free and Duty-Free Entry to Textiles and Apparel from Sub-Saharan Africa," Investigation 332-379, at www.usitc.gov/332S/ES3056.htm.

25. U.S. International Trade Commission, "Likely Impact."

26. Richard Stevenson, "Seeking Trade, Africans Find Western Barriers," *New York Times,* 26 May 2002, 3.

27. Honorable Amama Mbabazi, testimony before House of Representatives Ways and Means Subcommittee on Trade, 23 February 1999.

28. Office of the United States Trade Representative, "2002 Comprehensive Report," 4.

29. Text of the African Growth and Opportunity Act.

30. Cited in Charlene Barshefsky, "Advances for Africa," *Washington Times,* 25 June 1998, A21.

31. Cited in Paul Blustein, "Another Plea for More Aid to Poor," *Washington Post,* 19 November 2001, A18.

32. International Monetary Fund and International Development Association, "Heavily Indebted Poor Countries (HIPC) Initiative: Status of Implementation," 12 April 2002, at http://www.worldbank.org/hipc/Status_of_Implementation_0402.pdf.

33. Charles B. Rangel, "Africa As Forgotten Trade Partner," *Washington Times,* 10 June 1999, A21.

34. Rangel, "Africa As Forgotten Trade Partner."

35. Office of the United States Trade Representative, "2002 Comprehensive Report," 1.

36. U.S. Department of Commerce, "United States–Africa Trade Profile," March 2002.

37. U.S. Department of Commerce, "United States–Africa Trade Profile."

38. Office of the United States Trade Representative, "2002 Comprehensive Report," 3.

39. Office of the United States Trade Representative, "2002 Comprehensive Report," 6.

40. The Africa: Seeds of Hope Act is Public Law 105-385, and the Global AIDS and Tuberculosis Relief Act of 2000 is Public Law 106-264. For brief descriptions, see Congressional Research Service, "Africa Backgrounder: History, U.S. Policy, Principal Congressional Actions," at www.congress.gov/cgi-lis/web_fetch_doc?dataset=erp_prd.dst&db=rl&doc_id=xRL30029.

41. Congressional Research Service, "Africa Backgrounder: History, U.S. Policy, Principal Congressional Actions," at www.congress.gov/cgilis/web_fetch_doc?dataset=erp_prd.dst&db=rl&doc_id=xRL30029.

42. U.S. Department of Commerce. "United States–Africa Trade Profile."

43. Senator Lugar, speech on the Senate floor introducing AGOA.

III

THE ROAD AHEAD

10

The Threat of Terror

Kenneth L. Adelman

The twenty-fifth year of Dick Lugar's service in the U.S. Senate has differed sharply from any of the previous twenty-four. Terrorist attacks transformed America radically, while terrorist threats now endanger America gravely. We are citizens of a new nation, together facing a new threat—distinct from that imagined by the young Dick Lugar first arriving on Capitol Hill as senator, or even the yet-younger Lugar first arriving at Indianapolis City Hall as mayor.

Not all of this has been for the worse. Americans have come to share the basic values Senator Lugar and other like-minded Midwesterners have felt their whole lives (I admit being a regional chauvinist, hailing from Chicago).

Americans are now more determined, grateful for the nation's liberties and character. We are more purposeful, patriotic, and profound since September 11, 2001. The narcissism of the 1990s—so aptly represented and reinforced by the Clintons—has yielded to a far finer citizenry.

A Boston conductor friend speaks of "the gift of September 11." This initially jars, but he explains that since that cataclysmic event, both his performers and his audiences have revealed a depth in sensitivity he had never seen before—probably because they had seldom experienced it before.

The frivolous "me-me" 1990s were transformed into the purposeful opening of the twenty-first century. Such transformation has a historical precedent. The decade of the 1920s was marked by *The Great Gatsby* and President Warren Harding's overblown, Clintonian flourishes about his times "not [of] heroics but healing, not nostrums but normalcy, . . . not revolution but restoration, not agitation but adjustment, . . . not surgery but serenity, not the dramatic but the dispassionate," and, finally, "not experiment but equipoise."

Yet Harding's was a frivolous time, before the struggles of the 1930s and the triumphs of the 1940s. George Orwell in 1940 wrote an insightful article about the transformation then underway: "Nearly all Western thought since" World War I, he told, "has assumed tacitly that human beings desire nothing beyond ease, security, and avoidance of pain."

Yet, as Orwell explained, "human beings *don't* only want comfort, safety, short working-hours, hygiene, birth control, and, in general, common sense. They also, at least intermittently, want struggle and self-sacrifice, not to mention drums, flags and loyalty parades. . . . Whereas socialism, and even capitalism in a more grudging way, have said to people 'I offer you a good time,'" great people at historic times seek more than mere comfort.

They find meaning in epic battles for noble causes. First the British people, and then we Americans, became aroused and determined in our epic battles for civilization against the twin totalitarian barbarisms of Nazism and communism. The guiding principles which served those epic battles— "unconditional surrender," and then "containment" and "deterrence"—no longer fit today's epic battle for civilization against the threat of terrorism and reality of radical Islam.

Henceforth, the guiding principle of American national security, and foreign policy, is "preemption." Adopted officially as U.S. policy by President Bush, incrementally after September 11 and then quite explicitly during his commencement speech at West Point on June 1, 2002, this doctrine recognizes that acts of terrorism against civilians are too horrendous to wait until their completion. Vigorous action is needed before the dastardly crimes can be perpetrated. "If we wait for threats to fully materialize," President Bush said there, "we will have waited too long."

The intellectual foundation of preemption comes from an insight by Machiavelli when he compared deft statecraft to medical treatment. The more glaring the symptoms of any disease, he wrote in *The Prince,* the more obvious its diagnosis—but yet the more difficult its treatment. By the time a doctor is certain a patient has lung cancer, the time for effective treatment may have passed. The best presidents, like the best doctors, may have to act when the evidence is still inconclusive. Otherwise, the time for effective action may have passed.

Our wisest leaders joining Dick Lugar on the Senate Foreign Relations Committee, the Senate Armed Services Committee, their counterparts in the House, and especially those in the executive branch from the president down to all those responsible for our national security, must now ask not only, "What *is* happening?" but "What *could* happen?"

When millions of Americans, Israelis, Brits, and other democratic peoples are threatened by terrorists willing to die themselves in launching chemical, biological, or nuclear weapons, there is no one evident who can unconditionally surrender. Rather than rollback Nazi and Japanese aggression, or keep the expansive Soviet empire encaged, we must now preempt threats to our security and civilization. As the most sophisticated weapons come into the most despicable hands, we must take proactive steps to wipe out those weapons, or, better yet, those hands as well.

Containment and deterrence worked wonders when the prime aggressors we faced had a specific face and address. As President Bush said at West Point: "Deterrence, the promise of massive retaliation against nations, means nothing against shadowy terrorist networks with no nation or citizens to defend. Containment is not possible when unbalanced dictators with weapons of mass destruction can deliver those weapons on missiles or secretly provide them to terrorist allies."

Indeed, the identity of all those responsible even for September 11 remains unknown. Among them were Osama bin Laden and the nineteen hijackers. But they undoubtedly had many intermediaries we still cannot identify, more than a year later. Moreover, such an approach presumes rationality and a desire for self-preservation. Neither is evident among terrorists today.

Leaders in the Kremlin knew that an attack against us, our friends, and allies, would unleash a devastating reaction. And we could rely on deterrence while waiting out the inevitability of Soviet decay. As George F. Kennan wrote so presciently, over time communism's rot would erode that system and the power on which it rested. Meanwhile, fear of their own death and their society's destruction would keep Kremlin leaders from recklessness.

In today's world, no such assumptions hold. The terrorists' world will not rot much further over time, as it is already pretty rotten. Regardless, they care little about their societies. Rather, they are filled with inexplicable bile against civilization, and divine justification from the Koran.

In fact, no form of deterrence works any longer. Terrorists do not fear their own death, but indeed welcome it—with all those brown-eyed virgins awaiting them in the afterlife. And, again, they could care less about their own society's destruction.

Moreover, the traditional foreign policy approach of America, first enunciated by John Quincy Adams, of leading by example has become utopian. "We cannot defend America and our friends," said his successor George W. Bush on June 1, 2002, "by hoping for the best." Nor is the twentieth-century tool of U.S. national security—international arms agreements—any longer of much help. Again, President Bush: "We cannot put our faith in the word of tyrants who solemnly sign nonproliferation treaties and then systematically break them."

In the pre–September 11 world, preemption seemed downright dangerous. Hence, President Clinton could refuse to seize, or have slain, Osama bin Laden three times in the 1990s (according to the *London Sunday Times*) without debate (though with much regret now).

We witnessed the cost of that traditional approach on September 11. Now we know better. And so we must act better—by preemption. Here is how President Bush put it at West Point: "The war on terror will not be won on the defensive. We must take the battle to the enemy, disrupt his plans and confront the worst threats before they emerge. In the world we have entered, the only path to safety is the path of action. And this nation will act."

Our security requires such preemptive action. How dreadful it would be if America were dealt another devastating blow—perhaps even greater than September 11. More dreadful if we all realized that President Bush could have prevented it—in the new jargon, "preempted" it—but chose not to because of armchair nattering by Europeans or foreign policy elites.

Preemption thus has become the watchword of U.S. foreign policy out of necessity, not choice. And just as "containment" and "deterrence" could offer few precise policy prescriptions during Cold War crises, preemption encapsulates a thrust for policy actions—not the timing, type, or level of our actions. Some preemptive steps may be political or economic, but many must be military attacks. As then, reasonable people will disagree over which options, if any, to choose at any particular time.

In fact, preemption will prove far more controversial than containment. The former doctrine was primarily defensive and passive. We warned the Soviets against aggression and built barriers to dissuade them. Our new doctrine is primarily aggressive and proactive. *We* decide when we must move to combat potential terrorists. The level of evidence, timing, and scale of our attacks will be disputed.

We have come to realize what would happen if a terrorist cell gets possession of a nuclear, biological, or chemical weapon. It would, in essence, wreck havoc on America. Americans have been told by our top officials—Vice President Dick Cheney, Defense Secretary Donald Rumsfeld, and Homeland Security Chief Tom Ridge—that such an attack may even be inevitable. That is why the United States must go on the offensive in the war against terrorism.

Preemption can best begin by removing the world's most probable supplier of weapons of mass destruction to terrorists—Saddam Hussein—from office. In his stellar State of the Union Address in January 2002, President Bush included Iraq as one of the "axis of evil" states. The president has since repeatedly indicated that Saddam must be removed from office.

Since then, dire warnings have been sounded about the dangers and difficulties of liberating Iraq. Two knowledgeable Brookings Institution analysts, Philip H. Gordon and Michael E. O'Hanlon, concluded that the United States would "almost surely" need "at least 100,000 to 200,000" ground forces.[1] Worse: "Historical precedents from Panama to Somalia to the Arab-Israeli wars suggest that . . . the United States could lose thousands of troops in the process."

Granted, removing Hussein would differ from taking down the Taliban. And no one favors "a casual march to war." This is serious business, to be treated seriously.

And we took it seriously the last time such fear-mongering was heard from military analysts—when we considered war against Iraq twelve years ago. The "strategist" Edward N. Luttwak cautioned on the eve of Desert Storm: "All those precision weapons and gadgets and gizmos and stealth fighters . . . are not going to make it possible to re-conquer Kuwait without many thousands of casualties." As it happened, our "gizmos" worked wonders. Luttwak's estimate of casualties was off by "many thousands," just as the current estimates are likely to be.

I believe that defeating Hussein's military power and liberating Iraq would be a cakewalk for four simple reasons: (1) It was a cakewalk last time; (2) Iraq has become much weaker; (3) we have become much stronger; and (4) now we are playing for keeps.

Gordon and O'Hanlon mentioned today's "400,000 active-duty troops in the Iraqi military" and especially the "100,000 in Saddam's more reliable Republican Guard and Special Republican Guard," which "would probably fight hard against the United States—just as they did a decade ago during Desert Storm."

Many of us missed that. Instead, we saw gaggles of Iraqi troops attempting to surrender to an Italian film crew. The bulk of the vaunted Republican Guard either hunkered down or was held back from battle.

Iraqi forces are now much weaker. Saddam's army is one-third its size since then, in both manpower and number of divisions. It still relies on obsolete Soviet tanks, which military analyst Eliot Cohen calls "death traps." The Iraqi air force, never much, is half its former size. Iraqi forces have received scant spare parts and no weapons upgrades. They have undertaken little operational training since Desert Storm.

Meanwhile, American power is much fiercer. The advent of precision bombing and battlefield intelligence has dramatically spiked U.S. military prowess. The "gizmos" of Desert Storm were 90-plus percent dumb bombs. Against the Taliban, more than 80 percent were smart bombs. Unmanned Predators equipped with Hellfire missiles and Global Hawk intelligence gathering did not exist during the first Iraqi campaign.

In 1991 we engaged a grand international coalition because we lacked a domestic coalition. Virtually the entire Democratic leadership stood against President Bush. The public, too, was divided. This President Bush does not need to amass disparate small states as "coalition partners" to convince the Washington establishment that we are right. Americans of all parties now know we must wage a total war on terrorism.

Saddam Hussein constitutes the number one threat against American security and civilization. For, unlike Osama bin Laden, he has billions of dollars in government funds and scores of government research labs working feverishly on weapons of mass destruction—and just as deep a hatred of America and civilized free societies. Once President Bush clearly announces that our objective is to rid Iraq of Hussein, and our unshakable determination to do whatever it takes to win, defections from the Iraqi army may come even faster than a decade ago.

We can force a rapid collapse of Saddam's regime:

- by quickly knocking out all his headquarters, communications, air defenses, and fixed military facilities through precision bombing
- by establishing military "no-drive zones" wherever Iraqi forces try to move
- by arming the Kurds in the north, Shiites in the south, and his many opponents everywhere
- by using U.S. Special Forces and some U.S. ground forces with protective gear against chemical and biological weapons
- by stationing theater missile defenses to guard against any Iraqi Scuds still in existence
- by announcing loudly that any Iraqi, of any rank, who handles Saddam's weapons of mass destruction, in any form, will be severely punished after the war

Measured by any cost-benefit analysis, such an operation would constitute the greatest victory in America's war on terrorism. It would take "preemption" from the message of a West Point commencement address to the essence of U.S. foreign and national security policy.

In our transformed nation, Americans now appreciate what would happen once terrorists obtain "loose nukes." Millions have watched Ben Affleck and Morgan Freeman in the Tom Clancy movie thriller *The Sum of All Fears*. This story of a nuclear attack on Baltimore has a message which is echoed in the serious press. For instance, the May 25, 2002, *New York Times Magazine* blasted across its cover the following frightful sentence: "The best reason for thinking that a NUCLEAR TERRORIST ATTACK [their emphasis] won't happen is that it hasn't happened yet, and that is terrible logic."

Ace reporter Bill Keller ends his careful and lengthy examination, "A terrorist who pulls off even such a small-bore nuclear explosion will take us to a whole different territory of dread from September 11th. It is the event that preoccupies those who think about this for a living."

Such responsible reporting removes any excuse for the U.S. government *not* to act on the threat of a terrorist attack. It is a clear and present danger. Any conceivable reasons for the Bush administration's pre–September 11 lackadaisical attitude on terrorism are gone.

Besides the protection of Americans and democratic peoples, removing Saddam from power would have a positive effect on the most troublesome region of today—the Middle East. In a nutshell, it would bolster forces for moderation and peace between Israelis and Arabs, and give a body blow to the forces for radicalism and war against democracies.

My longtime mentor, Donald Rumsfeld, is fond of saying: When a particular problem is intractable, enlarge it. While that sounds incongruous, applying it to the Israel-Palestinian war, which has clearly become intractable, shows its profundity. The Bush administration could enlarge this local problem by moving beyond the status of Jerusalem, the legality of Israeli settlements, the right of return by displaced Palestinians, and sundry nits and nats of whatever cease-fires can be patched together.

It could undertake various actions against the longtime campaign to destroy Israel—and America, as a fellow prosperous and successful democracy. First, it could stop calling Palestinian kids "suicide bombers" and rather call them "homicide bombers." This White House spokesperson Ari Fleischer did for a while. But the administration soon reverted to the conventional terminology, which is misleading. For anyone committing suicide does so alone, without any inkling to harm anyone else. Here, rather, the goal is not to kill oneself, but to kill others. For a Palestinian kid to commit suicide, without killing Jews, is to be a failure.

Second, the administration should stop leaking that evidence does not exist linking Iraq to terrorism. According to those who are in the best position to know, the Czech intelligence agency, terrorist ringleader Mohammed Atta met in Prague a few months before September 11 with a leading Iraqi intelligence agent. Before that, Saddam had a key role in the World Trade Center bombing of 1993 (the mastermind of that Twin Towers attack now resides in Baghdad). There are satellite photographs of a commercial airplane fuselage in a terrorist training camp south of Baghdad. Saddam's links to terrorism include his gassing Iraqi citizens by the tens of thousands; ordering his goons to assassinate former president Bush (has any other head of state ever ordered an assassination of a former president of the United States?); and his generous doling out of cash to the Palestinian families of homicide bombers.

Third, the administration should stop considering Saudi Arabia "a peacemaker" proposing serious peace initiatives. Our responsible leaders should acknowledge that the Saudis have long been funding hatred toward Jews, Christians, Israelis, and Americans. These ideas create the conditions which motivate kids to blow themselves up in order to kill as many Israelis as possible. Saudis, too, give grants to the families of the homicide bombers.

Most controversial, I would hope that Senator Lugar's Foreign Relations Committee will stop recommending we keep funding Egypt to the whopping tune of $2 billion *per year*. The $100 billion of U.S. foreign aid handouts since the 1970s has given America little back but Egyptian hostility toward Israel and America. This "friendly" regime too has been funding the spewing of hatred by its state-funded mullahs, state-controlled press, and state-sanctioned academics.

All such steps can be advanced, and the dynamics of Arabian thought and politics transformed, by changing the Iraqi regime, forcing it to go from the worst to among the best governments in the region. A moderate, pro-Western, quasi-democratic, somewhat tolerant Iraq—an Iraq like the Kurdish one-third of the country now protected from Saddam Hussein's tyranny by American forces—could speed a popular revolution in Iran. And once these jumbo dominos fall, fundamental changes in Saudi Arabia and Egypt could easily follow. Furthermore, an Iraq producing oil at full capacity would ease any lingering reliance we have on Saudi oil.

The more Islamic states in the Middle East begin to resemble Turkey and Bangladesh—the less they continue to be pressured by, or attempt to imitate, Iraq and Syria—the greater are the chances for regional peace and stability. And the safer both Israel and America become.

Granted, this is a rather large order. It calls for farsighted and courageous leadership of the kind Senator Richard Lugar displayed when championing the Nunn-Lugar legislation to remove the threat from Russian weapons of mass destruction. It is an ideal agenda for Senator Lugar's next twenty-five years in the Senate. And the sooner, the better. For we surely do not have twenty-five years to analyze and agonize, debate and regurgitate these issues.

NOTE

1. *Washington Post,* 25 December 2001.

11

Intelligence and Its Uses

Robert R. Simmons

Richard Lugar was selected to serve on the Senate Intelligence Committee early in his Senate career. In fact, his assignment to the committee in 1977, as a freshman senator from Indiana, was unusual and reflected the confidence that the Senate leadership had in his abilities. Those abilities were substantial. Not only had he won a Rhodes Scholarship to study at Oxford University in the mid-1950s, but he had also served in Naval Intelligence in the late 1950s. Rumor had it that he used to arise at 2:00 A.M. every morning to read and memorize classified reports from around the world, and then brief the chief of naval operations, Admiral Arleigh Burke, and other high-ranking officials from memory. These skills, as well as a ready smile and a congenial personality, made him an effective member of the committee.

Senator Lugar served as chairman of the Subcommittee on Analysis and Production during his first eight-year term as a member of the committee and went on to be reappointed in 1993. As such, he is the longest-serving member of the committee. Long a believer in language and area studies, he worked to focus the intelligence community on developing these skills which are essential in both clandestine collection as well as in analysis and production. His moderate views and realistic approach to intelligence have been important to making critical decisions between national security and civil liberties.

As Dick Lugar knows, intelligence is a critical component of American national security policy. Good intelligence informs national security and those who make it. Poor intelligence, or the lack of intelligence altogether, degrades our policies and places our people, resources, and values at risk. This has been true since Revolutionary War times when Nathan Hale made espionage honorable by offering his "one life" in the service of his country. It is no less true today as the United States faces multiple risks from traditional sovereign states and nongovernmental international terrorist groups. One of the great challenges of the American intelligence establishment is to walk the fine line between producing intelligence in support of our national security and respecting those civil rights which make citizenship in this country such a special blessing.

The following comments address the challenges of this "fine line" in a world where America's most fundamental values—our freedom and our democracy—are at risk. They aim to describe what the United States needs to consider in order to improve its intelligence product in the post–Cold War era—an era in which counterterrorism and homeland defense are vital to the survival of our freedoms and democratic institutions.

NO PEACE DIVIDEND AT THE END OF COLD WAR

During the Cold War, the United States faced a reasonably predictable set of threats. We knew who our adversaries were, we were aware of their capabilities, and we directed our military, intelligence, and other resources toward thwarting their efforts. The United States planned and executed its strategy well and won the war. Current events have illustrated in a most cruel way that threats to America did not come to an end with the fall of Soviet communism. For better or for worse, Moscow's iron fist had restrained the aspirations of its client states and many would-be tyrants. As the Soviet Union collapsed and communism was exposed as a failed ideology, the landscape was cleared for the rise of other doctrines and ideologies. The resulting void has been filled, in part, by radical Islamism, which has been magnified throughout the Middle East and elsewhere around the globe. Radical Islamism represents a serious threat to the United States and its allies.

A variety of incidents throughout the 1990s should have convinced American leaders that although the Cold War was over, there were other profound dangers on the horizon that were confidently and determinedly moving our way. Those threats were accurately and persuasively assessed in the report of the National Commission on Terrorism "Countering the Changing Threat of International Terrorism." The report, known as the Bremer report, after Chairman L. Paul Bremer III, was released in 2000. It contained considerable wisdom, including the recommendation that Afghanistan should be designated a sponsor of terrorism. It would not be long before the world would realize that the writers of the report were most perceptive.

The commission noted that today's terrorists are less dependent on state sponsorship and are forming transnational relationships based on religious or ideological similarities and a common hatred of the United States. These factors make terrorist attacks more difficult to detect and prevent than in the past. They also make quality intelligence critical to upsetting the terrorists' efforts. Acquiring information about the identity, plans, and vulnerabilities of terrorists is enormously difficult. Yet, no other effort is more central to preventing and responding to attacks.

Another dilemma we face in fighting terrorism is that the terrorist has two critical asymmetries in his favor. First, a defender has to protect his complete range of vulnerabilities. To come even close to guaranteeing our security against an attack we would have to guard all our embassies, all public buildings, all parks and highways—in short, everything. This is clearly impossible.

The second asymmetry is that the cost of defense is far greater than the cost of offense. By spending several hundred dollars, a handful of terrorists with machine guns can create carnage at a mall, an airport, or a train station. Defending those sites effectively can cost hundreds of thousands, if not millions of dollars. Consequently, it is impossible to defend the entire spectrum of vulnerabilities. Solid and timely intelligence is needed to determine when, where, and how attacks will come.

A VARIETY OF WAKE-UP CALLS

The horrific terrorist assault against America on September 11, 2001, was not the first shot fired against us. It was perhaps impossible to envision a terrorist group attacking America in the manner it did that deadly day, but it was far from the first assault on America or against American citizens. If our intelligence community failed to foresee what was to occur, we must also acknowledge that our leaders had already emboldened our enemies by failing to respond to previous assaults and that our intelligence community had not been receiving the support it required to do its work.

A terrorist bombing in Riyadh, Saudi Arabia, in 1995 killed 5 U.S. military advisers; in 1996, 19 U.S. military personnel were killed in an attack on Khobar Towers, also in Saudi Arabia; in 1998, 224 people, including 12 Americans, were killed in simultaneous assaults on U.S. embassies in Kenya and Tanzania; and in November 2000, there was an attack on the USS *Cole* at port in Aden, Yemen.

While we might express shock at the magnitude of the September 11 attack, we have no right to be surprised at this offensive against America. The World Trade Center had already been the target of a truck bombing in 1993. What was different about September 11 was the scope and lethality of the endeavor, the coordination of the attack, and the callous dedication of the 19 hijackers who willingly killed themselves, the passengers, and crews of the aircraft they commandeered, and the thousands of persons working in and visiting the World Trade Center and the Pentagon that day.

Clearly, the end of the Cold War did not bring safety to a dangerous world. Instead, it opened a Pandora's Box of new and incomprehensible dangers and threats. America underestimates the wrath and resolve of global terrorist organizations at its own risk. It is the job of our intelligence community to

provide our leaders with information that will be used to frustrate our enemies before they can carry out their deadly plans.

Quality intelligence informs, warns, and protects. September 11 has
reestablished the understanding of the American people of the need for solid
intelligence. It falls on the shoulders of our leaders to reassess the means by
which we conduct and coordinate our intelligence responsibilities within the
boundaries of a free and open society.

The report on the Khobar Tower bombing incident illustrates the importance of making sure information is analyzed thoroughly and properly in
concert with our allies. Although the assault took place in June 1996, as early
as November 1995 security forces at Khobar had begun to record numerous
suspicious incidents that should have served as a warning that a terrorist attack was being planned.

Much of the activity was recorded along the perimeter of Khobar Towers
where Americans were housed. There were reports of persons looking
through binoculars at the facility. On one occasion an individual drove his
car into one of the concrete barriers along the perimeter, moving it slightly,
and then drove off. This may have been an attempt to determine how easily
the perimeter could have been violated.

In November 1995, and in January, March, and April 1996, air force security
police reported a number of incidents, including Saudis taking photographs
and circling the parking lot adjacent to the northern perimeter. Security police
were uncertain about the purpose of these actions. In March there was a report that a large quantity of explosives was to be smuggled into Saudi Arabia
during the Hajj. On March 29, a car was seized at the Saudi-Jordanian border
with eighty-five pounds of explosives concealed in the vehicle's engine com-
partment.

The Saudi response to these threats was to suggest that the existing
perimeter was sufficient against a baseline threat of a car bomb similar to the
previous Riyadh bombing. The Saudis offered to increase Saudi security pa-
trols inside and outside the compound.

The Bremer report comments:

> A substantial degree of the intelligence available to the United States on Saudi
> Arabia comes from the Saudis themselves. However, on politically sensitive
> topics—such as the level of activity of Saudi dissidents—there is reason to
> doubt the comprehensiveness of intelligence that is passed to Americans by the
> Saudis. . . . It is common belief among U.S. intelligence and military officials
> that information shared by the Saudis is often shaped to serve the ends of com-
> peting Saudi bureaucracies—interior and defense ministries, for example—
> from which it originates.

The Bremer report said, "While a number of incidents could have reflected
preparations for an attack on Khobar Towers, there was no specific intelli-

gence to link any of them to a direct threat to the complex." But given the bombing in Riyadh, the frequency of suspicious activity, the volatility of the region, and the nature of the Saudi government, it would have been appropriate for both U.S. and Saudi authorities to work under the assumption that an attack was being planned.

Saudi Arabia is situated in a region of the world where anti-American sentiments are powerful and where those extreme attitudes are fueled by schools that are sponsored by the same Saudi government that we rely on for assistance. While we refer to Saudi Arabia as a moderate Arab nation and consider it a friend, we must not permit ourselves to approach relations with Riyadh as if we were communicating with leaders in London. Unquestionably, more should have been expected and demanded of the Saudi government.

As the war on terrorism progresses, it will be essential that the United States receive as much assistance as possible from our friends, especially in the Middle East. But it is also imperative that the United States upgrade its human intelligence force. America cannot depend on uncertain friends who may be providing us with information that "is often shaped to serve" their goals and not ours.

THE IMPORTANCE OF HUMAN INTELLIGENCE

The Central Intelligence Agency has seen a significant reduction in staff since the end of the Cold War. By cutting support from the men and women who protect our nation, we have handed an advantage to our enemies around the world. While more resources are now being appropriated, and rightly so, to our military and intelligence communities, we must be prudent in the allocation of those resources. It is crucial that we keep in mind that those capabilities that will help peripherally are easily procured, but information that will be of greater value is more laboriously acquired. Human intelligence (HUMINT) is vital in the war on terrorism and it is a type of intelligence that is difficult for Americans to produce.

It is fairly simple to purchase satellites and other devices that can serve as America's eyes and ears from space and other places far from the object of our inquiry. Such platforms have yielded very valuable information. But as technology continues to spread to the most distant corners of the globe, it is becoming more difficult to obtain this type of data. Those whom we target are becoming more technically proficient, which means they are better equipped to evade our prying eyes and eavesdropping.

Aris A. Pappas and James M. Simon Jr., senior officers in the Intelligence Community Management Staff under the Director of Central Intelligence, warn that "[t]echnology is no longer a U.S. monopoly." U.S. intelligence has historically relied on the deployment of sophisticated technologies that our opponents did not have. This is no longer the case.

"Already two of our most important collection capabilities have been seriously affected," Pappas and Simon write.

> Satellite imagery is now commonly understood. Commercial interests, convinced that they can do a better job and provide necessary services to a wider customer base, have increasingly challenged the government's traditional dominance of imagery. Signals and communications intercept capabilities have been degraded by the digital and fiber optic revolutions and the marked increase in commercially available and effective encryption. The public availability of secure communications means that security is now affordable and accessible to terrorists, organized criminals and others.

America will remain a world leader in technology, but our ability to hold our advantage in intelligence gathering systems will decrease as the rest of the world gains access to readily available systems. The United States must develop new systems that will offer us closer looks at smaller transportable targets like terrorist groups and mobile missile sites. Our intelligence must be as nimble and quick as the target.

Pappas and Simon point to several technologies that may provide great rewards for our intelligence community. They could also produce great danger if they are developed and used by our enemies. First is nanotechnology, which offers new ways to get close to targets. This technology can offer unobserved penetration of a terrorist camp and enable the user to collect data and mount an attack. Potential applications include a laboratory on a chip to provide long-term detection of biological, chemical, radiological, and other weapons of mass destruction. This same technology could also give us miniature cameras for real-time video that can be used in precision targeting.

The second technology, Maxwell's Rainbow, is a reference to the spectrum beyond the visual and electromagnetic bands. This technology provides thermal, atomic, and other signatures, making it possible to look through camouflage, identify the function of underground facilities, and find chemical, biological, and nuclear weapons.

Human intelligence is a valuable means for collecting information against terrorist groups, but it is very difficult and dangerous to engage in such work. It is also necessary to direct resources toward a variety of disciplines, including the teaching of language skills and the immersion of operations officers into foreign cultures so that they can speak the language and interpret the culture as if it were their own.

Pappas and Simon warn that our human and technical collection procedures are in need of renovation or replacement. Most of our systems were designed to scrutinize a gradually evolving and massive target—the Soviet Union. Dramatic policy swings and unforeseen initiatives were not the standard during the Cold War. Warning was obtained by regularly monitoring large military forces to determine changes in their position or alert status. The sprawling and intermittent nature of today's threats requires more precise and constant monitoring.

These new realities demand we employ a larger, broadly deployed clandestine service that must be able to see further than externally obvious signs. We must keep in mind that seeing is not necessarily understanding. U.S. intelligence requires adequate knowledge to understand the social, political, and economic dynamics of our targets and to interpret what has been observed. In some respects this is a more difficult task. Terrorists develop their plans by scheming with small numbers of colleagues. Secrecy is vital to their success. The surest, and sometimes the only, way to know their minds and their plans is to penetrate their organizations and identify their operatives so they can be neutralized before they carry out their activities.

During the Cold War, our intelligence human resources were primarily directed toward the presence of Soviet personnel. Today, we need to recruit in more places and against more targets because terrorist groups are small and widespread.

To gain better human intelligence we must reinforce the CIA's Directorate of Operations (DO), the primary espionage organization of the U.S. government. From the last days of the Vietnam War through the end of the Cold War, the DO encountered substantial oversight and criticism, which provoked personnel layoffs, high turnover, increased regulation, and a fraying of morale.

In 1995, the CIA issued new guidelines in a response to concerns about alleged human rights violations committed by agency sources. The result is that the guidelines have deterred and delayed efforts to recruit potentially useful informants and provoked a decline in morale that had not been experienced since the 1970s. The 1995 guidelines should be rescinded. The world of espionage is neither kind nor gentle and oftentimes it is necessary to associate with unpleasant individuals.

In reference to this, Professor Richard K. Betts, director of the Institute of War and Peace Studies at Columbia University, rightly concludes that, "After the recent attacks, worries about excesses have receded and measures will be found to make it easier for the clandestine service to operate. One simple reform, for example, would be to implement a recommendation made by the National Commission on Terrorism a year-and-a-half ago: roll back the additional layer of cumbersome procedures instituted in 1995 for gaining approval to employ agents with 'unsavory' records—procedures that have had a chilling effect on recruitment of the thugs appropriate for penetrating terrorist units."

On this same topic, the Bremer report said, "Complex bureaucratic procedures now in place send an unmistakable message to CIA officers in the field that recruiting clandestine sources for terrorist information is encouraged in theory but discouraged in practice. Inside information is the key to preventing attacks by terrorists. The CIA must aggressively recruit informants with unique access to terrorists' plans. That sometimes requires recruiting those who have committed terrorist acts or related crimes, just as domestic law enforcement agencies routinely recruit criminal informants in order to pursue major criminal figures."

The Bremer report further states: "Recruiting informants in not tantamount to condoning their prior crimes, nor does it imply support for crimes they may yet commit." Indeed, even as we relax restrictions on recruitment of agents we must be careful not to provide a get-out-of-jail free card to those who might commit future crimes. The person best qualified to know and reveal the plans of a terrorist organization is a member of the organization. Yet, a CIA operative in the field who hopes to entice such a source faces a flurry of reviews by committees back in the office who begin with the view that enlisting such a source is a bad idea.

Even if the decision is finally made to go forward with the plan, the individual being solicited may have changed his mind or may have been discovered consorting with a CIA officer and been eliminated. If the vetting procedure takes too long, the possible attack that is under investigation may have already taken place. The Bremer Commission rightly determined that, however well intentioned, the 1995 guidelines constitute an obstacle to effective intelligence collection and should be rescinded.

The report also observed that the risk of personal liability arising from action taken in an official capacity discourages law enforcement and intelligence personnel from taking bold steps to combat terrorism. The authors of the report recommended that Congress "amend the statute to mandate full reimbursement of the costs of personal liability insurance for FBI special agents and CIA officers in the field who are combating terrorism."

In 2001, an amendment to correct this situation became law. Passage of this amendment was the right thing to do. Intelligence officers in the field are engaged in tremendously dangerous work and they deserve all the support a grateful nation can provide.

We will never know if a more robust human intelligence presence would have prevented any of the attacks listed at the beginning of this chapter. We do know, however, that the strategy that was in place during those years did not avert them and that Americans and others lost their lives as a result.

The construction of a global human intelligence network is a painstakingly time-consuming endeavor. It will invariably generate concerns regarding cost, the allocation of valuable resources, and usefulness. One must take for granted that many networks will never produce anything of substance, many of the sources employed will prove undependable, and we will join hands with a multitude of disreputable individuals. But the work must be done.

This strategy will require us to develop a wide range of individuals with expertise on the Middle East, Central and South Asia, and other regions that play host to terrorist groups. It will not be enough for our operations officers to be able to speak and write Farsi, Arabic, and Pashto—they will have to be fully fluent. This will not be a simple or swift venture but it is crucial that we meet these high standards.

An education in Middle Eastern languages, politics, and cultures should not begin when an individual seeks employment with the FBI or the CIA. As part of our overall effort to broaden America's knowledge of other cultures and languages, we should promote the idea of such in-depth studies in high schools and universities. This demands a dramatic change in our approach to education and, even should that occur, one which will not produce results for years. The time to begin implementing this strategy is now.

It will prove difficult, if not impossible, for American citizens to penetrate organizations like al Qaeda (although John Walker Lindh was certainly able to gain entry at a low level) but the war on terrorism demands that America and our allies make the effort to infiltrate nonstate actors. Our enemy has small and deadly cells throughout the world and recruits its soldiers from a wide variety of nations, primarily in Asia and the Middle East. While we may be able to identify the most dangerous source nations that present the most immediate threats, we cannot afford to concentrate on one or two countries. Until the aftermath of September 11, most Americans had probably not heard of Kabul. Today, there are probably few Americans who are not familiar with the name and most could probably locate the city on a map. Afghanistan has become the first frontline in the war on terrorism. There will be others.

As the events of September 11 remain fresh in our minds and as long as the war on terrorism produces tangible results, no doubt the American public will support the development of a first-class human intelligence network. It is vital that our leaders impress on the American people that, as President George W. Bush cautioned, "the war on terrorism will take us down a winding and dangerous road. It requires that our nation make a long-term and united commitment to the battle ahead."

A Congressional Research Service report released February 21, 2002, written by Richard A. Best Jr., accurately observes one of the dilemmas our nation faces. Best writes,

> A central issue for Congress is the extent to which it and the public are prepared to accept the inherent risks involved in maintaining many agents with connections to terrorist groups. Statutory law requires that congressional intelligence committees be kept aware of all intelligence activities; unlike the situation in the early Cold War years when some intelligence efforts were designed to be "deniable," it will be difficult for the U.S. government to avoid responsibility for major mistakes or ill-conceived efforts of intelligence agencies.

Best correctly notes that while there is a broad consensus that al Qaeda poses a genuine and serious threat to all Americans and to our national interests, we should not take for granted that the public or all members of Congress will view other similar groups in that same light. The intelligence community no doubt is sensitive to the reality that earlier alliances with anticommunist groups in Central America came under persistent public disapproval because some of these groups were responsible for human rights violations and because they were, or seemed to be, supporting repressive regimes.

Many members of Congress shared these criticisms. Consequently, intelligence agencies understood that they were operating under a fog of mistrust. Best observes that the attacks on America on September 11 may have produced a willingness on the part of the public to accept greater intelligence flexibility, but intelligence professionals will unquestionably want to ensure that the work of their agencies will not be put at risk by changes in public opinion. An intelligence strategy must be based on the need to collect and analyze data and to identify and disrupt threats to national security. It cannot be repeatedly modified to match the mood of the moment. It must be consistent and long-standing.

OPEN SOURCE INTELLIGENCE

American intelligence organizations need both open source and classified material to do their work. Intelligence is a product of the collection, processing, and analysis of all the information at one's disposal. Primary source materials are readily available to government analysts and anyone else with access to the Internet. This is open source information and it can be valuable in our efforts to understand those who wish to harm America.

Open source information has been ignored for too long. It is inexpensive to access, it represents a potentially huge source of information, and since the material is unclassified it can be used in public discussions with uncleared personnel. Open source material includes anything a reporter, a scholar, or the general public can access. This includes Internet websites, chat rooms, and public records that show ownership of a variety of assets, which can reveal from whom and to whom money is flowing.

America does not currently have a centralized office that gathers, analyzes, and distributes this type of data. Such information could be particularly useful in homeland security where it can be provided to every police chief, fire chief, and other first responders who do not have security clearances. In all other intelligence disciplines, we have groups of experts collecting information; we need to do the same with respect to open source information.

It would be a mistake to assume that open source information is of little value because it is in the public arena. Fragments of information viewed in isolation may not provide much of significance, but when a number of pieces are put together the puzzle becomes clearer. Open source information can and should be a critical part of any intelligence production.

For example, open source information has enabled America to shut down financial operations and cover organizations that fed terrorist groups. When various reports that include information gleaned from open sources are put together, we might develop a single report that can convey a very sensitive and important story. There are companies that have been awarded government contracts to assemble reports using open source material. When the reports have been delivered, they have often been stamped "Classified" because they point to America's interest in a certain topic. We must develop an infrastructure for capturing and taking advantage of the enormous wealth of public print and voice information that is available for the taking.

CYBERTHREATS

Technology can work for and against American interests. In his testimony before the House Permanent Select Committee on Intelligence on September 26, 2001, Dr. John Hamre, president and CEO of the Center for Strategic and International Studies, noted that the information age has reduced the power of states and elevated the power of individuals, small groups, and networks.

"Enemies of the United States, opponents of its armed forces, or those in opposition to U.S.-based multinational corporations can choose cybercrime, cybervandalism or cyberattacks against U.S. public or private interests, turning our reliance on information systems into a strategic vulnerability," Dr. Hamre warned. "Cyber vulnerability is magnified by the fact that 95 percent of all U.S. military traffic moves over civilian telecommunications and computer systems. A terrorist can combat U.S. military forces, disrupt a military operation, or hurt the U.S. economy by hindering our vulnerable civilian telecommunications systems."

Dr. Hamre said that in 1999 there were more than 22,000 attacks against unclassified military computer systems, representing a threefold increase over the number reported in 1998. Some experts suggest that only about 10 percent of the penetrations have been detected. Resisting a major assault on America's computer network is a daunting challenge. A large-scale assault, similar to September 11, coordinated with a cyber attack on the U.S. government and civil telecommunications infrastructure, would create extensive destruction. Such an assault might conceivably be timed to correspond with a major deployment of U.S. forces overseas or some other event critical to American security. Experts have warned that the disruption caused by such a cyber assault would likely be enhanced if there were a significant period of time between the attack and its discovery.

A key recommendation in the Bremer report addressed this issue. Without international cooperation, the United States cannot effectively secure its infrastructure from a cyber threat. Neither can any other nation. Since cyber terrorists using the Internet are not restrained by national borders, the United States should lead in the development of an international convention aimed at sharing information, providing early warning, and establishing accepted procedures for conducting international investigations of cyber crime.

New threats also require our intelligence and law enforcement agencies to work more closely with state and local governments and the private sector, as each is a key player in America's war on terrorism. America's cyber network filters into every corner of American life, from the Pentagon to government to businesses to police and fire departments to schools and to homes. America needs complete technical evaluation of the threats our computer network might face, as well as our ability to deter them and rebound should such an attack succeed.

Pappas and Simon point out that under current law "cyber intrusions are presumed domestic in origin unless demonstrated otherwise. This limits the participation of the U.S. intelligence community in detecting and tracking cyber crime." The world of cyberspace is a region where our domestic law enforcement agencies and our intelligence community should be working closely together. We have already taken several steps to bring those two communities to the same table. This must continue.

THE PATRIOT ACT AND NEW FBI REGULATIONS

War has been brought to the American homeland for the first time in 150 years, and as a result homeland security is a vital component of the war on terrorism. As the American people appropriately value the freedom and openness of our society, it is important that the rights guaranteed in the Constitution are protected. The PATRIOT Act, which has been enacted into law, is a powerful tool law enforcement can use against terrorists. At the same time, it preserves the guarantees of the Constitution.

The PATRIOT Act, an acronym for legislation to "Provide Appropriate Tools Required to Interrupt and Obstruct Terrorism," goes a long way toward bringing domestic intelligence gathering into the twenty-first century. It improves law enforcement sharing of information, strengthens our hand against border abuse by foreign terrorists, and recognizes that improvements in technology have rendered certain law enforcement techniques obsolete. For example, since criminals and terrorists often use a variety of cell phones for communication, the PATRIOT Act allows law enforcement to seek wiretaps for individuals, not individual telephones. Under the old law, in order to avoid a wiretap, a terrorist would switch phones. This law allows the legal process to catch up to technology.

Since the war on terrorism is being fought both at home and abroad, it is important that our intelligence gathering agencies and law enforcement agencies share information. The PATRIOT Act addresses this concern in a number of ways. For example, it amends the Federal Rules of Criminal Procedure, which governs grand jury secrecy, to allow the disclosure of certain information presented to a grand jury.

Prior to the PATRIOT Act, law enforcement officials were prevented from sharing information provided to a grand jury with the intelligence community. It is important that evidence and testimony submitted to a grand jury not leak out to the general public, but there is no reason to prohibit the intelligence community from confidentially reviewing material in matters involving foreign intelligence and counterintelligence. As our law enforcement and intelligence communities work to ensure the safety of American citizens, it would be unconscionable to prevent this sharing of critical information. The lives of our citizens may depend on it. The simple collection of information, from whatever source, is not a comprehensive and coordinated intelligence strategy. The PATRIOT Act works to address that problem by encouraging the analysis of shared information.

Testifying about his commission's report before the Select Senate Committee on Intelligence on June 8, 2000, L. Paul Bremer said,

> We also need more vigorous FBI intelligence collection against foreign terrorists in America and better dissemination of information. The FBI's role in collecting intelligence about terrorists is increasingly significant. Thus, it is essential that they employ the full scope of the authority the Congress has given them to collect that information. Yet, the commission believes unclear guidelines for investigations and an overly cautious approach by the Department of Justice in reviewing applications for electronic surveillance against international terrorism targets are hampering the Bureau's intelligence collection efforts. We recommend improvements in both of these areas.

This is an example of the "new thinking" we must adopt as we continue to prosecute the war on terrorism. The old strategies no longer fit current realities. The recent announcement that the FBI is becoming a domestic intelligence agency, dedicated to preventing future terrorist attacks and disrupting terrorist organizations within America, is an essential step in the war on terrorism. The FBI must work to prevent new domestic attacks. We will not win this war by suffering further assaults, then putting the accused on trial while pious pundits contemplate everything from the death penalty to the venue of the trial. Wars are not won in court. They are won on the battlefield. And for the first time since the Civil War, the battlefield is in the homeland.

Policy failures are as dangerous as intelligence failures. By changing the policies and purpose of the FBI, America is fortifying itself against its enemies. The FBI's traditional emphasis has been on investigating and prosecuting crimes that have already occurred. This reactive role is of no use in the war on terror, however, and the bureau's new forward-looking approach is fully warranted.

Past regulations prohibited FBI agents from collecting material from open sources, such as newspapers, unless they received permission to begin an investigation. Agents were especially hampered if a suspect group was operating as a religious, civic, or charitable organization. These restrictions provided our enemies with a competitive advantage. Preliminary inquiries, where agents collect information before enough evidence had been uncovered to merit a full investigation, could only be used to decide whether there was enough documentation to justify investigating a crime. The material could not be used to decide whether to open a broader investigation of groups involved with terrorism. Also, under the previous rules agents were prohibited from visiting public places. Agents avoided them not because they were forbidden by the Constitution but because of the lack of clear authority under administrative guidelines issued decades ago.

The new domestic threat environment demands that we think in new ways about national security. Since America will continue to wage a sustained, global war against terrorism, we must also be prepared to wage a sustained, domestic war against terrorism. The new guidelines reflect the need to locate terrorists and stop them before they strike. They expand the scope of criminal intelligence investigations, lengthen their authorization period, and ease approval and renewal requirements. This flexibility increases the FBI's terrorism prevention functions and helps agents in the field.

The new guidelines authorize agents to have normal access to public places for the purpose of detecting and preventing terrorist activities. Under the old regulations, FBI agents were hampered by ponderous rules requiring them to secure headquarters' approval before launching counterterrorism investigations. As a result, they lost opportunities waiting for headquarters to consider and review requests over a period of weeks and sometimes months. Moreover, the old regulations lacked clear direction to use lawful methods of inquiry and as a result agents declined to use these techniques when investigating crimes committed by affiliates of some political and religious organizations.

For example, in 1993, the FBI received information about terrorist activities planned by Sheik Abdel Rahman, who would later be convicted of plotting to bomb landmarks in New York City, including the World Trade Center in 1993. Because of ambiguity in the guidelines, the FBI did not call the sheik before a grand jury or conduct surveillance of his offices or the religious buildings where he met with colleagues. The new guidelines allow agents who are investigating suspected terrorists, even if they have ties to religious and political groups, to use the same investigative techniques they would use when investigating any other type of organization. FBI agents will now be freer to conduct surveillance at political rallies and at religious gatherings. While religious and political groups should not be singled out for harassment, neither should terrorists with ties to such groups receive immunity from lawful investigation. The new guidelines also increase decision-making authority in the field. Special agents in charge at field offices may now approve and renew terrorism enterprise investigations.

Our technological expertise secured a relatively painless victory in the Gulf War and our experience in Afghanistan has, thus far, been successful. The domestic war on terrorism will be more complex because we must balance civil rights with national security. There will continue to be those who will remind us of abuses of power that occurred decades ago. There is far too much at stake for us to meander back through time to an era that offers us no solutions for today's problems.

The FBI must work to interrupt terrorism in America precisely because our civil liberties must be preserved. Our enemies, at home and abroad, must recognize that their fate is not our fault, and their destiny is not our responsibility. If the war is not conducted successfully overseas, and if we are unable to detain dangerous individuals and thwart their efforts abroad, the war will surely return to our soil. If a few envelopes of anthrax were able to cause such disruption, consider what would happen to our people, our nation, and our civil liberties if something on a larger scale were to transpire.

Those who have voiced objections to the PATRIOT Act need to be heard, but all must understand that war has been declared on America. The American people are facing unique new challenges. In order to respond successfully, it is crucial that we afford our law enforcement and intelligence agencies the tools and authority they need to stop terrorists who seek nothing less than the destruction of America. Security and freedom are not adversaries; they are allies. We can only truly enjoy our freedoms when there is peace and security. No people can be free if they live under the threat of terrorism.

THE DEPARTMENT OF HOMELAND SECURITY

After a careful review, President George W. Bush proposed the creation of a permanent, cabinet-level Department of Homeland Security to unite agencies that must work together to prevent future attacks and to find and disrupt the terrorists that remain in America. His proposal—which has now been reflected in a law creating a new Department of Homeland Security—brings together the Coast Guard, the Customs Service, immigration officials, and other agencies that are essential to America's domestic security. It makes sense to unify the more than 100 different government organizations that had grown up to address security concerns. Our nation requires a single, unified security structure to improve protection against today's threats and be flexible enough to help meet the unknown threats of tomorrow.

But structure alone will not yield early warning or security. If the new organization is not accompanied by a thoroughgoing public acceptance that our domestic security efforts must be directed toward preventing terrorist activities, not toward avoiding hurt feelings and other inconveniences, then the changes will be cosmetic and nothing more.

We cannot possibly win the war on terrorism if we cannot bring ourselves to accept the nature of our enemy. If an individual robs a bank, the police will ask those present to describe the thief. If the witnesses tell the police the individual was a heavy-set white man, about six feet tall, we would not expect the police to begin searching for a black man, or a short, thin white man or a woman who appeared to be of Japanese descent. It is the task of investigators to determine a description of the individual and to dedicate their efforts to find a suspect who fits that description. This is not profiling; it is common sense.

The newly established Department of Homeland Security creates a unit with the mission of assembling and analyzing intelligence data from government sources, including the FBI, CIA, INS, Customs, and other agencies. This makes sense, but we need to bring this data together into what might be called a "fusion center" so that bits and pieces of information can be collected in one place for more effective analysis. It is critical that all of our intelligence agencies share their data with this new department. Nothing can be held back. Attorney General John Ashcroft recently said, "We welcome people from around the world to visit a land which we believe is a blessed land. We will continue to greet our international neighbors with goodwill. Asking some neighbors and visitors to verify their activities while they are here is fully consistent with that outlook." Reasonable individuals who are even modestly acquainted with current events would agree with that sentiment.

Our vigilance may cause inconvenience and bruised feelings. But our efforts must nevertheless be focused on the collection and analysis of information on those who wish us ill.

TO RISE TO THE CHALLENGE

Since September 11, American patriotism has made a welcome return to the national stage. Patriotism neither demands that we condemn other nations, nor does it require us to admire our own nation uncritically. It does demand that we understand why America is worthy of our allegiance. American principles, as enshrined in our Declaration of Independence and our Constitution, deserve our devotion and they are worth defending. We do not understand other nations and other cultures better by misunderstanding our own.

The terrorists who threaten us are not interested in a dialogue. As the jets that were hijacked on September 11 sped toward their targets, the perpetrators did not use cell phones to demand money. Their goal was death and destruction. We have become reacquainted with a lesson we never should have forgotten—that some people do not wish to talk, they simply wish to kill. The hollow phrase, "one man's terrorist is another man's freedom fighter," has no place in the vocabulary of those who appreciate what is at stake. The terrorists who attacked America were not freedom fighters. They had no interest in freedom.

The American people must keep fresh in their minds the reasons why we are fighting. The successful prosecution of the war on terrorism requires more than changes in force structure and in intelligence and law enforcement capabilities. It is not only our military strength that is being tested, but also our national will. Our media, our houses of worship, our schools, and our universities all have an obligation to speak out in defense of the freedoms we enjoy—the freedoms that make America what it is.

The collection and analysis which American intelligence operations provide is critical to our struggle. In 1929, Secretary of State Stimson ceased to fund military code-breaking activities with the declaration that, "Gentlemen do not read each others mail." But the world is not peopled only with "gentlemen" and reading the mail is sometimes the only way to divine evil intentions. Did Stimson's shortsightedness lead to Pearl Harbor? Were we similarly shortsighted prior to September 11, 2001?

From the time that Nathan Hale regretted he had "but one life to lose" for his country to the time that CIA case officer Johnny "Mike" Spann was killed on the ground in Afghanistan, Americans have relied on intelligence. Dedicated Americans have devoted themselves to the collection, analysis, and timely dissemination of intelligence to the president, the Congress, military leaders, and policymakers so that the nation may be defended and its policies informed. In the war on terrorism, intelligence is, now more than ever, the first and best line of defense.

12

Shaping a Strong Military

William S. Cohen

From his navy service during the Cold War to his Senate tenure and his accomplishments on the Senate Foreign Relations and Intelligence Committees, Dick Lugar's life of public service has been a model of intelligence and integrity. He is rightly listened to by presidents and prime ministers the world over. Among his foreign policy achievements, several are especially worthy of mention in an essay devoted to new security threats and our response to them. In 1991—immediately following the break up of the Soviet Union—Senators Lugar and Sam Nunn launched the Cooperative Threat Reduction program to dismantle and convert the post–Cold War Soviet nuclear stockpile to prevent its use by hostile countries or terrorist groups. Their efforts helped accelerate the collection and ongoing destruction of the 30,000 tactical nuclear weapons in the former Soviet Union, and prevented the creation of several new nations with nuclear weapons.

Before "homeland security" became a household term in the aftermath of the September 11, 2001, attacks, Senator Lugar also created a program (in 1996) to strengthen international border controls to prevent weapons and material smuggling. This program also provided training for policemen, firemen, and emergency responders in 120 of America's largest cities so that they can better react to terrorist attacks involving chemical, biological, or nuclear weapons.

TODAY'S SECURITY ENVIRONMENT

Senator Lugar's ability to predict threats and to act before they materialize has improved our security dramatically. In that spirit, this essay reviews a strategy for shaping the U.S. military of the future. To provide some context, the essay briefly examines the current security environment. Here, the news is both good and bad. On the positive side, in virtually every corner of the globe countries are moving toward democracy and freedom, seeking to cast their fate with the family of free nations. And in every single instance it has been the active engagement and presence of the U.S. military that has helped to make this possible.

In Europe, the circle of freedom, security, and prosperity is wider and stronger than ever. We continue to embrace new democracies as we enlarge and expand NATO, and we are working with the Russians to give them an opportunity to play a constructive role in European security through the new NATO-Russia Council.

When we look to the Asia Pacific region, we find broad recognition that the U.S. military presence does and will continue to serve as a pillar of regional security. We have fundamentally strengthened our long-standing security alliances and partnerships across the entire region. As examples, I would point to Japan, with updated modern guidelines for cooperation; to Australia; to Thailand; to the Philippines, with whom we signed and ratified a new visiting of forces agreement and with whom we are working to combat the spread of terrorism; and to Singapore, which now has completed a large facility that will accommodate the arrival of U.S. aircraft carriers. We are once again engaging China. Restoring our military-to-military contacts with China is important for keeping open lines of communication. The enduring U.S. military presence and our active engagement in Korea has helped bring about hope on that peninsula that a half-century of division might come to an end.

Countries in the Asia Pacific region are now working together to help provide for their own security. For example, states throughout the Asia Pacific region came together to create a peacekeeping mission in East Timor. This is a very positive development; but it is one which is occurring within the framework of broad security guarantees backed up by U.S. military forces.

In the Near East and Southwest Asia, our forces continue to defend and protect our vital interests throughout the region to make sure that the flow of oil continues unimpeded. We conducted a sustained air campaign in December 1998 with British and other forces to degrade Iraq's ability to deliver chemical, nuclear, or biological weapons and to threaten its neighbors. We continue to enforce no-fly zones in both the northern and southern parts of Iraq to prevent Saddam Hussein from threatening his neighbors and, indeed, portions of his own population

In the Western Hemisphere and in Africa, we have worked with individual states and regional groups to strengthen democracy and the civilian control of their military forces. For example, in Africa we instituted a program called the African Crisis Response Initiative, helping to train African countries to prepare for peacekeeping actions on the African continent, which will be critical to the future of Africa. In Central America, our forces provided massive humanitarian assistance in the wake of Hurricanes Mitch and George.

In short, because America's ideals are backed by America's military power, democratic principles are in the ascendancy in many parts of the globe. More countries are choosing the path of integration and political cooperation, and more of the globe's population lives under the flag of freedom than ever before. This is a time of great promise.

There are, however, serious threats emerging in today's world, and these threats must guide our efforts to shape the kind of military we need in the twenty-first century. It will not suffice simply to do more of the same. The new threats come in many forms. Shadowy transnational groups engage in terrorism, crime, and narcotics trafficking. "Rogue regimes" continue to threaten their neighbors and to export the tools of violence abroad, sometimes to distort locales. The flames of ethnic hatred no longer are contained by the realities of the Cold War; virulent nationalism, as we saw in the former Yugoslavia, is a source of instability in many quarters. A continuing cycle of violence in the Middle East forces difficult choices on policymakers. Instability, sparked by persistent poverty or health challenges such as AIDS in Africa, offers tough challenges. And continued uncertainties—suggesting signs of both hope and concern—are inherent in the evolution of Russia and China. Each of these situations will continue to present very significant challenges to American policymakers.

In what follows, I will focus especially on asymmetrical threats to American security. I do so because these new kinds of threats will force us most dramatically to expand how we think about security threats and how we organize our military forces. These threats, which will be with us for the foreseeable future, cannot be dealt with by traditional military operations against states with which we are at war. Rather, these threats are inherent in the rapidly evolving nature of technology and the ways in which technology permits small numbers of adversaries to do serious harm to our security and to our interests.

The United States is supreme in every conventional and strategic way to any other country, or any combination of countries. It is this conventional and strategic superiority that prompts adversaries to adopt unconventional or asymmetric warfare. We have seen this, of course, in the 1993 bombing of the World Trade Center, the U.S. embassy bombings in Kenya and Tanzania, the attack against the USS *Cole,* and the attacks on the Pentagon and World Trade Center in 2001. We will continue to see the spread of nuclear, biological, and chemical weapons capabilities, making such threats far more serious. More than two dozen countries, including Iraq and North Korea, either have or are in the process of acquiring weapons of mass destruction. Transnational groups aim to possess them as well. This is not hypothetical; it is a reality. Defending against the use of these weapons will be very difficult.

Moreover, we will likely see increasingly effective cyberterrorism against our "nervous system" in this cybernation—our banking, transportation, energy, and defense systems. We will see more attacks such as we saw in 1998 and 1999, in which unclassified but very sensitive information in the Defense Department was copied off our systems. We will face more assaults from professional cyberwarriors.

Finally, we will see the spread of missiles and missile technology. Here again, the threat is real and growing. North Korea is building and selling to others long-range missiles that would increase the range of weapons of mass destruction. Iran, which already possesses chemical weapons, is developing the Shahab-3 long-range missile. It will be followed by the Shahab-4 and -5. Were he free of United Nations sanctions, no doubt Saddam Hussein would expand with impunity his deadly programs to develop nuclear, biological, and the chemical weapons and the means to deliver them.

This is the grave new world that we are facing—a world in which highly lethal attacks on our forces and our citizens present a real and present danger. It is a world in which the traditional threat of retaliation will not be effective against attacks from shadowy transnational groups. Americans must be brought to understand and confront these dangers if we are to develop support to provide the resources and to devise the techniques and capabilities to defend against them.

When President Bush took office, many of our European allies questioned whether he would seek to pull America back from its strong engagement overseas. Events following his election show conclusively that America's security will continue to be best assured by our full engagement—diplomatically, economically, and militarily—around the world. The operations in Afghanistan proved that we lack the luxury of choosing the conflicts for which to prepare. U.S. Marines, trained to storm beaches in the Pacific or Southwest Asia, landed in Afghanistan and stormed the mountain fortresses of the Taliban and al Qaeda. U.S. Special Forces, replete with the latest high technology equipment, mounted horses to hunt down the enemy. U.S. forces must be ready to meet all kinds of missions. Our willingness to engage is absolutely vital; but we must know that we will be engaging against a wider array of threats than ever before.

A TRANSFORMATION STRATEGY

To shape our forces for today and tomorrow, we must continue our ongoing revolution in military affairs, shaping and transforming our military to meet new and asymmetrical threats. Our progress in recent years has been impressive—the military has become lighter, more lethal, faster, and more flexible, and we are continuing to experiment with radical new approaches to warfare. But we still have work to do.

As we forge ahead with this transformation, we must do so with a strategy that integrates activities in six areas:

1. Service concept development and experimentation efforts that make use of promising technologies to perform critical tasks;
2. Joint concept development and experimentation to harmonize service capabilities and develop joint solutions, ensuring that future joint force commanders have the tools needed to meet key operational challenges;
3. Implementation processes in the services and joint community to rapidly identify the most promising new concepts and capabilities that emerge from experimentation and put them on a fast-track toward incorporation in the force;
4. Science and technology efforts focused on areas that can enhance U.S. military capabilities to meet projected challenges, with close ties between technologists, innovators, and warfighters;
5. Efforts to encourage international transformation activities; and,
6. Exceptional people with the right skills for the twenty-first century and attitudes nourished in a culture that encourages bold innovation and leadership.

In order to be prepared for the challenges of the future, the military must learn from all available sources, including public- and private-sector models; war game experiments; computer-assisted simulations; and field trials that simulate future operational capabilities. Each of the services will have its own roles and its own challenges in this endeavor.

The Army

On October 12, 1999, the army articulated a vision to meet the challenges of the twenty-first century: "Soldiers on Point for the Nation . . . Persuasive in Peace, Invincible in War." The army's vision is a force that combines the decisive warfighting lethality of today's mechanized forces with the strategic responsiveness of today's light forces.

Achieving the army's vision requires comprehensive transformation of the entire army—from the operational force to the institutional army. The transformed force will be responsive, deployable, agile, versatile, lethal, survivable, and sustainable. As an objective measure of force responsiveness, the army will need the capability to deploy a brigade anywhere in the world 96 hours after liftoff, a warfighting division in 120 hours, and 5 divisions in 30 days.

The Navy

The strategic vision *From the Sea* drafted in the early 1990s shifted the navy's focus to the littorals; *Forward . . . From the Sea*, adopted in 1997, defined this vision within the context of naval forces which are forward-based throughout the spectrum of operations, from peacetime presence to crisis and war. The navy's new *Maritime Concept* provides the organizing principles for the new capabilities and concepts needed to ensure access forward with combat-credible forward presence and knowledge superiority. *Maritime Concept* exploits access to cyberspace to provide a superior knowledge-position relative to opponents, which allows U.S. forces to act with timely and decisive effect. Accordingly, the navy is transforming to a knowledge superior networked force in order to dictate the operational tempo across a battlespace that includes sea, air, land, space, and cyberspace.

Network-centric warfare is therefore a key organizing principle for the navy. This does not change the underlying tenets of warfare; rather, it assists commanders in making rapid and well-informed decisions. In the future, speed of command—the ability to make timely, correct decisions inside an adversary's detection and engagement time line—will be as important as command of the seas to achieve full-spectrum dominance across the battle-space and to conduct effects-based warfare. Additionally, new mission areas—such as projecting defense ashore with Theater Missile Defense (TMD) and precision land-attack deep into enemy territory—establish requirements for new capabilities and concepts. These are being explored and developed through an extensive concept development and experimentation program, as well as several complementary near-term transformation efforts that draw on newly available technologies.

The Marine Corps

Marine Corps Strategy 21 is the capstone strategy of the Marine Corps. It is reflected in the revised Marine Corps operational concept, *Expeditionary Maneuver Warfare*, which provides an overarching framework for full-spectrum capabilities and which evolved from *Operational Maneuver from the Sea*. It provides the basis for a Marine Corps organized, trained, and equipped to conduct expeditionary operations in a joint and combined environment within the complex spectrum of twenty-first-century conflict. It describes a Marine Corps of enhanced strategic agility, expanded operational reach, and improved tactical flexibility.

Twentieth-century amphibious operations moved through distinct phases, pauses, and reorganizations. Twenty-first-century expeditionary forces will be capable of moving directly from far offshore to objectives deep inland, uninterrupted by topography or hydrography, achieving greater surprise and complicating the adversary's defensive problem. In conjunction with the navy, marines will provide an early forcible entry capability from the sea. The ability to strike critical vulnerabilities and unhinge an adversary will be achieved through the combination of the Landing Craft Air Cushion, the Advanced Amphibious Assault Vehicle, and the V-22 Osprey tilt-rotor aircraft. The new concept focuses on the full spectrum capabilities of the Marine Corps, the employment of scalable Marine Air-Ground Task Forces (MAGTFs), to include the Marine Expeditionary Brigade, and the various means through which marine forces integrate with joint and combined task forces. The MAGTF will be able to reorganize and reorient rapidly in response to changing tactical opportunities throughout the full spectrum of future operational environments, while able to operate flexibly from expeditionary locations at sea or ashore.

The Air Force

The air force's new vision, *America's Air Force: Global Vigilance, Reach and Power*, is the aerospace answer to the *Joint Vision 2020* challenges and is designed to provide the nation with an integrated aerospace force. People are its foundation, aerospace is its domain, and the key to dominating this domain is the Expeditionary Aerospace Force (EAF). The core competencies needed by the EAF for such domination remain aerospace superiority, information superiority, global attack, precision engagement, rapid global mobility, and agile combat support. The air force views transformation as a sustained and determined effort that focuses on developing and fielding critical future capabilities, ensuring that America keeps the key asymmetric advantage of aerospace power vis-à-vis all potential adversaries.

In the place of the Cold War construct of fighter wing equivalents, the air force is reorganizing combat forces into ten Air Expeditionary Forces (AEFs) that are versatile, tailorable, and highly responsive. Each AEF will be capable of deploying a full spectrum of air-to-air, air-to-ground, command and control, and support capabilities. This restructuring involves organizational, cultural, and operational changes designed to improve management of global engagement activities and to enhance the air force's warfighting capability. AEFs will be able to sustain operations with a reduced forward-deployed footprint by exploiting the seamless integration of information support and weapons technologies.

JOINT CONCEPT DEVELOPMENT AND EXPERIMENTATION

As the executive agent for joint warfighting concept development and experimentation, U.S. Joint Forces Command (USJFCOM) aims to ensure that the joint warfighter's voice is heard and advocates joint alternatives for meeting key operational needs. Working closely with the services to leverage their robust transformation efforts, USJFCOM is responsible for joint concept development and experimentation that is a critical source of the ideas and innovation necessary to transform the department's military forces.

JFCOM's concept development and experimentation plan is organized around three axes that correspond to the near, mid, and far term. The first axis, enhancement of the current force, is aimed at the 2000–2010 time frame and focuses primarily on achieving near-term improvements to existing forces that constitute critical prerequisites for achieving longer-term transformation goals. The near-term experimentation agenda revolves around improving joint doctrine and organization, logistics, command and control, intelligence, surveillance, and reconnaissance capabilities.

The second axis of JFCOM's campaign plan looks beyond the systems and capabilities of the current force to determine what should begin to replace them between 2010 and 2020. These concept development and experimentation efforts focus around expanding and refining JFCOM's Rapid Decisive Operations (RDO) concept. The challenge of the RDO concept is to enable U.S. forces to accomplish their operational and strategic objectives in days and weeks across global distances against a competent regional adversary. This adversary may possess numerical superiority, an ability to shape the battlespace due to having a home field advantage, advanced antiaccess capabilities, a competent information operations capability, a willingness to sustain and inflict significant combatant and noncombatant casualties, and a significant ability to learn and adapt. JFCOM expects that this notional adversary will attempt to deny us access to the theater of operations and, if that fails, then attempt to draw U.S. forces into a protracted war of attrition.

The third axis of JFCOM's joint concept development and experimentation effort is focused on 2020 and beyond, and considers those concepts and technologies that have the potential to effect revolutionary transformation of the joint force. To support this third axis of experimentation, Joint Forces Command has established an Innovation and Transformation Center that has joined with key components of the defense science and technology community, the Department of Energy, selected industries, and the academic community to begin an exploration of highly advanced technologies and concepts. In 2000, this body began its work at an initial session at the Johns Hopkins Applied Physics Laboratory, in the area of future robotic systems and the possibilities for autonomous operations. In 2001, the effort will continue with consideration of the trends and possibilities in nanotechnologies, biocentric operations, and alternative energy sources.

RAPID IMPLEMENTATION

The Pentagon is pursuing new processes for committing resources to key emerging capabilities and promising operational concepts faster than the normal programming and budgeting process would allow. One such effort is the Army's Warfighter Rapid Acquisition Program (WRAP), a fund of approximately $50 million per year used to procure rapidly relatively low-cost but high-leverage systems that performed well in experimentation, such as the Rifle-Launched Entry Munition. The WRAP effort has reduced acquisition cycle time for systems by an average of twelve months. The army has used this account to implement results from its Force XXI advanced warfighting experimentation and, more recently, to defray some costs associated with converting initial brigades to the new medium weight design. The Marine Corps and the air force are establishing similar rapid acquisition programs. In the future, the Defense Department will consider whether such a rapid acquisition program is needed to implement new capabilities emerging from joint concept development and experimentation efforts.

Developing new technologies that create revolutionary military capabilities is a key element of the military's transformation strategy. New information systems, married with technological advances in other key areas including stealth platforms, unmanned vehicles, and smart submunitions, are essential to the efforts to exploit the revolution in military affairs.

Coalition building is also an important part of shaping the National Military Strategy. U.S. forces must plan, train, and prepare to respond to the full spectrum of crises in coalition with the forces of other nations. As the U.S. military transforms its capabilities with new technologies and operational concepts, careful design and collaboration will be needed to preserve our combined operations capabilities with friends and allies.

The military must also recruit, train, and retain people with the broad skills and good judgment needed to pursue dynamic change in the twenty-first century. Having the right kinds of imaginative, highly motivated military and civilian personnel, at all levels, is an essential prerequisite for achieving success in the Pentagon's ongoing military transformation. The Pentagon is and must continue to focus its efforts on three critical populations: young people with needed skills and attitudes, innovators, and current leaders. Each of these populations will play a vital role in ensuring that U.S. military forces are best shaped to respond to the threats of the twenty-first century.

CONCLUSION

The world of today presents us with many dangerous challenges. There is no silver bullet to address them. But the transformation strategy outlined above offers the best prospect of defending against multiple threats, whether anticipated or unanticipated, conventional or asymmetric. The United States—working together with existing allies and building relationships with new ones—has the skill, strength, and ingenuity to make this world safe, secure, free, and democratic for this and future generations. As we do this, we are continuing to build on the legacy of Dick Lugar and his vision for America and its role in the world.

13

A Global Coalition against Terrorism

Sam Nunn

The gravest danger in the world today is the threat from nuclear, biological, and chemical weapons. The likeliest use of these weapons is in terrorist hands. Preventing the spread and use of nuclear, biological, and chemical weapons should be the central organizing security principle for the twenty-first century.

In October 2001, top U.S. government officials received a highly classified intelligence report, warning that terrorists had acquired a 10-kiloton nuclear bomb and planned to smuggle it into New York City, where it could—if detonated—destroy much of lower Manhattan and kill tens of thousands of people.

This intelligence report—thank God—was later judged to be false. But it was never judged to be impossible or implausible. This should focus our attention on two fundamental questions:

1. If the report had been accurate, and the bomb had gone off, what would we wish we had done to prevent it?
2. Why aren't we doing that now?

Standing with President Putin at the White House in November 2001, President Bush said: "Our highest priority is to keep terrorists from acquiring weapons of mass destruction." At their May 2002 Moscow Summit, President Bush said: "President Putin and I agree that the greatest danger in this war is the prospect of terrorists acquiring weapons of mass destruction. Our nations must spare no effort at preventing all forms of proliferation."

These are encouraging words, but if this is our priority, what is our strategy? Where are we putting our resources? Have we rallied our friends and the world behind this "highest priority" to meet this "greatest danger"?

This is not just an American question. This is a global question. If a catastrophic terrorist strike could hit New York, it could hit Paris, St. Petersburg, London, Tokyo, or Moscow. The world must answer this challenge, beginning with Russia and the United States. The clock is ticking.

Unfortunately, we have not done enough—not individually or collectively. The key achievement of the May 2002 Moscow Summit was to sign a treaty to reduce by two-thirds the number of warheads on each side over the next ten years. This is an important accomplishment. But there is more urgent work to be done. We are in a new arms race. This time the United States and Russia must be on the same side. Terrorists and certain states are racing to acquire weapons of mass destruction, and we ought to be racing together to stop them. We have to think anew.

Reducing warheads is our joint response to the *reduced* nuclear threats *between* Washington and Moscow. But do we have a joint response to the *rising* terrorist nuclear threat that *targets* Washington and Moscow? I would have to say: "not yet" . . . which is somewhat better than "n-yet."

Ten years ago, a communist empire broke apart, leaving as its legacy 30,000 nuclear warheads and enough highly enriched uranium and plutonium to make 60,000 more; 40,000 metric tons of chemical weapons; missile-ready smallpox; and tens of thousands of scientists who know how to make weapons and missiles, but don't know how to feed their families.

Russia's dysfunctional economy and eroded security systems have undercut controls on these weapons, materials, and know-how—and increased the risk that they could flow to terrorist groups or hostile forces. Russia's early warning system has also seriously eroded, and some have suggested that their command and control, which for years helped prevent a calamitous mistake, is no longer assuredly reliable.

As these new threats have multiplied, both the United States and Russia have continued to invest large resources in nuclear strategies left over from the Cold War days: the maintenance of strategic forces with thousands of nuclear warheads ready for immediate launch. In today's multipolar world with its multiplicity of new threats, it no longer makes sense for either nation to stake its security so disproportionately on its ability to launch promptly a nuclear attack with thousands of warheads. These nuclear postures do not fit the demands of the day. They are not relevant in stopping proliferation, they compress decision time for each president to a matter of a very few minutes, they make an accident or misjudgment more likely, particularly with Russia's diminished weapons survivability and decreased warning, and they multiply the consequences of a mistake by either Russia or the United States.

The threats we faced during the Cold War—a Soviet nuclear strike or an invasion of Europe—were threats made more dangerous by Soviet strength. The new threats we face today—false warnings, accidental launch, the risk of weapons, materials, and know-how falling into the wrong hands—are threats made more dangerous by Russia's weakness. We addressed the Cold War's threats by confrontation with Moscow. There can be no realistic comprehensive plan to defend America against weapons of mass destruction that does not depend on cooperation with Moscow.

We have taken important steps, but we need giant strides. Over the last ten years, the United States through the Nunn-Lugar program has worked with Russia, Kazakhstan, Ukraine, and Belarus to recover and destroy 456 ballistic missiles, 383 ballistic missile launchers, 95 bombers, 483 long-range air-launched cruise missiles, 380 submarine missile launchers, 305 submarine-launched ballistic missiles, and 22 strategic missile submarines. In addition, 194 nuclear test tunnels have been sealed, and close to 6,000 warheads on strategic systems aimed at the United States have now been deactivated. The United States and Russia cooperated in preventing the birth of three new nuclear powers—one of the great accomplishments of the Clinton administration.

To reduce threats to our own security, we have helped the Russians secure their nuclear weapons and materials to prevent theft and accidents; helped them convert nuclear weapons facilities to civilian purposes; and helped them employ hundreds of their weapons scientists in peaceful pursuits. We also passed legislation in 1996 that created the framework for homeland defense. It has helped 150 U.S. cities prepare for the possibility of biological and chemical attacks and authorized the Defense and Energy Departments to carry out research and development on means to detect weapons of mass destruction. Funds were also authorized to purchase equipment capable of detecting and interdicting weapons of mass destruction and to assist border guards in eastern Europe and the former Soviet Union in blocking the unauthorized transfer of weapons of mass destruction.

These were not the accomplishments of one political party. The original Nunn-Lugar legislation was authored by a Republican and a Democrat; passed with Republican support by a Democratic Congress and signed by a Republican president. Later, the same legislation was passed with Democratic support by a Republican Congress and signed by a Democratic president. Nunn-Lugar-Domenici had similar support. We need to build on this record of bipartisanship to take the added steps compelled by the present dangers we face.

Missile defense is one such issue. The proliferation of missile technology, as well as the proliferation of nuclear, biological, and chemical weapons, poses the danger that a rogue state could develop the capability to launch a nuclear missile at a U.S. city. From my perspective, this threat is not an immediate danger, but it cannot be dismissed because it is more distant or because it would—for the attacking nation—amount to national suicide. I believe, however, that protecting our deployed military forces is a much more urgent threat, and mobile theater defense should be our priority focus.

Over the long run, to the extent that we can develop the means to shield ourselves from attack through a limited missile defense, we should do so— so long as it does not leave us more vulnerable to threats that are more likely, more immediate, and more potentially devastating. We must understand that threat reduction, diplomacy, cooperation, military power, and intelligence are our first line of defense against the spread of weapons of mass destruction and against terrorism. National missile defense is our last line of defense if all else fails. We have to guard against overinvesting in our last lines of defense and underinvesting in the first. The cost incurred should be proportional to the threat deterred.

If we are to develop any enduring consensus on this subject, missile defense must be debated as a technology, not a theology—as *part* of a security framework, not the whole of it. Our goal should not be to deploy a particular defense, but to reduce an overall threat. If we remember this, we have a chance to find common ground on this most contentious of all issues in the new security framework.

The fight against terrorism, nuclear force posture, nonproliferation, and missile defense each address separate elements of the response to the threat of weapons of mass destruction. But they should not and must not be formulated into separate *policy*. The character of one has a strong influence on the effectiveness of the others. That is why they must be considered not separately, but jointly, and woven into a comprehensive defense against weapons of mass destruction—in any form, from any source, on any vehicle, whether triggered by intent or accident by a rogue state or a terrorist group.

To be effective and comprehensive, we must also integrate the *missing* link—the link between changes in our offensive and defense systems and the essential cooperation required from Russia and others to prevent the spread of weapons, missiles, and materials, and to strengthen the global coalition against terrorism.

As Senator Lugar has said, "Funding for limited missile defenses [should] be embedded in a revised and more all-encompassing non-proliferation strategy . . . to prevent countries from acquiring weapons of mass destruction . . . in the first place."

The United States cannot secure dangerous materials, limit the spread of weapons of mass destruction know-how, gather accurate and timely intelligence, eliminate terrorist cells, or apply pressure to rogue regimes without the active cooperation of allies and former adversaries, including Russia and China. Any security initiative that undercuts this essential cooperation could leave us less secure, not more.

In sorting out our priorities, we must elevate facts above fear and analysis above emotion, and be sure that we are making the most of our resources. This must start with an objective, comprehensive intelligence estimate that assesses each major risk, ranks each major threat, and helps us devise a broad strategy that confronts the full range of significant dangers in a way that defends against one without making us more vulnerable to another. This approach would give the most weight and the most resources to threats that are the most immediate, the most likely, with the greatest consequences. In the absence of an infinite budget, relative risk analysis must be the beginning point in shaping our strategy and allocating our resources—to defend our citizens at home and abroad.

If the United States and Russia begin working together as partners in fighting terror and the threat from weapons of mass destruction, and encourage others to join, the world will be a different place for our children and grandchildren. We face a major challenge, but also a historic opportunity. Time and circumstance have given us a chance to shape new relationships and to build a new security framework, so that the pain of today will not be known by the children of tomorrow.

The United States and Russia have ceased to be enemies. We are talking, but not yet acting, as security partners. In a sense, we have ended one era in our relations, but we haven't fully begun another. Every day we delay, we place ourselves in greater danger.

Our situation, I believe, is captured in the pages of *War and Peace*. Count Tolstoy describes young Nikolai Rostov in his first cavalry charge against Napoléon's troops. He was knocked off his horse during the charge and scrambled to his feet in time to see French soldiers running at him with bayonets. His first instinct was that they must be coming to help.

Then, he began to think to himself: "'Who are they? Are they coming at *me*? Can they be running at *me*? And why? To kill *me*? *Me* whom everyone is so fond of?' He thought of his mother's love for him, of his family's and his friends', and the enemy's intention of killing him seemed impossible . . . for over ten seconds he stood rooted to the spot, not realizing the situation."

There is a warning for us in this passage from *War and Peace*. If we stay rooted to the spot, not realizing the situation, we are likely to see more war than peace. We must overcome our disbelief that there are terrorists dedicating their time, energy, and money to acquiring weapons of mass destruction so they can kill millions of people. As unthinkable as that is, we have to respond. We may not be able to make these terrorists less evil, but we can make them less powerful. We must keep them from acquiring weapons of mass destruction.

How difficult is it for terrorists to acquire a nuclear weapon? That depends on how difficult we make it. It becomes obvious from analyzing the terrorist path to a nuclear attack that the most effective, least expensive way to prevent nuclear terrorism is to secure nuclear weapons and materials at the source. Acquiring weapons and materials is the *hardest* step for the terrorists to take, and the *easiest* step for us to stop. By contrast, every subsequent step in the process is *easier* for the terrorists to take, and *harder* for us to stop.

Once they gain access to nuclear materials, they have completed the most difficult step. That is why the defense against catastrophic terrorism must begin with securing weapons and fissile materials in every country and every facility that possesses them.

This threat includes, but extends well beyond Russia and the former Soviet Union. Some 20 tons of civilian HEU exists at 345 civilian research facilities in 58 countries, yet there are no international standards for securing these nuclear materials within these countries. We are talking about the raw material of nuclear terrorism, stored in hundreds of facilities in dozens of nations—some of it is secured by nothing more than an underpaid guard sitting inside a chain-link fence. Addressing this is a global security imperative.

A wide alliance of nations must work together to identify, account for, and secure all—as soon as possible. This will not happen without active leadership from Russia and the United States.

President Bush has said: "In the breadth of its land, the talent and courage of its people, the wealth of its resources, and the reach of its weapons, Russia is a great power, and must always be treated as such." Russia today is a great power in another sense as well. Russia is in a unique position to make the world more secure by helping to safeguard weapons and materials at home and around the world. Russia has enormous technical and scientific expertise for the task. Russia has influence in some important capitals where most other nations do not.

Russians are known as gifted strategic thinkers—from the battlefield to the chessboard. It should be obvious that when the world faces a global security threat—and there is a particular nation whose people have excelled in every area of creative human endeavor—from art and music, to literature and science—then the people of that nation should be fully deployed against the threat. If the world's gravest threat is not opposed by the world's greatest talent, we will have failed to do all we can to protect the future for our children.

With my long-time colleague Dick Lugar, we have been working to conceive and to build the architecture to meet this challenge. There are six essential steps to consider as we begin to map out a new strategy for global security in the twenty-first century.

(1) The first step is to put our own houses in order—identifying, accounting for, and securing weapons and materials in Russia and the United States. Both the United States and Russia should pledge to ensure that nuclear, chemical, and biological materials and weapons in both countries are safe, secure, and accounted for with reciprocal monitoring sufficient to assure each other and the rest of the world that this is the case. This would require rapid security upgrades, accelerated blend-down of weapons materials, and consolidation of weapons materials in fewer sites.

(2) The United States and Russia should insist on accurate accounting and adequate safeguards for tactical nuclear weapons, including a baseline inven-

tory of these weapons and reciprocal monitoring. Tactical nuclear weapons have never been covered in arms control treaties. We can only guess at the numbers in each other's inventories. Yet these are the nuclear weapons most attractive to terrorists—even more valuable to them than fissile material, and much more portable than strategic warheads. The relations between our two heads of state are warm. Our perception of our common interest is closer than it has ever been. If this new relationship is to improve our security, then it must be able to melt the suspicion that has kept us for so many years from an accurate accounting and assured protection of these weapons. As President Putin said on his visit to the United States in October 2001: "People expect U.S. and Russian politicians to leave behind double standards, empty suspicions and hidden goals and engage in an open, direct, and fruitful dialogue. . . . The Cold War must no longer hold us by the sleeve." I agree; the Cold War will continue to hold us by the sleeve until we deal with tactical nuclear weapons.

(3) Both President Bush and President Putin should order their military leaders, in joint consultation and collaboration, to devise operational changes in the alert status of their nuclear forces that would reduce toward zero the risk of accidental launch or miscalculation and expand the decision time available to each president before he would be forced to make the fateful decision to launch. This process should begin with an operational stand down of the weapons now scheduled for reductions.

(4) The United States and Russia should combine our biodefense knowledge and scientific expertise and apply these joint resources to defensive and peaceful biological pursuits. The two nations could promote a bilateral effort to cooperate on our research agendas and build on what both nations know. This is an endeavor that should begin with Russia and the United States and expand to include the rest of the world.

(5) Both presidents should pledge that the May 2002 Moscow Treaty will be supplemented by additional agreements to ensure transparency, verifiability, irreversibility, and stability. The goals of stability and irreversibility would be substantially advanced by agreeing to dismantle nuclear weapons from each nation's stockpile.

(6) My sixth point includes the others and goes beyond them. It is the heart of the new initiative Dick Lugar and I have launched. The United States and Russia should build a Global Coalition against Catastrophic Terrorism. The Global Coalition would be based on the fundamental premise that the greatest dangers of the twenty-first century are threats all nations face together and no nation can solve on its own. The most likely, most immediate, most potentially devastating threat is the terrorist use of weapons of mass destruction. The best way to address the threat is to keep terrorists from acquiring nuclear, biological, and chemical weapons. And we must never forget: the chain of worldwide security is only as strong as the link at the weakest, least-protected site. That is why the coalition must be global.

It would begin with the United States and Russia, but quickly expand to include nations such as China, India, and Pakistan. It would involve every state with nuclear weapons and weapons-usable materials—and would assist each state in establishing standards and cooperative programs for inventory control, safety, and security. It would improve border and export controls, and train international teams to respond in the event of terrorist nuclear explosion or the loss of control of nuclear weapons or materials.

To deny terrorists access to dangerous biological materials without hindering important medical research, the coalition would establish standards for safeguarding biological materials in scientific practice. It would devise approaches for limiting the spread of biological weapons know-how and developing effective measures to prevent bioterrorism and minimize the effects of any attack. It would direct more resources and attention to global infectious disease surveillance and prevention—improving worldwide efforts in detecting and reporting disease outbreaks, and bringing forth an effective global response. In addition to the moral imperative of stepping up the fight against infectious disease around the globe, we now have a security imperative as well.

These ideas represent the outlines of a Global Coalition against Catastrophic Terrorism that could emerge from U.S.-Russia cooperation, and *only* from U.S.-Russia cooperation. The idea of Russia and the United States leading something so ambitious might prompt some to say: "Nunn is Don Quixote, dreaming the impossible dream. What about the frictions in U.S.-Russia relations? What about Iran, Iraq, chemical and biological weapons compliance, NATO expansion, missile defense, Chechnya, Jackson-Vanik—or even chicken parts?"

My answer is to end where I began. To put these issues in perspective, we must again ask this question: If terrorists succeed in destroying Washington or Moscow with weapons of mass destruction, what would we wish we had done to prevent it? Why aren't we doing that now?

One nation cannot win this fight alone. As the Russian proverb says: "One person on the battlefield is not a soldier." Two nations cannot win the fight alone either. But the actions of many nations often follow from the actions of a few—particularly when the actions of the few are in the interest of the many.

The United States and Russia have done more than all other nations combined to build up the world's deadly supply of weapons and materials. *We must now build them down.* As we do, we will gain the authority and credibility we need to ask other nations to do their part to reduce this global threat. Together, we must inspire the world to come together in a way it never has before—to prevent a danger it has never faced before.

14

Responsibility and Foreign Affairs

Mark Blitz

What should be the purpose of our foreign policies? Why might someone spend time away from private interests or domestic politics to become engaged in them? What prevents such engagement from becoming a field for imperial ambition as it has been historically from the Athenian Alcibiades to contemporary tyrants?

In one way or another, the response to these questions involves the way we protect equal liberty or equal rights. I intend to organize my discussion around one element of this liberty, namely, the place of responsibility in our political life generally and our foreign affairs in particular. Responsibility is, of course, not the only phenomenon worth exploring here, but properly understood it is especially significant because it is central in the actual exercise of our rights. It enables us to look beyond liberties and rights statically described to our form of government actively in motion. The practical conclusion of my analysis will be that our foreign policies should foster responsible freedom, our own and to a lesser extent that of others. Seeing things as a responsible man sees them, moreover, should be the standard for our judgments and involvement. The clash of responsibilities is a—perhaps the—safeguard of liberty. My theoretical point will be that a link exists between the virtues that American life tries to enhance in its citizens and the virtues that we require to make our institutions function well. End and form work together, and the virtue of responsibility is a central element in both. This is as true in foreign as in domestic matters.

REALISM AND IDEALISM

It may seem obvious that our foreign policies should promote responsibility. Who would be mad enough to say they should foster the opposite? Blithe disregard, wild adventurism, feckless frittering away of power and substance—these are platform planks that not even a Democrat could knowingly love. Yet, much of what we do abroad is not very different from what would result were irresponsibility our conscious guide. Policies shaped by economic interest alone, for example, or by national interest otherwise narrowly construed treat others' religion, hopes for liberal freedom and possible democratic institutions as odd irritants to be dismissed, ignored, or wished away. People who themselves would not yield an ounce of liberty for a pound of flesh repeatedly act as if others will. The endless surprise when economic ties and mutual advantage do not always lead others to gaze lovingly when Americans wander into sight is an example of this mistake. A shock to "realism" has been a recurring feature of our Mideast affairs from Iran to Afghanistan.

Iran, of course, took its hostages during the administration of our most famously moralistic president since Woodrow Wilson. Jimmy Carter's moralism and moralism generally led us to wield power with guilt and therefore poorly, to cede our authority to international bodies or make nervous excuses when we do not, and to overlook our interests. No serious or responsible politician should entertain disinterested or legalistic obedience to the Kyoto Accords, the International Criminal Court, or their thousand cousins of the past (such as the Law of the Sea) or future. A moralistic belief in internationalism, in fact, is often inseparable from the visible or unconscious wish to divest ourselves of the responsibility that comes with our power, if not from that power itself.

Although both realism and moralism lead to foolish disregard of reality and inattention to power or inability to use it, neither leads or has yet led us to wild adventurism. Their irresponsibility is the wishful thinking of hard or soft men, not boldly reckless or even tyrannical action. Perhaps liberals were honest when they treated President Reagan's Strategic Defense Initiative as the height of recklessness—made worse by its being poised against the "evil" empire. Perhaps they mean it when they fear President Bush's "axis of evil" will tempt him to extreme measures. I myself believe that neither of these charges is intended seriously. I doubt that those who oppose(d) attacking Iraq really believed it to be recklessly wild (as opposed to something they themselves might not have done) or that anyone but a deterrent theologian actually believes the common sense of strategic defense to be outlandishly extreme and not merely uncomfortably new and expensive. I doubt as well that liberals and conservatives who opposed intervention in Bosnia, Haiti, or even Somalia truly believed it to be boundlessly excessive and not just imprudent. The overstatement in all these cases is more political than genuine.

I emphasize these points because the absence of wild adventure or extremism even in what some consider our most excessive foreign policies teaches us something about responsibility. The classic forms of irresponsible adventurism are present in tyrants' wishes to shatter and dominate or in proud men's hopes to make themselves imperial gods or figures of noble renown. We think of Alexander conquering the Persians, of Alcibiades fighting for Sparta against his Athenian homeland, of Napoleon's conquest of Europe, of the murderous lives of Stalin and Hitler.

The significance of America's domestic freedom from such characters should not be underestimated. At the country's beginning it could hardly be taken for granted. It was a staple of political rhetoric to claim that Hamilton, Burr, or Jefferson wished to be another Bonaparte.[1] As it turned out, however, our foreign (and domestic) affairs began to operate within the horizon of and for the protection of equal rights. The design of the founders forced political ambition and activity in the milder direction in fact that they had intended in principle. It is a political blessing that here the tall trees are always based in the egalitarian forest. We nonetheless need something of the spirit of noble pride if we are to meet the threat of tyrannical figures from abroad. The Roosevelts and MacArthur, not to mention Washington and Lincoln, are necessary (or rise to the fore) in our direst circumstances or when our way of life is founded and secured. One of the remarkable features of American statesmanship is how we successfully redirect outstanding political capacity to liberal democratic ends without so stunting these capacities that we inevitably find them shriveled when we wish to see them in bloom.[2] Whatever the irresponsibility of our actions, fostering tyranny is infrequently among them.

RESPONSIBILITY AS VIRTUE

I believe that by examining responsibility we can begin to understand what substitutes democratically for political or even imperial excess, provides a standpoint that overcomes the mistaken extremes of realism and idealism, and explains more ordinary—if still exceptional—attention to foreign affairs. If the importance and breadth of responsibility is demonstrated by nothing else, it is indicated by the fact that both Presidents Clinton and Bush, both Democrats and Republicans, make it a central element of their rhetoric and intentions.[3]

"Responsibility" is a virtue. It is therefore similar as an element of character to courage, moderation, generosity, and acting justly. As a virtue it belongs to a more natural or commonsensical perspective than does "morality" as we discuss it under Kant's influence or the narrowness of a self-interest that modern philosophers isolate from the natural search for happiness. Virtues as, classically, Aristotle understands them in his *Ethics* comprise character, the dispositions to choose what reason tells us to choose concerning that things that usually matter to us—pleasures, fear, wealth, reputation, and so on.[4] To be moderate is the habit of choosing to enjoy pleasure (and therefore enjoying it) in the right way and degree, at the right time with the right people. "Practical" reason tells us what these right ways are. Because virtue, character, involves enjoying pleasure, wealth, and honor, it neither ascetically or moralistically sets aside our passions nor acts as if the only real things are accumulations of wealth to satisfy material interests.

Responsibility is a virtue in this sense but one more suited to the modern world of the founding fathers than to the ancient world of Aristotle himself. It supplements as do modern virtues such as industriousness, toleration, and kindness the other elements of character and largely replaces one of their peaks.[5] This peak is what Aristotle called greatness of soul, or great pride, the disposition to choose or seek the greatest practical honor for oneself, political rule, and to deserve it. Just as this virtue helps account for political excellence, so does the vice of overweening or misplaced pride (the extreme ambition to stand in an undeserved place of honor and the related imprudence) go far toward explaining political tyranny.[6]

The novelty of responsibility is indicated first by the fact that the term is used initially at the time of the American founding (primarily to discuss institutions) and second by the fact that being responsible is a phrase that we can apply to practically anyone in any line of work.[7] Greatness of soul, however, is rare. So, at the same time that taking on great political responsibilities is akin to great pride, it is also akin to and indeed merely extends the more ordinary responsibilities of democratic characters in democratic societies. This wider application and relative novelty of the term suggest that responsibility is connected to the modern notions of happiness and the purpose of politics that begin with Machiavelli, are developed by John Locke and later Enlightenment thinkers, and culminate practically in America's principles and constitution. We will now examine responsibility in more detail.

THE SUBSTANCE OF RESPONSIBILITY

Responsibility first indicates accountability, a moral trait connected to punishment and guilt. Responsible officials are those on whom to pin the blame, the ones to sue, condemn, and denounce. Responsible officials, however, are also the ones we expect to help when we are in trouble or to fix what is broken. So, "responsibilities" are not merely things for which we are morally accountable but tasks or jobs we are supposed to complete. The whole panoply of punishment and guilt in which a good heart, good intentions, or proper repentance can expiate or justify sins or mistakes is only half the story, or less, because people who should responsibly do their jobs complete what they set out to accomplish and leave no loose ends untied. Failure with a good heart is still failure. Not getting the job done even though (or because) one acted by the book or in the "right" way is disappointing and sometimes disastrous.[8] Rather than punishment and blame, accomplishment and success are the essence of this other half or more than half of responsibility. In fact, it is often easier to dodge blame or verbally accept it than actually to finish things effectively.

Of course, although being held to account and being effective are different they can be linked: we are accountable to our employer for succeeding and not merely trying. But such specific accountability is an insufficient condition for responsible effectiveness. The physician or mechanic who fails with good intentions is not the responsible physician or mechanic who actually pays attention intelligently and in detail, trains himself to the degree that is necessary, and finishes his work well and on time.

RESPONSIBILITY AND RIGHTS

Responsibility is a central element of character among free peoples. For, together with certain opinions and practices about equality, law, and political institutions, it expresses what it takes to secure and exercise one's rights. Let us see how this is so.

The habit of responsibility enables someone to work freely to satisfy both his future and present interests. In fact, although we usually are effective by doing jobs for others (those to whom we are accountable) we first learn to be responsible for our own good. Being responsible is how we treat ourselves when our success depends so much on ourselves, when we take the long view of ourselves, when we, as it were, invest in ourselves. When parents urge children to be responsible, they have in mind studying so one can be successful in the future, being careful so one has a future, and preserving property (for example, not wrecking cars) so it can be used tomorrow. Urging responsibility, indeed, is what makes parents so serious and boring, enemies of the immediately self-indulgent and playful. We want teenagers to take their medicine when they get in trouble (that is, to be accountable) but what we really wish is that they consider their resources and tasks seriously enough that they do not get in trouble in the first place. Preparing oneself to be effective is the substance of responsibility to oneself: Through this preparation I do not serve any particular interest, but myself as a free man capable of serving many interests. At the same time, by being responsible I work for others' interests, and respect them as free men also capable of enjoying many interests.

We can see, therefore, how responsibility is similar to duty or ordinary justice (for example, doing what one is paid for) in much of its substance. It differs, however, because of the voluntary and secular essence of modern liberal democracies. Obligations and tasks do not only or primarily come from heaven, are not enforced by divine institutions, and are not tied to specific professions, estates, or guilds that one rarely leaves. Rather, most activities are voluntary, and the basis of obligation must be consistent with the primary grounding of human affairs on natural rights that belong to the self. Responsibility, the habit of effective attention to one's work and to oneself as a steady chooser and accumulator of substance and success, is an appropriate means in this new situation to serve oneself while serving others.

In this way, responsibility correctly understood links moral good and self-interest because it is neither mere moral accountability apart from results nor a disposition to favor one's immediate interests at the expense of one's longer term freedom and a success that helps others. Responsible behavior aids others, not only oneself, but as effectiveness it also serves one's own interest through jobs well done, payments for them, and the steady growth of one's own character and efforts. As a goal—securing of the good character that allows the active exercise of one's rights—and as a means to satisfying interests and others' ends, it helps overcome both the ineffective or even slavish unreality of excessive realism and the fecklessness of moralism.

RESPONSIBILITY AND POLITICS

This point will become clearer if we stretch our understanding of responsibility, and if we then consider more carefully its link to securing equal individual rights and its (consequent) difference from great pride. For, responsibility is not only the disposition to do one's jobs successfully. This considers all one's actions as voluntary, yet defined—one fulfills the contract, attends to one's children's education, and helps one's patients. Such responsibility is a disposition that is akin to or part of justice or ordinary pride. But responsibility also involves taking on the tasks that belong to no one in particular, the ones where my interests are no more engaged than are anyone else's. The responsible men and women who, say, seek positions on school boards, lobby the local government, or organize their fellow employees to complain to higher-ups show this kind of responsibility. Responsible men and women not only execute their own jobs, they take on the jobs that belong to no one in particular—they are the opposite of the notorious free rider. Nonetheless, although they take on common tasks they do not characteristically do so altruistically, but serve their own as well as others' good.

This kind of responsibility is especially interesting because it brings us close to the virtue and ambition of outstandingly political men. Nonetheless, because such responsibility originates in, protects, and makes effective voluntary choice, equal rights, and the activities that flow from them, it is broadly egalitarian. As such, it does not stem from the desire to outrank all others, to win every victory, to be outstanding as only few can be outstanding. Nor, however, does it fulfill itself or believe it fulfills itself only in complete moral or intellectual perfection, because it tends toward specific effectiveness. It is rooted neither in absolute honor nor purity. Responsibility in the broadest sense, I am suggesting, involves more than just doing one's own tasks. It sometimes is directed to the tasks that belong to no one, not only to one's own ability to accumulate and be effectively free. It is the heart of actively engaging in politics, including seeking and conducting oneself in political office in a manner consistent with equal rights and not grounded on majestic pride or religious duty.

The fact that political responsibility is desirable and that it exists do not altogether explain how it arises. How is it coherent with and even prompted by more ordinary effectiveness? Politically, it arises consistently from this efficacy because the care, seriousness, skills, firmness, and attention to the future that make up or stem from responsibility need not be limited to the field of one's own self-interest. In fact, with sufficient intelligence, energy, and passion it is likely that some will seek larger and larger fields on which to be successful and come to consider themselves as a certain type of character who acts in certain ways—the ones who deliver, get things done, and secure the future generally. More than calculation, it is this democratic habit, prudence, and regard for oneself as broadly effective that lead people to care for what is common. Such care or excellence occurs in unequal degrees, however, because talents and energy differ. Responsibility follows along a continuum that moves from securing self-interest to engaging in ordinary public tasks that belong to no one in particular (for example, voting) to devoting much of one's life to the public. Identical actual responsibility for all men in all things would deprive us both of sufficient freedom and the greatest abilities. Yet, this variability among people in private effort and public responsibility is based on equal rights. It is neither aristocratically permanent nor tyrannically encompassing, but democratically competitive.[9]

RESPONSIBILITY AND INSTITUTIONS

However important character is, it is insufficient by itself to limit the pretensions of political activity, encourage it properly, or direct it always to the common good. Our opinions about the justice of equality in rights and the worth of self-government form us to some degree independently of our characters. The qualities that become the virtue of responsibility can also become a disposition merely to successful selfishness when these qualities lose or never find their connection to a view from which I see myself primarily as a free being equal to others in my rights. Responsibility as the virtue that activates constructive immediate and long-range expressions of equal liberty will too easily give way to grasping calculation when equality in rights is misunderstood or subjugated to the simple satisfaction of animal desires. Or, it will become misconceived as excessive accountability to abstract, uncompromising duties if the link between equal rights, satisfying interests, and holding property is misconceived or ignored.

In addition to good opinion, good character, and the healthy pursuit of interests, good laws and institutions also are needed to direct private and political efforts properly, to, for example, enhance the competition that restricts privilege and calls forth industry. Good results depend on the proper channels. Nonetheless, unless rights actually are exercised responsibly, neither political institutions nor private competition will be activated properly. Responsible character must supplement, indeed it partially causes, good laws and right opinion. As Publius writes in the *Federalist Papers,* ambition must counteract ambition among office holders who live up to their responsibilities. Despite what scholars sometimes seem to suggest, the institutions within our government do not check each other automatically. Successful public and private life require the clash and (partial) resolution of enterprising efforts to meet new circumstances and farsighted compromises to treat more usual yet important concerns. Merely balancing interests, moreover, will often fail to achieve the public good because public efforts should be directed toward securing rights and the conditions for their free use, not the dominance of this or that group of interests to which liberties might be sacrificed. Although the public efforts of political men serve their interests, moreover, these efforts surely differ from maximizing them privately. Leading the attempt to secure sufficient funding and intelligent curricula for schools, for example, has as much or more to do with securing conditions for the intelligent and responsible use of others' freedoms as it does with enhancing one's own.[10]

So, important as are right opinion and sound institutions, certain virtues, responsibility chief among them in our modern American case, are needed to bring these opinions and institutions to life.

RESPONSIBILITY AND FOREIGN AFFAIRS

I have argued that the phenomenon of responsibility suggests a link between morality and interest because responsibility supports and expresses the exercise of one's equal rights for the purpose of satisfaction, especially satisfaction of one's immediate interests. It therefore promotes a people in tune with equal liberty and competition. The just limits to one's aggrandizement do not become effective automatically, as we have said, but require legally secured competitive markets and competitive politics working through separated powers. Political attention to the common good is also not automatic, for it depends on the unusual (though not extreme) responsibility of some few. The question before us now is what responsibility—both as a goal to seek and as a standpoint from which to judge—indicates about directing foreign affairs.

I will mention six areas, three concerning ways and means, and three that are more immediately substantive. First is to remind ourselves of the significant place of Congress and not only the executive in foreign affairs. The Constitution indicates preeminence for the president as commander in chief, but this preeminence stands within overall shared responsibility for budgets and treaties.[11] Such shared responsibility is nothing new. Serious discussions in Washington's and Adams' administrations of policy toward France and Great Britain and of raising an army and navy were hardly confined to the executive alone. They were central also to the legislative debates, public opinion, and electoral politics of the day. Jefferson's Louisiana Purchase was a bold assertion of executive enterprise, but it could not have been assimilated without legislative compromise and support. Responsible legislators to this day must work with the executive to secure effective programs and useful appropriations. They are the ones who must derail inappropriate treaties and other potential mistakes. They also often take larger steps because the character and views that lead them to perform sometimes thankless public tasks also drive them to examine territory the executive has not yet occupied. The Nunn-Lugar Act is a good example from recent years. Congressional responsibility properly understood checks executive pretension, works together with the executive to meet necessities, and sometimes presses forward where the president himself has not taken the lead.

Second, as I suggested earlier, is to be cautious of internationalism. By internationalism I mean ceding authority to international bodies as opposed to working with allies toward a common goal. To allow international courts and political entities serious authority is to restrict freedom, for to promote freedom practically is to promote the habit of its use: to encourage freedom is to support the growth and exercise of responsibility. To advance the exercise of responsibility, therefore, is to begin along a path that encourages all people to engage to some degree in public affairs and several to engage in it significantly. Increased internationalism, however, makes government ever more remote from citizens and restricts active attention. Bureaucrats, those elected by no one or those who do not believe in free government in the first place, are the ones who make decisions. The spectacle of tyrants excluding the United States from international human rights bodies is appalling. The tendency of some European governments to decide that the citizens of other democracies should not be subject to these countries' own laws is disturbing.[12] Judicial measures are promoted in international bodies whose norms and procedures are alien to our own. Legislative and bureaucratic activities are conducted at far removes from effective representation. Whatever gain internationalism brings in security is countered by a loss in self-government, not only ours but also that of other free countries. National governments are imperfect, but their imperfections are by and large worsened not improved by the remoteness of international regimes. In fact, the size, distance, unclear goals, and potential dominance of these groups is such that the difficulties I have mentioned would exist even were international bodies collections of perfectly republican governments, as of course they are not. Free governments must be composed of actively free citizens.

Third is prudent or responsible intervention in areas beyond our immediate interests. By responsible intervention I mean intervention measured carefully by our resources, the importance and urgency of the situation, others' need for self-reliance, and our own understanding of ourselves as standing for what is right. Responsibility obviously argues against feckless gestures and unbalanced use of resources. It also points away from a moralism that is disconnected from our own interests and fails to see others' freedoms in the context of theirs. In its broader political meaning, however, it also precludes mere calculation (because we connect interests to rights) and excessive control (because we are concerned with others' self-government). Self-interest alone will not induce us to take risks to help others attain their freedoms even though these freedoms may help us in the long run.[13] To measure possible intervention in this way, however, provides at best a standpoint for judgment, not a formula for application. It is a standpoint not terribly far from the considerations that we have brought to bear throughout our history, and especially as our power has grown.

This leads to the substantive question of the purposes of our policy, and here we should have in mind both "idealism" and "realism" considered responsibly. From the beginning of the United States, our founders believed that regimes based on equal rights would dominate the future. The differences between, say, Jefferson and Adams in policies toward Great Britain and France did not mean that either thought that regimes based on standards other than those of equal rights were as just as those that are. No multiculturalism clouded their principled view. In my judgment, it still is wise actively to promote equality of rights, religious tolerance, representative government, majority voting, and separation of powers. Responsibility in others should be our central goal in dealing with them. Such promotion—whether through prudent intervention, aggressive public diplomacy, or as the result of private action—has several advantages. It may seem to foster, but actually it restricts our potential arrogance by reminding us that what is distinctive about us are principles that cover others as well as ourselves. It gives us a task and direction beyond self-interest narrowly conceived. And conducted intelligently it promotes rather than risks our security because it expands our circle of friends. Our liberal principles, moreover, permit and indeed encourage reasonable diversity in practices and beliefs not just among our own citizens but for the citizens of other countries who choose to be formed by them. Their spread is therefore not venally "imperialistic." It is nonetheless true that free government will color these practices in ways similar to the manner in which the responsible character of liberally acquisitive citizens colors earlier notions of duty and obligation.

I conclude with the points that strong defense and careful attention to economic interests also stem from the perspective of responsibility. For, this perspective is attentive to interest both in itself and a necessary element of effective principle. Security is brought about by strength not weakness or indifference, and security is a condition of freedom. John Adams once wrote that the peace missions he sent to France during his presidency "were the most disinterested and meritorious actions" of his life. "I reflect upon them," he continued, "with so much satisfaction that I desire no other inscription over my gravestone than: 'Here lies John Adams, who took upon himself the responsibility of the peace with France in the year 1800.'"[14] As Adams saw it, he could discharge this responsibility effectively only because at the same time we were beginning to build a navy strong enough to give others a reason to join us in our peaceful quest. Thoughtful American statesmen always have been aware that responsible statesmanship demands sufficient resources. It cannot rely solely on goodwill or purity of intention and surely not on wishful thinking.

NOTES

1. Consider, for example, material quoted or summarized in David McCullough, *John Adams* (New York: Simon and Schuster, 2001).

2. Consider John Keegan, *The Mask of Command* (New York: Penguin, 1988); Lord Charnwood, *Abraham Lincoln* (New York: Henry Holt, 1917); and various biographies of Winston Churchill, such as Roy Jenkins, *Churchill* (New York: Farrar, Straus and Giroux, 2001) and Robert D. Kaplan, *Warrior Politics* (New York: Random House, 2001).

3. Consider their inaugural addresses and many other statements.

4. Consider Aristotle, *Ethics*, Books 1–5.

5. See *The Federalist* 23, 63, 70, 77, 79; John Locke, *A Letter Concerning Toleration*, ed. James H. Tully (Indianapolis: Hackett, 1983); and Jean Jacques Rousseau, *Second Discourse*.

6. Far is not everywhere. In order to complete a picture of, say, communism or Nazism, we must also consider other causes such as Plato's discussion in the *Republic* of the connection between tyranny and boundless eros, and the peculiar role of misplaced "theory." One might consider (and contrast) the works on Hitler and the Nazis of Ian Kershaw, Michael Burleigh, and Daniel Goldhagen, and the works on Stalin and the Soviet Union of Adam Ulam and Robert Conquest.

7. See *The Federalist* 23, 63, 70, 77, and 79.

8. Consider for all these issues and their interconnection the controversy (current at the time this essay was completed) concerning the reaction of various elements of the FBI to early warnings of what became the September 11, 2001, attack. See Eric

Lichtblau and Josh Meyer, "Missed Memo Stirs More Trouble at FBI," *Los Angeles Times*, 25 May 2002, A1.

9. I do not mean to suggest that there is a hard and fast distinction between responsibility, duty, great pride, and love of honor. In any given modern case, the somewhat different motivations of these types may be hard to tell apart, and in some responsibility may seem the less accurate designation. Churchill surely seems closer to being a great souled man than to being a paragon of responsibility. Yet, even his pride is limited by the circumstances and goals of modern liberalism, modern technology, and modern responsible government. Harry Truman seems more a slightly outsized version of ordinary responsibility than an example of greater political passion, yet his war service, historical studies, and ambition all point in a direction much more public-spirited than the norm. The point is that to the degree these cognates of responsibility still exist in deed and not only in word they now emerge and flourish primarily from the point of view of responsible character and are therefore limited by and connected to interest and equal rights. Responsibility is central in linking democratic pride and interest, in not descending to interest alone but also in directing pride away from tyranny or fantasy. It is the element in the liberty-loving character that partially explains why we are political at the same time we are apolitical.

10. I have examined these topics in other papers. Consider here, Mark Blitz, "Virtue Ancient and Modern," in *Educating the Prince*, ed. Mark Blitz and William Kristol (Lanham, Md.: Rowman and Littlefield, 2000); Mark Blitz, "Responsibility and Public Service," in *Active Duty: Public Administration As Democratic Statesmanship*, ed. Peter Lawler, David Schaefer, and Robert Schaefer (Lanham, Md.: Rowman and Littlefield, 1998); Mark Blitz, "The Problem of Practice—Foreign Policy and the Constitution," in *Foreign Policy and the Constitution*, ed. Robert A. Goldwin and Robert A. Licht (Washington, D.C.: American Enterprise Institute Press, 1990); and Mark Blitz, "The Character of Executive and Legislative Power in a Regime Based on Natural Rights," in *The Revival of Constitutionalism*, ed. James Muller (Lincoln: University of Nebraska Press, 1988).

11. Consider article I, sections 7, 8, 9, and 10, and article II, sections 2 and 3 of the Constitution.

12. We should consider with concern the measures taken and threatened against Henry Kissinger and Ariel Sharon. Several recent works by Jeremy Rabkin are a good guide to this general issue. Representative are his testimony at the hearings on "International Justice," Committee on International Relations, U.S. House of Representatives, February 28, 2002; "The International Kangaroo Court," *The Weekly Standard*, 25 April 2002; and "Human Rights Agenda versus National Sovereignty," which is part of Freedom House's Freedom in the World survey for 2000–2001, at freedomhouse.org.

13. Self-interest, however, can sometimes go surprisingly far. Presumably, for example, it was the ground for much of France's help during our battle for independence from Great Britain.

14. From David McCullough, who refers to Ralph Waldo Brown, *The Presidency of John Adams* (1975; reprint, Lawrence: University Press of Kansas, 1981), 174. Brown himself finds the quotation in Zoltán Haraszti, *John Adams and the Prophets of Progress* (New York: Grosset and Dunlap, 1964), 263.

A Foreign Policy Chronology of Richard G. Lugar

April 4, 1932	Richard Green Lugar is born in Indianapolis, Indiana
1950	Graduates first in class, Shortridge High School, Indianapolis, IN
1954	Graduates first in class, Denison University, Granville, Ohio
1954–1956	Rhodes Scholar, Pembroke College, Oxford University; MA, in politics, philosophy, and economics
September 8, 1956	Marries Charlene Smeltzer
1957–1960	U.S. Navy (including service as intelligence briefer for Admiral Arleigh Burke, Chief of Naval Operations)
November 5, 1963	Elected to the Indianapolis School Board
November 7, 1967	Elected mayor of Indianapolis and serves two terms (1968–1975)
1971	Elected president of the National League of Cities
November 2, 1976	Unseats incumbent Vance Hartke to gain election to the U.S. Senate
January 3, 1977	Sworn in as U.S. Senator from Indiana; begins an eight-year term on the Senate Select Committee on Intelligence
January 1979	Joins the Senate Committee on Foreign Relations
November 2, 1982	Reelected to a second term in the Senate
January 1983	Becomes chairman of the Subcommittee on European Affairs, Senate Committee on Foreign Relations
September 1983	Leads Senate adoption of the Congress-Bundestag exchange program for U.S. and German high school students

January 1985   Becomes chairman, Senate Committee on Foreign Relations

January 1985   Named cochairman of the newly formed Senate Arms Control Observer Group

July 31, 1985   Under the leadership of Chairman Lugar and House Foreign Affairs chairman Dante Fascell, Congress passes its first foreign assistance authorization bill since 1981

January 30, 1986   President Reagan announces he will send an official delegation to monitor the upcoming Philippine presidential elections; Secretary of State George Shultz asks Lugar to lead the delegation

February 5–10, 1986   Leads the U.S. election observer team in the Philippines

February 11, 1986   Meets with President Reagan and tells him that the Philippine Parliament is "cooking the results" of the election

February 24, 1986   Ferdinand Marcos leaves the Philippines and the United States immediately recognizes the Aquino government

October 2, 1986   The Senate votes 78–21 to override President Reagan's veto of the Comprehensive Anti-Apartheid Act, a bill to impose U.S. sanctions on South Africa

May 27, 1988   The Senate ratifies the Intermediate Nuclear Forces Treaty, for which Lugar served as a floor manager, by a vote of 93–5

1988   Publishes *Letters to the Next President*, a primer of basic principles on presidential foreign policy leadership

November 8, 1988   Reelected to a third Senate term, receiving 68 percent of the vote

August 30, 1990   In an address to the national convention of the American Legion, Lugar calls for the removal of Saddam Hussein from power

November 13, 1990   On three network news shows, Lugar calls for a special session of Congress to authorize the use of force against Iraq

January 12, 1991   The House and Senate vote to approve the use of force against Iraq; in a Senate floor speech, Lugar says, "Our votes today express our determination to prevail. The moment of accountability has come."

November 25, 1991   Nunn-Lugar legislation to safeguard and dismantle weapons of mass destruction in the former Soviet

	Union and to provide alternative employment for weapons scientists passes the Senate by a vote of 86–8
December 12, 1991	Nunn-Lugar Cooperative Threat Reduction Act is signed into law
February 15, 1992	Accepts an appointment to serve on the Board of Directors of the National Endowment for Democracy; continues in this capacity until 2001, during which time he serves as the lead Senate proponent of the Endowment's work
March 1992	Senators Nunn and Lugar travel to Russia and Ukraine to meet with government officials to promote acceptance and implementation of the Nunn-Lugar program
Spring 1992	Publishes "The Republican Course," an outline of Republican foreign policy principles, in *Foreign Policy*
October 1, 1992	The Senate votes 93–6 in favor of ratification of the START Treaty, which was managed on the Senate floor by Lugar
January 1993	Is reappointed to the Senate Intelligence Committee; serves an additional ten years, becoming the longest-serving member in the committee's history
November 8, 1994	Reelected to a fourth Senate term, receiving 67 percent of the vote, the first Indiana senator to be elected to a fourth term
November 1994	In an operation known as Project Sapphire, the Defense Department uses Nunn-Lugar funds and authority to purchase and remove 600 kilograms of weapons-grade uranium from Kazakhstan
January 26, 1996	The Senate votes 87–4 in favor of ratification of the START II Treaty, which Lugar managed on the Senate floor
May 1, 1996	Surpasses the tenure of Daniel Vorhees to become the longest-serving Senator in Indiana history
June 27, 1996	The Senate passes the Nunn-Lugar-Domenici Amendment creating a program to train emergency personnel to respond to nuclear, biological, or chemical weapons attacks
October 1996	Nunn, Lugar, and Defense Secretary William Perry meet with officials in Russia and Ukraine regarding the progress of Nunn-Lugar; they witness the destruction of land- and sea-based missile launchers
December 2, 1996	Senators Lugar and Lieberman send a letter to President Clinton asking that he "reverse the decade-long erosion in foreign affairs spending"

January 7, 1997 — Introduces S.1413, a bill to limit ineffective unilateral economic sanctions

April 24, 1997 — The Senate votes 74–26 in favor of ratification of the Chemical Weapons Convention, of which Lugar is a lead Republican proponent

April 30, 1998 — The Senate consents to the ratification of the Protocols to the North Atlantic Treaty of 1949 on the Accession of Poland, Hungary, and the Czech Republic by a vote of 80–19; Lugar had been one of the Senate leaders in pressing for NATO expansion during the previous six years

November 1998 — During a trip to Russia and Ukraine, Lugar visits the closed nuclear city of Mayak and the biological weapons facility at Obolensk; he also witnesses Nunn-Lugar dismantlement operations involving a DELTA nuclear submarine and a Blackjack bomber

December 20, 1998 — Publishes a *Washington Post* editorial entitled "Why Saddam Must Go"

January 1999 — With former CIA director James Woolsey, publishes an article in *Foreign Affairs* entitled "The New Petroleum," outlining the breakthroughs in cellulosic biomass technology and arguing for rapid development of this fuel to reduce U.S. dependence on foreign oil

March 18, 1999 — Introduces the Africa Growth and Opportunity Act (AGOA), a bill expanding trade with African countries; the bill attracts a bipartisan group of fourteen cosponsors and lays the groundwork for passage in 2000 of an omnibus trade bill including the AGOA legislation.

April 23, 1999 — Along with then-Senate minority leader Daschle, represents the Senate at Capitol Rotunda ceremonies honoring the three newest members of NATO: Poland, Hungary, and the Czech Republic

February 29, 2000 — Lugar's National Sustainable Fuels and Chemicals Act of 1999 passes the Senate unanimously; the bill, which is signed into law several months later, provides for accelerated research into fuels derived from biomass

August 27, 2000 — It is announced that Lugar and former Senator Sam Nunn have been nominated for the Nobel Peace prize for their work in helping secure Russia's nuclear, chemical, and biological arsenals; the pair is renominated for the award in 2001 and 2002

November 7, 2000	Reelected to a fifth Senate term with 67 percent of the vote
June 13, 2001	In a speech to the Center for Strategic and International Studies, Lugar calls for an aggressive second round of NATO expansion that would "seize this unprecedented opportunity to expand the zone of peace and security to all of Europe"
August 19–September 4, 2001	Visits Latvia, Estonia, Lithuania, Bulgaria, and Romania to discuss NATO expansion with leaders of those countries; he also visits Nunn-Lugar dismantlement sites in Ukraine and Russia
September 7, 2001	Receives an honorary doctor of strategic intelligence degree from the Joint Military Intelligence College at Bolling Air Force Base
December 12, 2001	Calls for the United States to use all diplomatic, economic, and military means at its disposal to safeguard and destroy weapons of mass destruction around the world to keep them out of the hands of terrorists
March 4, 2002	In a speech to the Council on Foreign Relations, calls for NATO to transform itself to address the war on terrorism and the possible terrorist use of weapons of mass destruction
March 18, 2002	Introduces the Nunn-Lugar Expansion Act, which would authorize the Defense Department to apply Nunn-Lugar money and expertise to respond to proliferation threats outside the former Soviet Union
January 2003	Becomes chairman, for a second time, of the Senate Committee on Foreign Relations

Index

About the Contributors

Kenneth L. Adelman is host of DefenseCentral.com, national editor of *Washingtonian* magazine, and cofounder of an executive training firm Movers and Shakespeares (which uses lessons of the Bard for modern executives). He was assistant to Defense Secretary Donald Rumsfeld from 1975 to 1977, deputy U.S. representative to the United Nations, and arms control director under President Reagan. Ambassador Adelman is the author of five books and numerous articles on foreign and national security policy.

William J. Bennett, who is currently codirector of Empower America, has served as chairman of the National Endowment for the Humanities, as secretary of education, and as the nation's "drug czar." He has written and edited fourteen books, including the best-selling *The Book of Virtues*. Dr. Bennett writes and speaks widely on political, social, and educational issues. His most recent book is *Why We Fight: Moral Clarity and the War on Terrorism*. Dr. Bennett's essay is based, in part, on that book and on his previous essay entitled "Morality, Character and American Foreign Policy" published in *Present Dangers: Crisis and Opportunity in American Foreign and Defense Policy* (2000).

Jeffrey T. Bergner is president of the government relations firm Bergner, Bockorny, Castagnetti, Hawkins, and Brain. Prior to that, he served as staff director of the Senate Committee on Foreign Relations and as chief of staff to Senator Richard Lugar. Dr. Bergner serves on a variety of not-for-profit boards including the Hudson Institute and the Asia Foundation. He is currently adjunct professor of national security studies at Georgetown University. He writes and speaks widely in the fields of politics, international affairs, and political thought.

Mark Blitz is the Fletcher Jones Professor of political philosophy, chair of the Department of Government, and director of research at Claremont McKenna College. He has served as associate director of the U.S. Information Agency and as a senior professional staff member of the Senate Committee on Foreign Relations. He has served as director of research at the Hudson Institute, and has taught at Harvard University and the University of Pennsylvania. He is the author of numerous books and articles on political philosophy and public affairs.

Zbigniew Brzezinski is counselor at the Center for Strategic and International Studies and professor of American foreign policy at the Nitze School of Advanced International Studies, Johns Hopkins University. He also serves on the board of directors of a variety of not-for-profit organizations dedicated to philanthropic causes and to the promotion of freedom. Dr. Brzezinski served as the national security advisor to the president from 1977 to 1981. He has taught at Harvard University and Columbia University. He has written widely in the field of foreign affairs and has been honored in the United States and abroad.

William S. Cohen serves as chairman and chief executive officer of the Cohen Group. He served as a member of Congress from 1973 to 1979 and as U.S. senator from Maine from 1978 to 1997. In the Senate, he served on both the Armed Services Committee and the Intelligence Committee. He served as secretary of defense from 1997 to 2001. Cohen has been actively involved in the work of the Council on Foreign Relations, the Center for Strategic and International Studies, the School for Advanced International Studies, and the Brookings Institute. He is the author of nine books of nonfiction, fiction, and poetry.

Carl Gershman is president of the National Endowment for Democracy, a position that he has held for seventeen years. Prior to that, he served as senior counselor to the U.S. representative to the United Nations. Mr. Gershman also served as resident scholar at Freedom House and as executive director of Social Democrats, USA. Mr. Gershman has written and spoken widely on foreign policy issues. He is coeditor of *Israel, the Arabs and the Middle East* and the author of *The Foreign Policy of American Labor*.

Chuck Hagel is U.S. senator from Nebraska. He currently serves on the Committees on Foreign Relations; Banking, Housing, and Urban Affairs; Energy and Natural Resources; Budget; and Aging. He also serves on the Congressional-Executive Commission on China and the NATO Observer Group. Prior to his election to the Senate in 1996, Senator Hagel worked as an investment banker and cofounded Vanguard Cellular systems. He served with distinction in the U.S. Army in Vietnam, earning two Purple Hearts. He has served on the boards of a variety of civic, educational, and charitable organizations.

Lee H. Hamilton is the director of the Woodrow Wilson International Center for Scholars. Prior to becoming director of the Wilson Center, Mr. Hamilton served for thirty-four years as a U.S. representative from Indiana's Ninth Congressional District. During his tenure in the House of Representatives, he served as chairman and ranking member of the Committee on International Relations, chairman of its Subcommittee on Europe and the Middle East, and chairman of the Permanent Select Committee on Intelligence. He is the recipient of numerous civic and educational awards, including fifteen honorary degrees.

William G. Lesher serves as president of the consulting firm Lesher and Russell. He has served in various U.S. government positions including assistant secretary of agriculture for economics; chief economist to the Senate Committee on Agriculture, Nutrition, and Forestry; and legislative assistant to Senator Richard Lugar. He served in the U.S. Army from 1970 to 1972. Dr. Lesher writes and speaks widely on agricultural, natural resource, and trade issues.

Sam Nunn is cochairman and chief executive officer of the Nuclear Threat Initiative. He is also a senior partner in the law firm of King and Spalding. Prior to his current positions, he served as U.S. Senator from Georgia from 1972 to 1996. During his tenure in the Senate, Senator Nunn served as chairman of the Armed Services Committee and as a member of the Select Committee on Intelligence. Among his legislative achievements are the Department of Defense Reorganization Act and the Cooperative Threat Reduction Program, also known as the Nunn-Lugar Program. Senator Nunn also currently serves as distinguished professor of the Sam Nunn School of International Affairs at Georgia Tech and chairman of the Center for Strategic and International Studies.

William Perry is the president of William Perry and Associates, a Washington-based firm providing consulting services to governments and the private sector throughout the Western Hemisphere. He also serves as president of the Institute for the Study of the Americas and is a senior fellow at the Center for Strategic and International Studies. Mr. Perry has served as a senior professional staff member of the Senate Foreign Relations Committee and as director of Latin American Affairs at the National Security Council. He is the author of numerous books and articles on Latin American political and security affairs.

Charles B. Rangel is the representative from New York's Fifteenth Congressional District. He serves as the ranking member of the Committee on Ways and Means, as deputy Democratic whip of the House of Representatives, and as dean of the New York State congressional delegation. He has worked actively to foster trade, especially with the Caribbean region and with Africa. He was a principal sponsor of the African Growth and Opportunity Act. Congressman Rangel served in the U.S. Army in Korea from 1948 to 1952, and was awarded the Purple Heart and the Bronze Star.

Robert R. Simmons is the representative from Connecticut's Second Congressional District. He is a member of the House Armed Services Committee, where he serves on the Special Oversight Panel on Terrorism. Congressman Simmons' previous government positions include ten years of service as an operations officer for the Central Intelligence Agency and as staff director of the Senate Select Committee on Intelligence. He was awarded the CIA Seal Medallion, its highest civilian award. Mr. Simmons served in the U.S. Army and is the recipient of two Bronze Stars.

James Woolsey is a partner at the law firm of Shea and Gardner. He has served in a variety of senior U.S. government posts, including director of Central Intelligence, ambassador to the Negotiation on Conventional Armed Forces in Europe, undersecretary of the navy, and general counsel to the Senate Committee on Armed Services. He has also served as a delegate to the U.S.-Soviet Strategic Arms Reduction Talks and to the Nuclear and Space Arms Talks. In addition to practicing law, Mr. Woolsey serves on the board of directors of numerous corporations and as trustee of many civic organizations.

Casimir A. Yost is director of the Institute for the Study of Diplomacy at Georgetown University, a position he assumed in 1994. Prior to joining the institute, Mr. Yost was executive director of the Asia Foundation's Center for Asian Pacific Affairs in San Francisco. He has served as president of the World Affairs Council of Northern California and as a member of the professional staff of the Senate Committee on Foreign Relations. Mr. Yost has also worked for Citibank of New York in the Middle East and South Asia.